Russian
Transnational
Entrepreneurs
Ethnicity, Class and Capital

Alexander Shvarts

LIBRARY AND ARCHIVES CANADA CATALOGUING IN PUBLICATION

Shvarts, Alexander, 1975-
    Russian transnational entrepreneurs : ethnicity, class and
capital / by Alexander Shvarts.

Includes bibliographical references and index.
ISBN 978-1-897160-38-1

1. Jews, Russian--Ontario--Toronto--Economic conditions.
2. Jews, Soviet--Ontario--Toronto--Economic conditions.
3. Minority business enterprises--Ontario--Toronto.
4. Entrepreneurship--Ontario--Toronto. I. Title.

HD2358.5.C32T67 2010   338'.0408991710071354   C2010-903592-5

Cover design and layout by de Sitter Publications.
Cover images fromfotolia.com.
        The morning flight © Oleksandr Bondar
        Mature businessman looking at camera © diego cervo

de Sitter Publications
111 Bell Dr., Whitby, ON, L1N 2T1
CANADA

deSitterPublications.com
289-987-0656
info@desitterpublications.com

TABLE OF CONTENTS

LIST OF TABLES

LIST OF APPENDICES

**Appendices available online at
www.desitterpublications.com/TransnationalEntrepreneurs**

PREFACE

One of the most interesting results of the collapse of the former Soviet Union is the emergence of successful cosmopolitan entrepreneurs from former Soviet republics who have immigrated to countries, such as the United States and Canada, and settled in metropolitan areas like Toronto and have made millions establishing businesses in their new host countries. I have chosen to study successful cosmopolitan entrepreneurs from the former Soviet Union because this group has immigrated from a place where the free market economy and privatization did not exist prior to the 1980s, so the important intellectual issue, is how did immigrants who grew up most of their lives in a state-controlled communist system where entrepreneurship was forbidden learn to become so adept at starting businesses in a market economy when they moved to Toronto. One of the central questions that this book aims to address is: How did experiences in the former Soviet communist economy and in the transitional economy affect the role that human capital, financial capital, and social capital played in establishing businesses in Toronto. This study is based on thirty two interviews that I have conducted with two cohorts of immigrants from the former Soviet Union, those who immigrated to Toronto in the late 1970s and early 1980s and those that immigrated in the late 1980s and 1990s. To address how Russian immigrants established businesses in Toronto, I used three bodies of literature, including (1) transitional economy, (2) ethnic and class dimensions of entrepreneurship, and (3) transnationalism to examine how each of the following factors: 1) social capital, 2) financial capital, 3) human capital, and 4) home country experience, specifically experience in the former Soviet communist economy and experience in the transitional economy affected the Russian entrepreneur at each stage of business development in Toronto.

CHAPTER 1

INTRODUCTION

One of the most interesting results of the collapse of the former Soviet Union is the emergence of successful cosmopolitan entrepreneurs[1] from former Soviet republics who have immigrated to countries, such as the United States and Canada, settling in metropolitan areas like Toronto and making millions establishing businesses in their new host countries (for discussion of successful cosmopolitan Russian entrepreneurs, see Yurchak, 2003 and Lynch and Valeri, 1996). This book focuses on successful cosmopolitan entrepreneurs from the former Soviet Union because this group comes from a place where the free market economy did not exist before the 1980s. It is important to understand how people—who grew up in a context where entrepreneurship was forbidden and where privatization did not exist prior to the 1980s (Gold, 1995a: xii)—could develop entrepreneurial skills and how they could transfer these skills to establish successful businesses in the modern context of market capitalism in Toronto. The majority of the immigrant entrepreneurs from the former Soviet Union that I interviewed were Jews. Soviet Jews are white Europeans, so they are members of the racial majority group in Canada and the United States, which makes them different from most new immigrants, who are from Asia, Latin America and the Caribbean, who encounter prejudice and discrimination (Gold, 1995a: xii). Jews from the former Soviet Union come from a country where until recently most of life's basic necessities were delivered by the government. Soviet émigrés are not accustomed to the many freedoms that Canadians, and many other immigrants, take for granted, such as opening a business. Expecting to improve their career prospects and those of their children and attain economic well-being, more than 250,000 Jews have emigrated from the former Soviet Union since 1971 (Markus and Schwartz, 1984: 71). By 1983, more than 75,000 of these had resettled in the United States and over 8,000 had chosen to settle in Canada, with approximately 6,000 coming to Toronto (Markus and Schwartz, 1984: 72). After four decades of emigration, there are now sizeable communities of Jews from the former USSR in several nations and three continents, including Western Europe, North America and Israel (Tress, 1994).

According to Statistics Canada, at the time of the 2006 Census, there were 20,920 recent Russian immigrants in Toronto. Many researchers have noted that in the US and Canada there is an overrepresentation of the foreign born in the business population and some groups have entered business ownership in numbers disproportionate to their group's size (Chan and Cheung, 1985: 143; Aldrich and Waldinger, 1990: 112). Despite their numbers, there has been relatively little research on this group (Gold, 1995a: x). In Canada there has been very little systematic research which focuses on immigrant entrepreneurs from the former Soviet Union, and no studies have explored the effects of transnational business linkages between Russians in major immigrant receiving countries, such as Canada and in their sending countries.

This research considers how the experiences in the former Soviet communist economy and the transitional economy affected the role of human capital, financial capital, and social capital in establishing businesses in Canada. It looks at the effects of transnational business linkages, which for Russian immigrants is unique from other immigrant groups because it reflects the unique cultural patterns and structural characteristics of the former Soviet Union. In short, the unique historical, economic and political environment of the former Soviet Union provided favourable conditions for entrepreneurship.

This study is based on 32 interviews that I conducted with two cohorts of immigrants from the former Soviet Union, those who immigrated to Toronto in the late 1970s and early 1980s and those who arrived in the late 1980s and 1990s. I chose these two cohorts because I expect that those who immigrated in the late 1970s and early 1980s came to Toronto with virtually no entrepreneurial experience and no financial capital because they came before the market transition in the former Soviet Union, making them more likely to use networks within their ethnic community in Toronto to establish businesses within the enclave economy or to rely on networks to access the mainstream Canadian economy. I expect that those who immigrated in the late 1980s and 1990s were more likely to come with entrepreneurial experience and financial capital because they lived in the former Soviet Union during the market transition; they will be more likely to use networks and connections formed during the transitional Russian economy of the 1980s and 1990s to establish transnational businesses in Toronto.

Purpose of Research

To address how Russian immigrants have established businesses in Toronto, I will examine how social capital, financial capital, human capital, and home country experience, specifically experience in the former Soviet communist economy and experience in the transitional economy have affected Russian entrepreneurs at each stage of business development in Toronto. I approach these four factors through the three following critical lenses: the transitional economy, ethnic and class dimensions of entrepreneurship, and transnationalism. I use the central postulates of each of the three approaches to determine how these major factors influenced and shaped business practice and success in Toronto for the two cohorts of Soviet immigrants. I focus on two phases of entrepreneurship and the founding of a business: (1) Pre-Start-Up - Motivation and Idea Development and (2) Start-Up - Planning and Organizing the Founding of a Firm. As has been noted elsewhere, these phases are important to entrepreneurship (Greve, 1995: 3; Carter et al., 1996; Kamm & Nurick, 1993).

Paths to Entrepreneurship

Through an analysis of interview data and biographies of entrepreneurship, I will discuss the diverse paths to self-employment for Russian immigrants and show the influence of human capital, social capital, financial capital, and home country experience. These paths represent opportunity structures that are linked to the structural problems faced by all new immigrants, including these particular immigrants from the former Soviet Union, when starting a business. People with varied amounts of class and ethnic resources take diverse paths to entrepreneurship, and I focus on these diverse paths to explain why immigrant groups turn to self-employment.

The first path to entrepreneurship can be explained using the disadvantage theory of entrepreneurship. This theory asserts that immigrant groups go into business because they are disadvantaged in the general labour market due to poor English, inferior education, lack of host country credentials and licenses and discrimination (Kim, 1981).

The second path can be explained using a cultural theory of entrepreneurship, which posits that immigrants become entrepreneurs because they identify closely with and are socially and culturally attached to their ethnic group, living and interacting on a regular basis with their ethnic group (Light, 1980), or they choose entrepreneurship because they want to make enough money to return to their origin country (Bonacich, 1973), or entrepreneurship is a collective response to structural disadvantage (Light, 1980).

The third path to entrepreneurship can be explained using opportunity theory; when immigrants are working in salary jobs and there is an opportunity to start a business, they may decide to leave their salaried position. They will consider such things as the number of businesses already in the field, technological requirements, and capital requirements. If they find that the market is underserved, they may decide to open a new company to meet the market demands (Aldrich and Waldinger, 1990). This path is consistent with the ethnic and class dimensions of the entrepreneurship approach, namely, that the inclination toward business and the relative success of entrepreneurial efforts by immigrants is influenced by their class resources, including financial and human capital, specifically the money that they have made and the experience they have accumulated in previous salaried jobs (Light, 1984; Waldinger et al., 1990). This path is also consistent with a transnationalism approach if the immigrants started transnational businesses as a result of their ability to more easily access the business opportunities generated by cultural frontiers and they have the international social capital, networks, and bilingual skills to support international business (Lever-Tracy et al., 1991: xi, 113 in Light, 2007: 90; Wong, 1998: 95 in Light, 2007: 90).

The fourth path can be explained using ethnic economy theories of entrepreneurship, which state that participation in the ethnic sub-economy promotes self-employment because entrepreneurs receive assistance from other co-ethnics (Portes and Bach, 1985), who may help them get a job in a co-ethnic firm and then help them start a business (Bonacich and Modell, 1980). The first, second, and fourth paths to entrepreneurship are consistent with the ethnic and class dimensions of an entrepreneurship approach, which considers that the inclination toward business and the relative success of entrepreneurial efforts on the part of immigrants is based on a balance of class resources: financial, human, and cultural capital and ethnic resources, the latter including ethnic social networks and social capital (Light, 1984; Waldinger et al., 1990).

The fifth path to entrepreneurship can be explained using business background theory, which asserts that immigrant groups choose to be self-employed because they have business backgrounds in their country of origin (Light, 1984; Portes and Bach, 1985). This path is consistent with a transitional economy approach (Pontusson, 1995: 119; Nee, 1991: 267), which posits that immigrants who experienced the transition to a market economy in the former Soviet Union are more likely to have set up businesses in the former Soviet Union; as a result, they arrive in Toronto with business experience and financial capital.

Why Russian Businesses in Toronto are Worthy of Study

Findings from previous research show that medium and large businesses are typically run by native-born Canadians and established immigrants who have worked their way to the top. My research, however, demonstrates that as a result of globalization, Russian immigrants establish not only small businesses (ie, family-owned ethnic businesses[2] in an enclave market where they provide retail goods and services to co-ethnic or minority consumers [see Bates, 1994; Razin, 1992; Teizeira, 1998, in Lo and Wang, 2007: 65]), but also medium and large businesses. The latter generate yearly revenue of over one million dollars in a diversity of industries, many of which have transnational links to Russia.

Global political and economic restructuring and the international population movement of the last two decades have drastically altered the market. Contemporary ethnic economies, which include medium-sized and large firms, go beyond retailing and ethnic enclaves to command transnational networks (Li, 1998, in Lo and Wang, 2007: 65). In the past, medium and large businesses were mainly the territory of native-born Canadians and well-established immigrants. More recently, global movements of ideas and technology, and people and resources, have created a very different scenario. Many immigrants now come with human and financial capital, as well as management experience and business knowledge (Fong and Luk, 2007b: 65). The Russian immigrants I interviewed all came with a great deal of human capital; most of the second cohort who immigrated in the late 1980s and 1990s came with financial capital, management experience and business knowledge. My findings suggest that for my interviewees, self-employment represents an opportunity for economic advancement.

Why Russian Immigrant Entrepreneurs are Worthy of Study

Russian immigrant entrepreneurs are especially interesting because of their home country experience in the former Soviet communist economy and the transitional economy, both of which prove to be critical to their business development in Toronto. Russian immigrants are distinct from other immigrant groups because the Soviet system had decades of restrictions on self-employment. Nevertheless, as I will demonstrate, they were able to combine elements from the Soviet era and the transitional economy to establish businesses in Toronto. Russian entrepreneurs are distinct from other immigrant entrepreneurs because they learned to engage in business during communism in either the "command style" or black market economy, or they honed their entrepreneurial skills in the transitional economy. In either case, they successfully transferred these skills to Toronto.

Entrepreneurship was not entirely absent under state socialism in the former Soviet Union. There was a private sector, a hidden or second or black market economy, on the periphery of the socialist economy. Private economic activity was officially banned, but there was underground economic activity (Havrylyshyn, 2006: 36). In an economy of full employment under socialism, most people participated in the second economy part-time, while holding a secure state-sector job. Others used their state jobs as a starting point for full-time private enterprise later, taking advantage of the equipment, facilities, and materials of their state jobs.

The socialist private sector was the training ground for entrepreneurship in the post-communist era in the following ways. First, Soviet-period price and supply distortions generated underground capitalists, who in a market economy would probably have been legal traders (Rona-Tas and Lengyel, 1997: 10-11). Second, in the command-administrative economy, enterprise managers needed to behave in entrepreneurial ways to acquire financial resources and materials for their firms in conditions of chronic shortage and stifling bureaucratism. Third, they acquired skills in dealing with party and state officials. Fourth, as marketization proceeded, state enterprise managers had to demonstrate exceptional entrepreneurialism to keep their firms afloat (Bonnell and Gold, 2002: xix). The legacies of communal cultural traditions and the Soviet economic system, along with the economic chaos of contemporary Russia, make flows of goods and services through personal networks a dominant mode of exchange among organizations and individuals (Berliner, 1957; Kryshtanovskaya and White, 1996; Ledeneva, 1998). Routines and practices, organizational forms, and social ties retained from the socialist period are valuable resources and the basis for credible commitments and coordinated actions in the post-socialist period (Nelson and Winter, 1982).

Socialist entrepreneurial skills proved crucial for the development of private business in the first post-Soviet years (mid-1980s). They provided a new pragmatic understanding of work, time, money, skills, and professional relations; hybrid understandings of the official plans, rules, laws, and institutions of the party-state were particularly essential to the growth of private firms. These socialist entrepreneurial skills influenced business success abroad for immigrants. The immigrants from the first cohort I interviewed – those who grew up in the command-administrative economy in the Soviet Union – were more likely to use their socialist entrepreneurial skills in Toronto.

Why Soviet Jewish Immigrants are Worthy of Study

Soviet Jews are distinct from other immigrant groups because they immigrated from the Soviet Union, which, until its recent demise, was the world's oldest and most highly developed communist nation (Gold, 1995a: xi). Jews who have settled in the United States and Canada since the mid-1960s have arrived in two distinct flows. The first group, who entered from about 1972 to 1986, came from a functioning and highly restrictive communist nation. Since about 1986 – the beginning of Glasnost[3] – thousands more have emigrated from a country with increased freedom and uncertainty (Gold, 1995a: 1). Since 1974, an increasing proportion of Jews have opted to migrate to North America, and an indeterminate number who initially chose Israel have now moved to the US and Canada (Markus and Schwartz, 1984: 71-2).

In many ways, the Soviet Jews I interviewed stand out from earlier waves of Jewish immigrants. They have high levels of education, and they lived under communism for generations. Unlike most North American Jews, they have had minimal exposure to formal Jewish training and Jewish religious life and no experience of a highly organized Jewish community.

The Jewish community of Toronto expected that former Soviet Jews would identify with the existing Jewish community, living in a Jewish area, affiliating with a synagogue, providing children with a Jewish education, participating in Jewish communal organizations and activities, observing certain rituals, festivals, and life cycle events, supporting Israel, and giving financial support to the community through voluntary contributions (Markus and Schwartz, 1984: 72). But Soviet Jewish émigrés have not shown a willingness to express their ethnic identity through joining established Jewish communal organizations (Markus and Schwartz, 1984: 72).

One factor which may help explain the Soviet Jewish émigrés' lack of identification with the North American Jewish community is the strong positive association of former Soviet Jews with the Soviet Union and with the dominant Russian culture. After all, they had no opportunity to satisfy their Jewish interests in the Soviet Union (Markus and Schwartz, 1984: 79). Thus, their decision to migrate to Toronto is not related to their need to identify with a Jewish community (Markus and Schwartz, 1984: 80). In fact, the Jews from the Soviet Union show a commitment to aspects of their Soviet Russian cultural heritage; meanwhile, the established Jewish community favours adherence to the Jewish cultural heritage as it has evolved in Toronto (Markus and Schwartz, 1984: 81).

Soviet Jews arrived in Toronto convinced that the established community should and could do considerably more, especially in the area of employment. Many considered this a precondition for identification with the community. When the help they anticipated was not forthcoming, feelings of bitterness surfaced. Aggravating the situation was the growing awareness among members of the Jewish community that the demands made in the economic sphere by immigrants were not matched by an interest in Judaism and/or Jewish cultural life (Markus and Schwartz, 1984: 81). The Soviet Jewish émigrés' strong identification with Russian culture and their ambivalence regarding their Jewish heritage weakened the possibility that in the process of adaptation they would voluntarily establish roots in the Jewish community (Markus and Schwartz, 1984: 82).

In the Soviet Union, Jews gained social and occupational mobility by accepting the dominant linguistic and cultural patterns of Soviet society. Many Jews shed their Jewish identity and passed as Russians. They were thus denied access to experiences that would allow them to relate to an organized Jewish community, such as knowledge of their history and familiarity with Jewish traditions. Their ability to succeed in Soviet society depended on whether they were able to deny and hide their Jewishness and assimilate into the dominant culture (Markus and Schwartz, 1984: 84). Soviet Jews were highly assimilated to Soviet society and generally knew little about the Jewish religion, Jewish culture or Jewish history (Gold, 1995a: 71). It could be expected, therefore, that once in Canada they would repeat the adaptation pattern successfully applied in the Soviet Union and acculturate in the dominant secular patterns by learning English in a secular environment and working outside the Jewish community. As a result, Soviet Jews are not likely to join Jewish institutions in Toronto (Markus and Schwartz, 1984: 82). Markus and Schwartz's Toronto study (1984) shows that, despite initial material and social support from Jewish communal organizations, the respondents had little interest in continuing the association.

Many ethnic groups have a level of institutional completeness that gives their members an advantage for mobilizing resources (Aldrich and Waldinger, 1990: 130; Breton, 1964). Unlike many ethnic groups, Soviet Jews have a lack of institutional completeness in Canada; they have not developed large ethnic enclaves in the US or Canada as have Cuban and Korean entrepreneurs (Gold, 1988: 427; Min, 1986; Portes and Bach,

1985). Unlike earlier immigrants, Russian Jews have not been forced to band together to survive (Light, 1972; Glazer and Moynihan, 1963; Portes and Rumbaut, 1990).

While the Soviet Jewish enclave is united by language, immigration experience, estrangement from North American Jews, and shared notions of ethnic identity, it is also segmented. There are pervasive feelings of distrust and individualism within the community, which causes many émigrés to distance themselves from co-ethnics (Gold, 1995a: 90). Regionalism is also a source of division because émigrés from Russia (especially Moscow and St. Petersburg) generally feel themselves to be above those from the Ukraine. The divisions and ambivalent feelings towards fellow immigrants help explain the small number of formal organizations among Soviet Jews (Gold, 1995a: 92). Gold found that some Russian Jews who experienced communism are tired of being forced to join organizations, so in North America they want to be free of all organizations (Gold, 1995a: 93).

Even though they do not form many formal organizations and they tend to be segmented, recent Soviet Jewish immigrants have established communities where they share a common language, values, customs and experiences (Gold, 1995a: 93). They tend to settle in common areas, often in existing Jewish neighbourhoods, but Soviet Jewish enclaves are loose networks of émigrés representing a wide variety of occupations, regional origins, degrees of religious influence, and outlooks on adjustment to North America (Gold, 1995a: 94). Interaction among members is frequent in the ethnically owned delicatessens and Russian Jewish nightclubs where émigrés spend long evenings celebrating religious and secular events in a style that combines their Russian, Jewish and American identities (Gold, 1995a: 94, 99).

Even so, Soviet Jews have not merged with North American Jews nor set up strong, community wide formal organizations. These new immigrants, who are skilled and educated, have fewer reasons for organizing their communities than the immigrant Jews of an earlier generation who had few resources beyond their own organizations for satisfying basic needs. Most Soviet Jews now prefer the company of fellow émigrés in an informal context that emphasizes Russian culture (Gold, 1995a: 116). As noted above, because they come from a country where the government, until recently, controlled all organizational life, Soviet

Jews regard any type of organization with cynicism, despite the potential benefits that could be achieved through collective action (Gold, 1995a: 119).

Soviet Jews are well-equipped for the task of adjusting to North American life because they are highly educated, have urban experience, and possess the skills and resources needed to find jobs, all of which help them achieve economic self sufficiency (Gold, 1995a: 22-3). Once they learn English and understand how the North American job market works, they tend to do quite well (Gold, 1995a: 47).

Why the Case of the Former Soviet Union is Worthy of Study

The conditions both in the former Soviet Union and in the transition era were unique. Market transition can be implemented at different speeds and through a wide variety of policies. In Russia, a series of radical institutional reforms dismantled the system of far-reaching state control over the economy, leading to the rapid rise of private ownership and the market-based allocation of resources and consumer goods (Gerber, 2002b: 631).[4] However, the Russian transition differed from European countries, such as Hungary. For instance, Russia retreated to primitive barter relations and a subsistence existence, while Hungary consolidated its money economy. Russia criminalized the economy, while Hungary had an emergent rule of law. In Russia, there was a huge concentration of power in oligarchs; Hungary had a diversified economic structure, where small producers began producing goods and offering services on price-regulating markets in agriculture, the service sector, the construction industry, and some industrial branches (Eyal et al., 1998: 177; Burawoy, 2001: 1109). Unlike other European countries, Russia chose unlimited "voucher" privatization that allowed mediated participation as a method of property transformation (Laki and Szalai, 2006: 324, 340). In Russia, Ukraine and most other CIS countries, new laws allowing free enterprise coexisted for many years with Soviet-period laws and were considered illegal until the mid-1990s (Havrylyshyn, 2006: 35).

After the 1980s, the state sector downsized; many state firms entered into contracts with foreign companies, and new opportunities for entrepreneurship emerged. Official control was completely withdrawn, so people could now start private businesses and control the entire budget of their business. By the time the USSR had collapsed at the end of the 1980s, the second economy shifted an ever-expanding proportion of the benefits of economic activity away from the state into private hands, paving the way for self-employment to grow unimpeded in Russia for the first time. The success of Russian entrepreneurs in cities like Toronto was likely influenced by these unique historical circumstances. In particular, Russian immigrants who lived in Russia during the transition or who returned to Russia from Toronto at that time took advantage of privatization schemes and developed networks with state officials, former managers of state enterprises, and new Russian entrepreneurs (known as 'New Russians'). They were then able to use these contacts to develop businesses in Toronto.

Research Contributions

This research makes the following contributions:

1. I differentiate business development into two stages: pre-start-up and start-up stage. The success of immigrant entrepreneurs in the two phases of entrepreneurship is influenced by a combination of the following factors: 1) social capital, 2) financial capital, 3) human capital, and 4) home country experience, specifically experience in the former Soviet communist economy and experience in the transitional economy. In order to understand how the above four factors influence the success of immigrant entrepreneurs in the two phases of entrepreneurship, it is necessary to combine the following three theoretical approaches: transitional economy, ethnic and class dimensions of entrepreneurship, and transnationalism.

2. Past studies have not placed enough emphasis on how social context in the origin country influences business success in the host country. Therefore, an aim of this study is to demonstrate how past Russian cultural traditions and institutional arrangements have influenced business practices and success in Toronto, specifically during the pre-start up and start-up phase. I explore a seemingly contradictory phenomenon, namely, how people who grew up in a context where entrepreneurship was

forbidden and where privatization did not exist prior to the 1980s, could develop entrepreneurial skills and how they could then transfer these skills to establish businesses in the modern context of market capitalism in Toronto. It is this historical context which makes Russian entrepreneurs unique.

3. I focus on an emerging phenomenon: immigrants are arriving with a great deal of human capital, some with financial capital as well, and are establishing medium and large sized businesses. The Russian immigrants I interviewed had a substantial amount of human capital, and most of the second cohort had financial capital, management experience and business knowledge. In contrast to past research, which found that medium and large businesses would be run by native-born Canadians and established immigrants, my research demonstrates that as a result of globalization, the tendency of the immigrants that I interviewed from Russia was to establish not only small businesses in an enclave market, but also medium and large businesses in a diversity of industries, many of which have transnational links to Russia.

4. Finally, based on my findings, I indicate five diverse paths to entrepreneurship taken by the immigrants from both cohorts, and I demonstrate how human capital, social capital, financial capital, and home country experience, specifically socialist entrepreneurial skills learned in the former Soviet communist economy and in the transitional economy, have influenced the paths taken to establish successful businesses in Toronto.

NOTES

[1] *Entrepreneurs* will be operationally defined as respondents who are proprietors (owners and operators) of a firm or business enterprise or otherwise self-employed (Greenfield et al, 1979). An *entrepreneur* is commonly defined as one who owns, launches or takes over an existing business, manages, and assumes the risks of an economic venture by investing in or registering a firm (Greve and Salaff,, 2003: 2; Salaff, Greve, and Wong, 2007: 107; Aldrich et al., 1989; Walken, 1979). This definition is consistent with the North American research tradition and Revenue Canada's Tax rules (Salaff, Greve, and Wong, 2007: 107).

[2] The definition of ethnic businesses is limited to that of Portes and Jensen (1989), being those businesses owned and operated by people of a certain

ethnicity – either first or second generation Canadians – with no reference to their clientele (Lo and Wong, 2007: 66). Ethnic business networks don't have to be limited to a spatially bounded area and are often not geographically clustered (Greve and Salaff, 2005: 9; Fong 1994; Wong, 1998; Li, 1999). Ethnic business firms may get a range of economic inputs they need inside or outside the ethnic economy (Greve and Salaff, 2005:17).

[3]   Glasnost refers to the policy introduced by Prime Minister Mikhail Gorbachev in the Soviet Union during which many of the strict regulations which had been maintained from the time of the Revolution in 1917 were relaxed (Gold, 1995: 1).

[4]   Russia experienced a recession in the 1980s, which contrasts starkly with the strong growth experienced in China after the introduction of market reforms (Gerber, 2002b: 633).

CHAPTER 2

Research Methodology - Research Design and Data Collection

In this chapter, I describe the research design and the methods used in the empirical part of the study.

Overview of Research Methods Used to Collect Data

I use in-depth interviewing, the technique of many classic studies of immigrant communities and immigrant entrepreneurship (Bonacich and Modell, 1980; Portes and Bach, 1985; Gold, 1995a; Zhou, 1992). I follow the method used by Bretell and Alstatt (2007) in their study of immigrant entrepreneurs to demonstrate: (a) the active decision-making and agency of immigrants who go into business for themselves; (b) the resources (ethnic and class) they draw upon; and (c) the diverse paths to and experiences of self-employment for immigrant entrepreneurs from the former Soviet Union. This method allowed me to capture a rich and detailed image of the experience of immigrants – one with a human face – and to understand immigrants as social actors. Although my emphasis is on individuals and agency in entrepreneurship, I address the interplay of resources as well as structural contexts, such as work experience in the former Soviet Union, within which individual decisions were made and which influenced entrepreneurial practices in Toronto. My findings reveal immigrants who take control of their lives and who accumulate not only ethnic and class resources but also the experiential and motivational resources necessary to realizing the goal of self-employment (Bretell and Alstatt, 2007: 394).

The empirical data is derived from face-to-face in-depth interviews with 32 immigrants from the former Soviet Union who became entrepreneurs by starting private companies/businesses in Toronto.

The year of birth or age of each respondent is important because I was interested in immigrants who immigrated when they had attained an education and job experience in the former Soviet Union. The place of birth allows us to investigate the entrepreneurial experiences developed within the origin country that helped them establish businesses in Toronto. Education and the field in which it was achieved provide human capital variables. Previous occupation before coming to Toronto indicates work experience and is another human capital variable. Knowing the number of countries they lived in outside the USSR before coming to Canada (especially Italy and Israel) allows me to determine whether immigrants attained work experience (human capital) before coming to Canada and if they built networks or acquired financial capital that would help them establish businesses in Toronto.

Research Sample

I obtained my respondents from a non-probability snowball sample in the Greater Toronto area. I first identified several people with relevant characteristics and interviewed them. These subjects were asked for the names of other people with the same attributes. Starting with only a few informants, I was able to identify a larger sample of two cohorts of immigrants from the former Soviet Union, those who immigrated to Toronto in the late 1970s and early 1980s and those who arrived in the late 1980s and 1990s. I interviewed 23 immigrants from the earlier cohort and 9 from the later.

This book focuses on Russian immigrants who consider themselves, and are considered by others, to be successful because they have businesses generating revenue of over $1 million per year. Several studies of businesses have found that survival odds and signs of prosperity improve once the $1 million in sales level is attained (Timmons, 1986: 226).

I also interviewed immigrants from both cohorts who consider themselves unsuccessful; they started private companies/businesses, but either went bankrupt or were forced to sell because their businesses were not generating enough revenue. The immigrants who considered themselves unsuccessful in establishing businesses included those who left a salaried job and those who opened up businesses in the former Soviet Union that failed because of competition, legal changes, and the dangers of doing business in Russia.

Although this is a non-probability snowball sample, the fact that the interviewees have no family ties provides some assurance that the sample will not be skewed.

All immigrants from the former Soviet Union whom I interviewed came to Toronto with a high education and excellent skill sets. So the human capital of most entrepreneurs was vast; they had accumulated on average 5 years of work experience before starting their business, and all had at least a bachelor's degree. Most had technical and professional degrees, mostly in engineering and science subjects. Their ages ranged from 38 to 74 years, and they immigrated to Toronto between 1975 and 2002. On arrival, their average age was 34 years, and the typical family comprised 2 parents and 2 children. Their marital status

Table 1:
Characteristics of Businesses Established by
Russian Immigrants in Toronto

Type of Industry	Percentage (%)
Construction/Engineering	14
Food	10
Software/Technology	10
Metals	4
Science/Medical/Environmental	10
Stocks/Investments/Sales	10
Arts	6
Automobile	10
Manufacturing	10
Importer of Chemical Products	4
Media	4
Telecommunications	4
Relationship to Business	**Percentage (%)**
Owner	87
Owner/Manager/Founder	80
Number of Employees	**Percentage (%)**
Less than 10	53
More than 10	47

is important; it may play a role in the decision to start a transnational business and leave families behind while conducting business overseas. The overall composition of the sample was predominantly middle-aged men, starting their enterprise on average in their mid-30s and early 40s, married, with an engineering or science degree. Most did business as sole proprietors who registered their own capital ventures.

The following table shows the characteristics of the businesses these immigrants established in Toronto.

The majority of the sample identified themselves as enterprise owners or as a combination of owner, manager, and founder; thus, they are categorized as entrepreneurs, not managers. About half of the businesses had fewer than 10 employees; the other half had more than 10. The businesses were scattered throughout a variety of fields, the largest number being based in the construction, engineering, and manufacturing industries. The second largest category included the food, software/technology, science/medical/environmental, stock/investments/sales, and automobile industries. The smallest number of entrepreneurs was in the metals, arts, chemical, media, and telecommunications industries.

Information about Interviews

All interviews took place between August 2006 and June 2007. All were conducted in English, except two, which were conducted in Russian. The first person I interviewed was Abe, my father-in-law, who referred me to several entrepreneurs who had immigrated from the former Soviet Union, and who were his personal acquaintances through friendship or business. I called them and mentioned I was Abe's son-in-law; as a result of my relationship to Abe, they were happy to be interviewed. These entrepreneurs referred me to additional respondents from their social networks. It was easy to develop good rapport with all respondents because I am a Russian-Jewish student who immigrated to Toronto from the Ukraine in 1981; they felt comfortable sharing their experiences, including their lives as Jews in the former Soviet Union and their knowledge of immigration and settling in Toronto. They knew that my parents had similar experiences. Interviews were conducted either at the entrepreneur's place of business or at their home. They lasted 2 to 3 hours and were recorded on a voice recorder. After signing the consent form which detailed the voluntary nature of the interview and the audio-taping procedure, I obtained the participant's demographic information. The interviews were transcribed ad verbatim after completion. Quotations used throughout the study are taken directly from interview transcripts.

Interview Schedule

I used a semi-structured, interview schedule consisting of a number of questions, both open- and close-ended. I constructed a tentative interview schedule but altered it several times as interesting themes and topics appeared. The interview schedule reflects a categorical approach—a script of questions under each category or theme. Most questions were open-ended, so responses varied considerably. In many cases, in follow-up questions, interviewees were invited to elaborate on their answers.

The interview schedule was separated into the following categories:

- Individual demographic characteristics
- Employment background
- Immigration characteristics
- Immigrants' background in the former Soviet Union and the skills learned for entrepreneurship
- Launching, establishing, and running a business in Toronto
- Relationship between ethnic and class resources and immigrant entrepreneurship
- Social networks in Toronto
- Relationship between transnationalism and immigrant entrepreneurship
- Implications for Canadian citizenship/immigration policy and international trade policy

The interview schedule is presented in Appendix B.[1]

Data Analysis

Before the data analysis could be carried out, the interviews were transcribed ad verbatim with the help of a research assistant. The majority of the data analysis was conducted after all interviews were completed. I conducted some preliminary analysis while waiting—sometimes weeks or months—for an interview with transnational entrepreneurs who frequently traveled to other countries to conduct business. However, this gave me time to familiarize myself with the data before starting a new round of interviews. I coded the data both manually and using the qualitative research data analysis software program called Hyperresearch.

Operationalizing Theories and Variables

I drew upon three bodies of literature to examine how social capital, financial capital, human capital, and home country experience, specifically experience in the former Soviet communist economy and experience in the transitional economy, affected the Russian entrepreneur at each stage of business development in Toronto. The three bodies of literature include: transitional economy; ethnic and class dimensions of entrepreneurship; and transnationalism. I focused on five diverse paths to entrepreneurship, including disadvantage explanations, cultural explanations, business background explanations, ethnic economy explanations, and opportunity explanations, to demonstrate how human capital, social capital, financial capital, and home country experience influenced the path taken.

Variables in sociology are measurable concepts that can have more than one value. For example, I use education to measure human capital. In this section, I will describe the variables used in the questions (see Appendix B for questions) and discuss the indicators used for each (to see questions asked for each theory and/or variable, see Appendix A).[2]

1. Transitional Economy Approach: According to this approach, institutional changes determine the strategies of economic actors by virtue of the opportunities and constraints that they provide (Pontusson, 1995: 119). This perspective considers how the transition to a market economy in the former Soviet Union influenced entrepreneurial activity in both Russia and Toronto. It views the structural changes that followed the dismantling of the command economy as creating opportunities and incentives for entrepreneurial activity (Nee, 1991: 267).

Entrepreneurs were asked whether they were able to take advantage of the transition to a market economy and establish successful businesses in the former Soviet Union. If they obtained entrepreneurial experience by setting up businesses, they were more likely to use this experience to set up businesses in Toronto, because according to Nee's market transition theory (1996: 945), the structural changes that followed the dismantling of the command economy created opportunities and incentives for entrepreneurial activity. Entrepreneurs were asked if they lived in Russia during the transition or returned to Russia at that time; such immigrants were more likely to have established transnational social networks, in the form of connections with state enterprise directors and business groups that took over large formerly state-owned enterprises during the covert privatization of 1988-91, the massive swift voucher privatization of 1992-94, and the loans-for-shares auctions of 1995-9.[3] They could use these networks in Toronto to open transnational businesses.

2. Ethnic and Class Dimensions of Entrepreneurship Approach: According to this approach, the factors conventionally identified as directing immigrants toward entrepreneurship, such as ethnic and class resources, are also relevant in shaping their business success. The inclination towards business and the relative success of immigrant entrepreneurial efforts has been viewed as a balance of class and ethnic resources (Light, 1984; Waldinger et al., 1990). All groups possess class resources, including financial, human, and cultural capital and ethnic resources; these include ethnic social networks and social capital, but the balance varies from group to group.

(2a) Social Capital and Ethnic Social Networks: Entrepreneurs make extensive use of ethnic social networks for resources when starting and running a business. Social capital constitutes the ability of the individual to mobilize those resources on demand (Portes, 1995). In the literature on minority entrepreneurship, social capital

is illustrated by the use of co-ethnic employees, markets, suppliers, community sources of capital, advice and information, as well as membership in ethnic and/or community organizations.

To determine the importance of ethnic social networks and social capital for entrepreneurship, respondents were asked if they had any social networks in Canada, such as an established community of earlier Russian immigrants, before they left the former Soviet Union. This question sought to determine if they had direct social assistance or advice about employment and business opportunities in Toronto; according to the ethnic and class dimensions of entrepreneurship approach, the most salient feature of early business efforts by immigrant groups is their dependence on an ethnic community for support (Chu, 1996; Portes, 1998). Entrepreneurs were also asked if they contacted members from the Russian or Jewish community about business related matters, such as information about business opportunities, the feasibility of their business, places where they could get financing, and access to customers; this approach considers that the ethnic community provides immigrants with a support system that provides opportunities to start businesses (Salaff et al., 2007: 99; Nee, 1987, in Fong and Lee, 2007: 149; Aldrich & Zimmer, 1986, in Salaff et al., 2007: 101). In Chapter 6, I discuss whether the entrepreneurs obtained any aid, such as seed capital from their ethnic community and if they were members of any ethnic business organizations that provided benefits for their business, such as important social networks. According to the literature on ethnic entrepreneurship, ethnic groups regularly provide their members with financial capital through personal loans, relying on reputation and enduring relationships as collateral, what Light and Bonacich (1988) call ethnic facilitation.

Entrepreneurs were asked if they became members of professional trade organizations before or as soon as they started their businesses and if these helped them develop business contacts. They were also asked if they developed network contacts by working for established companies in their field or by attending trade shows and industry events. According to the ethnic and class dimensions of entrepreneurship approach, colleagues from earlier jobs can provide new business entrants with expertise, lines of credit, and links to suppliers and customers (Waldinger, 1986, in Salaff et al., 2007), and share specialized knowledge

(Salaff et al., 2007: 100). Entrepreneurs were asked if they opened their businesses within an ethnically identifiable neighbourhood, hired co-ethnic employees, used co-ethnic suppliers and targeted their businesses to customers from their ethnic group, because according to the literature, information about permits, laws, management practices, reliable suppliers, and promising business lines is typically obtained through personal networks linked to ethnic communities (Aldrich and Waldinger, 1990: 128). Immigrants who did not establish a business within the ethnic community were asked why they did not target their businesses to the Russian enclave community, whether they disliked doing business with Russian co-ethnics, and why they did not hire co-ethnic employees.

(2b) Financial Capital: Money and wealth are the two main forms of financial capital (Light and Gold, 2000: 84-5).

      According to the ethnic and class dimensions of entrepreneurship approach, motivated entrepreneurs need access to financial capital and other resources to take advantage of perceived opportunities (Aldrich and Zimmer, 1986: 3). Therefore, entrepreneurs were asked if they brought money with them from the former Soviet Union; they were also asked whether they immigrated to Toronto through Italy or Israel and if they worked in these countries. If so, had they accumulated money they could use as seed capital to open a business? Looking in the other direction they were asked if they were able to take advantage of the transition and establish successful businesses in Russia, which meant they were able to arrive in Toronto with financial capital. In Chapter 6, I also discuss how the immigrants chose where to obtain financing to determine if their human capital, in the form of years of education, work experience and high occupational skills were recognized by the banks and the government, or if they had to obtain financing from private investors or from ethnic community members. Table 9 (Sources of Financing) shows how many respondents received financing from banks, the ethnic community, private investors not part of the ethnic community, personal financing, or several sources.

(2c) Human Capital: Human capital refers to an individual's investment in personal productivity; education and work experience are the basic forms.

According to the ethnic and class dimensions of entrepreneurship approach, human capital as measured by education and work experience increases rates of entrepreneurship (Light and Gold, 2000: 87), aids business startups (Borjas, 1986, 1990; Sanders and Nee, 1996), and creates favourable conditions for long-term business success (Marger, 2001: 450; Portes et al., 2002: 288). In this study, I separated these two aspects of human capital into Russian and Canadian education and work experience. Table 3 (Education Attained by Immigrant Entrepreneurs in the Former Soviet Union) determines the types of degrees attained by the respondents. Table 4 (Work Experience Attained by Immigrant Entrepreneurs in the Former Soviet Union) shows how many respondents had fewer than 3 years and how many had more than 3 years of work experience in the former Soviet Union before coming to Toronto. Immigrants were also asked if they held jobs or opened businesses in other countries, such as Israel and Italy, because, as already noted, work experience in other countries influences entrepreneurship in Toronto. Table 6 (Work Experience Attained by Immigrant Entrepreneurs in Toronto) shows how many respondents had fewer than 5 years and how many had more than 5 years of work experience in Toronto before starting a business. Table 7 (Types of Jobs Held by Immigrant Entrepreneurs in Toronto) shows the types of jobs immigrants had before starting a business to determine where they acquired their work experience.

With respect to the second variable, education, I consider how the degrees attained by the immigrants correspond to their businesses. Immigrants educated in Toronto were asked if their education helped them get good positions in prominent firms, allowing them to develop the skills, knowledge, experience, and contacts required to start a business. Entrepreneurs were also asked how their experience in the Toronto labour market helped them develop the skills, knowledge, experience, and contacts required to start a business; I asked this question because all immigrants in the first cohort had limited access to relevant home country business experience because Soviet black market experience is different from Canadian business experience, and the latter is important to the success of a Canadian enterprise. Finally, they were asked if they attained any work experience outside the former Soviet Union or Toronto which helped them open a Canadian business.

(2d) Class-Specific Cultural Capital - Home Country Experience:
The occupational culture of the bourgeoisie includes the skills, knowledge, attitudes, and values transmitted in the course of socialization that bourgeoisies need to run a market economy; this is characteristic of bourgeoisies around the world and distinguishes bourgeois from non-bourgeois co-ethnics. Entrepreneurship is the occupational culture of bourgeoisies (Light and Gold, 2000: 92). Cultural capital, in the form of skills, knowledge, attitudes, and values needed for entrepreneurship can be obtained from the education system in Toronto, from experience in the labour market in Toronto, or from the education system in Russia, or from the black market economy in Russia, or from the market transition in Russia.

To measure cultural capital, I considered the skills and knowledge immigrants acquired from the education system, experience in the second economy or black market economy, the primary or command-administrative economy in the former Soviet Union, and the market transition in Russia. The Soviet experiences proved important in Toronto because people in the former Soviet Union were engaged in self-employed black market activity while working as salaried employees of the state where they learned socialist entrepreneurial skills (Kurkchiyan, 1999: 84). Immigrants were asked how much work experience they had and in which fields they worked before coming to Toronto to determine if they started businesses in their field of expertise in Toronto. They were asked which skills they learned while working as salaried employees of the state and while illegally involved in the black market economy (a principal source of income that was applied to legal entrepreneurship in Toronto).

3. Transnationalism Approach: According to the transnationalism approach, many migrants to different countries engage in transnational entrepreneurship. Drawing on transnational ties for social capital, they bring together resources from many institutional fields, making contacts from past professional relations in their country of origin. Bilingual immigrants with international social networks have natural advantages in trade promotion (Lever-Tracy et al., 1991: xi, 113 in Light, 2007: 90). They notice business opportunities generated at cultural frontiers and have the international social capital that supports international business

(Wong, 1998: 95 in Light, 2007:90). According to the literature
on transnationalism, immigrants can join previously unconnected
direct and indirect ties in their countries of origin and destination
(Landolt, 2001, in Salaff et al., 2007: 102), and globalization has
expanded the share of immigrants who notice and exploit international trading opportunities, making use of international social
capital (Fukuyama, 1995; Walton-Roberts and Hiebert, 1997;
Levitt, 2001: 62; Cohen, 1997: 176; Massey et al., 1993: 446 in
Light, 2007: 90).

The variables used to measure transnationalism in this
study include engagement in transnational business practices and
possession of transnational social networks. Entrepreneurs were
asked if they lived in Russia during the transition or returned to
Russia at that time; these immigrants were more likely to have
transnational social networks, in the form of connections with
state enterprise directors and business groups that took over large
formerly state-owned enterprises. They were asked if their
Toronto companies had contracts with state firms which provided
the capital investment they needed. They were also asked if they
received information about promising business avenues through
their networks in Russia and Toronto and if they found reliable
suppliers in Russia where they could import a variety of materials
at low prices, making a large profit by selling them in North
America.

The entrepreneurs were asked if they achieved success by
importing/exporting raw material, semi-processed products, manufactured durable and non-durable goods, by acting as intermediaries between potential buyers in North America and suppliers
in the former Soviet Union, or by setting up transnational manufacturing firms with production based in the republics of the
former Soviet Union and distribution in North America. The literature on transnationalism and entrepreneurship has focused on
these varieties of transnational entrepreneurship (Portes and
Guarnizo, 1991; Gold, 2001; Itzigsohn et al., 1999; Landolt,
2001; Levitt, 2001; Light et al., 2002). Table 10 (Paths to Entrepreneurship) determines whether their paths to entrepreneurship
influenced their likelihood of establishing a transnational business. I also asked whether the immigrants made frequent trips to
the former Soviet Union to conduct business while their families
stayed in Toronto; this helps measure whether these transnational

entrepreneurs have undertaken international income-seeking endeavours not merely to survive economically but to elevate their socioeconomic status.

4. Paths to Entrepreneurship: People with varied amounts of class and ethnic resources have diverse paths to entrepreneurship. In this book I focus on the following five paths to entrepreneurship to explain why immigrant groups turn to self-employment.

(a) Cultural Explanations: The orthodox (Light, 1980) interpretation of cultural entrepreneurship assumes that different ethnic groups have been endowed with different cultural and psychological qualities which account for their success or propensity to engage in business enterprise. The sojourner hypothesis, an aspect of the orthodox cultural theory, asserts (Bonacich, 1973) that some immigrant groups, have a high proportion of members who do not intend to settle permanently in the host society but plan to return to the homeland. They migrate to make money; this explains why they turn to self-employment. Light's (1980) reactive interpretation of cultural entrepreneurship considers the collective nature of the response to structural disadvantage. Reactive cultural theories argue that cultural traits are important in encouraging business activity when other factors in the social environment make business enterprises appealing and viable (Gold, 1995a: 56).

(b) Disadvantage Explanations: Disadvantage theory maintains that certain immigrant groups go into business because they are disadvantaged in the general labour market due to their poor English, inferior education, lack of host country credentials and licenses, and their experience of discrimination (Kim, 1981).

(c) Business Background Explanations: Business background theory (Light, 1984; Portes and Bach, 1985) asserts that the penchant for self-employment shown by certain immigrant groups is linked to a concentration of business backgrounds in the country of origin.

(d) Ethnic Economy Explanations: Ethnic economy theory claims that participation in the ethnic sub-economy promotes self-

employment because entrepreneurs receive assistance from co-ethnics (Portes and Bach, 1985), who help them get jobs in co-ethnic firms and then help them start a business (Bonacich and Modell, 1980).

(e) Opportunity Explanations: Opportunity theory says that when immigrants are working in salaried jobs and an opportunity comes up to start a business, they may opt to leave the salaried position. After looking at such things as the number of businesses already in the field, technological requirements, and capital requirements, if they find the market is underserved, they open a company to serve market demands (Aldrich and Waldinger, 1990).

I will now discuss some indicators and variables I used to determine which path respondents took to entrepreneurship. In Table 5 (Reasons for Leaving the Former Soviet Union), I determine how many respondents left the former Soviet Union because there were no opportunities in their field, they were experiencing discrimination, they wanted to create a better life for themselves and their children, or they didn't want to live in a communist system. Each plays a role in the path taken to entrepreneurship. Immigrants were asked if they held jobs or opened businesses in other countries, such as Israel and Italy, before immigrating to Toronto. According to the business background theory, such work experience will influence entrepreneurship. They were asked if they were able to take advantage of the transition and establish successful businesses in Russia, allowing them to come to Toronto with business experience. In Table 7 (Types of Jobs Held by Immigrant Entrepreneurs in Toronto), I determine what types of jobs immigrants held before starting a business to determine how this may have affected the path to entrepreneurship.

Table 8 (Paths Taken by Immigrants to Entrepreneurship) shows the reasons why immigrants left their professional jobs to start businesses. If they chose entrepreneurship because they identified closely with and were socially and culturally attached to their ethnic group, this supported the orthodox cultural theory of entrepreneurship (Light, 1980). If they chose entrepreneurship because they wanted to make enough money in Toronto to return to Russia, this supported the sojourner hypothesis (Bonacich, 1973). If they opted for entrepreneurship as a collective response to structural disadvantage and they perceived and experienced discrimination, this provided support for the reactive cultural theory of entrepreneurship (Light, 1980). If immigrants selected entrepreneurship because they experienced disadvantages in the labour market as a result of a lack of Canadian education or their credentials from the former Soviet Union were not accepted in Canada, this supported the disadvantage theory of entrepreneurship (Kim, 1981; Min, 1988). If they indicated that they chose entrepreneurship because they had accumulated business experience and were self-employed before coming to Canada, this provided support for the business background theory of entrepreneurship (Light, 1984; Bonacich, 1973). If immigrants chose entrepreneurship because they participated in the ethnic economy and members from the co-ethnic community helped them with advice and resources to start their business, this backed up the ethnic economy theory of entrepreneurship (Bonacich and Modell, 1980; Lovell-Troy, 1980; Portes and Bach, 1985; Wilson and Portes, 1980). If they preferred entrepreneurship because they found opportunities within the organization where they were working on a salary to serve unfulfilled market demands by starting a business, this supported the opportunity theory of entrepreneurship (Aldrich and Waldinger, 1990: 116).

In Chapter 6, I discuss how human capital, social capital, and opportunities differed for the five paths to entrepreneurship taken by immigrants from both cohorts. As noted, Table 9 (Sources of Financing) shows where they got their money to start a business. Entrepreneurs were also asked if they had taken employment with co-ethnics with validated credentials while they were waiting to validate their own credentials; according to the ethnic economy theory, immigrants who are unable to go into business shortly after arrival take jobs in firms owned by co-ethnics; in return for loyalty and hard work, the owner will aid employees in times of emergency and provide opportunities for advancement, such as helping start a business (Cobas, 1986: 104). In Chapter 6, I also discuss how entrepreneurs gained experience in the Toronto labour market; I note how this experience helped them develop the skills, knowledge, and contacts necessary to start a Canadian business. In Table 10 (Paths to Entrepreneurship and Establishing Transnational Businesses), I determine whether the paths that they took to entrepreneurship influenced their likelihood of establishing a transnational business by finding out how many from each path started a transnational business.

Internal Validity

I tested for internal validity, checking whether results were credible, by comparing my findings to other studies of entrepreneurship with similar concepts and theoretical perspectives.

External Validity

I tested for external validity, the degree to which results can be applied to other contexts or settings, by being as explicit as possible about how I conducted the study and the contexts within which I collected data. This will help other researchers determine whether and to what extent my results can be applied in other contexts. However, generalization is not the main goal of my research; rather, it is exploratory, and the primary goal is to determine how various theories about entrepreneurship can help explain the specific case of immigrants from the former Soviet Union turning to entrepreneurship.

Reliability

I tested for reliability, whether findings can be repeated or replicated by another researcher, by first checking whether findings were accurate by sending some interviews back to the respondents for comments. Interviews were transcribed ad verbatim, and all respondents agreed that they were transcribed accurately. Second, because I had a research assistant who read and coded the interview transcripts with me, we were able to check each other's work for accuracy. Lastly, I have thoroughly described how I conducted the study and have explained my methodological choices.

Objectivity

I tested for objectivity, the degree to which results are unbiased, by first checking and rechecking the data. I compared data from different interviews to see if the information presented was consistent. Second, I wanted to ensure that my evidence was not merely used to confirm my preconceptions and theoretical approaches; therefore, I sought out evidence that contradicted some of my preconceptions and theories. In the empirical chapters, I discuss empirical data which contradict some theories and make certain cases unique. Lastly, I consulted with colleagues throughout the process so that I could get a critical perspective on my research findings.

Limitations of the Study

As only 32 people were interviewed, findings cannot be generalized to all immigrants from the former Soviet Union who established businesses in Toronto. There are also variables that I do not control for, such as the place of departure from the former Soviet Union, or the effect of age and gender. I deal with these limitations by focusing my study on two cohorts of immigrants, those who immigrated to Toronto in the late 1970s and early 1980s and those who arrived in the late 1980s and 1990s. Both come from similar socioeconomic backgrounds, allowing me to compare how their success in two phases of entrepreneurship (pre-start-up and start-up) is influenced by a combination of social capital, financial capital, human capital, and home country experience. A final limitation is that the study is only focused on Toronto, so the findings may not extend to other cities. However, as I studied entrepreneurs throughout the entire Greater Toronto Metropolitan area, I explored differences between those who established businesses in downtown areas and those in suburban areas, so the sample is not homogenous.

NOTES

[1] Appendix B is available at www.desitterpublications.com/TransnationalEntrepreneurs.html.

[2] Appendix A is available at www.desitterpublications.com/TransnationalEntrepreneurs.html.

[3] Those with access to sociopolitical capital in Russia enjoyed higher chances of creating viable businesses because they could obtain political and administrative favours and protections (Yang, 2002: 143).

CHAPTER 3

Literature Review

Introduction

I drew upon three bodies of literature to examine how social capital, financial capital, human capital, and home country experience, specifically experience in the former Soviet communist economy and the transitional economy affected Russian entrepreneurs at each stage of business development in Toronto. More specifically, I considered literature on (1) the transitional economy; (2) ethnic and class dimensions of entrepreneurship; and (3) transnationalism.

I selected the tripartite approach because individual-level explanations that focus on a certain kind of personality and competence are inadequate in explaining the founding and success of a business. A tradition of economic thought considers the entrepreneur a creative force (RonaTas and Lengyel, 1997: 5), arguing that the true entrepreneur makes creative decisions that others might not make, and sees opportunities that others might miss (RonaTas and Lengyel, 1997: 5). The focus on personality traits links achievement aspirations, individualism, competitive drive and risk taking, the work ethic, and future business success (Salaff, Greve, and Wong, 2001: 11). For instance, Hong Kong's rapid development is often explained by personality and cultural characteristics that support successful Chinese entrepreneurship (Redding, 1990).[1] Because of their similar backgrounds, individual level explanations may lead to the expectation that new Russian immigrants are prime candidates for ethnic entrepreneurship, but personality and culture do not explain how people who grew up in a similar environment in the former Soviet Union have different rates of entrepreneurship after immigrating to Toronto.

I also selected the three areas of literature because past studies of ethnic businesses have focused on self-employment participation patterns (Light and Rosenstein, 1995b, in Luk, 2007), economic returns of participating in the ethnic economy (Portes and Zhou, 1996, in Luk, 2007), and social networks among ethnic businesses (Saunders and Nee, 1996, in Luk, 2007). These studies have not paid enough attention to the context of the country of origin and the role of the global economy on facilitating the setting up of businesses and the successful running of businesses in the host country.

In the literature review, I outline the theoretical assumptions of each approach, and present their empirical findings. I use the central postulates of each of these three approaches to extrapolate explanations regarding how these four major factors influenced and shaped business practice and success for immigrants from the former Soviet Union.

1. Transitional Economy Approach

According to the transitional economy approach, institutional changes determine the strategies of economic actors by virtue of the opportunities and constraints that they provide (Pontusson, 1995: 119). This perspective focuses on how the environment influences entrepreneurial activity. For example, Victor Nee (1996: 945) views the structural changes that follow the dismantling of the command economy as primarily creating opportunities and incentives for entrepreneurial activity. According to Nee (1991: 267), "the growth of markets expands the range of opportunities outside the boundaries of the distributive economy, changing the structures of opportunity and incentives and stimulating entrepreneurship." Transitional economy approaches argue that structural and institutional features of economies cause elite advantage to vary (Gerber, 2002b; Wu and Xie, 2003; Zhou, 2000).

Institutional theory, a variant of the transitional economy approach, emphasizes the influence of the social, political and cultural environments on entrepreneurial activity (Hill, Martin, and Vidinova, 1997: 231). This perspective is particularly appropriate for the analysis of transformation in post-socialist societies (Scott, 1995) where economic, political and social institutions have been intentionally transformed in the movement from socialism to capitalism (Hill, Martin, and Vidinova, 1997: 231), but employment cultures and structures deriving from the socialist era continue to influence expectations and patterns of behaviour in present entrepreneurial practices (Hill, Martin, and Vidinova, 1997: 232).

In the sociological literature, researchers draw two contra-dictory conclusions about who will take advantage of the new market institutions, who will benefit most from them, and as a con-sequence, how this institutional change will transform the social structure of post-communist societies. They offer contradictory suggestions as to who will become an entrepreneur and who will thrive in a post-communist transitional economy. Given these con-tradictions, it is interesting to consider how the transitional econ-omy influenced and shaped the business practice and success of immigrants from the former Soviet Union in Toronto, specifically during the pre-start and start-up phase of the business.

Elite Reproduction Theory

Elemer Hankiss was the first to point out that transforming the old cadre elite into new propertied bourgeoisie might guarantee a safe and peaceful transition from communism to capitalism. The *Political Capitalism theory* states that people in the *nomen-klatura* before 1989 were able to retain power and privilege during the post-communist transition by converting their former political power into private wealth (Eyal, Szelenyi, and Townsley, 1998: 115). Agreeing with Hankiss, Szalai suggested that "large enterprise management began to transform into a propertied bourgeoisie during the early stages of post-communist develop-ment through a series of management buy-outs" (Szalai, 1990: 169-176 in Szelenyi, Szelenyi and Kovach, 1995: 698). The advantages of the old communist elite were based on political assets and social networks. During the transition, cadres were able to convert political capital to economic capital (Hankiss, 1990; Stark, 1990; Staniszkis, 1991), thus entering a new prop-ertied class. They were also able to use old social networks to amass capital gains. According to this hypothesis, party member-ship positively affected the transition to entrepreneurship after 1989 (Robert and Bukodi, 2000: 152). According to the elite reproduction thesis, the majority of the members of the elite who were already directing state firms continued to occupy elite posi-tions in economic enterprises after the transition (Hanley, Yer-shova, and Anderson 1995: 666).[2]

In Russia, the relative absence of constraints on asset appropriation due to regime instability and an unregulated and rapidly occurring privatization program created a new propertied and corporate elite of incumbent officials with greater opportunities to maintain control of public assets as they were privatized or to obtain personal ownership of assets and enter the emerging market economy with large business advantages (Walder, 2003: 907-8). These managers moved into a newly privatized business oligarchy with origins in the Communist-era elite. Elite insiders in the former Soviet Union had almost exclusive access to the kinds of financial instruments, asset transactions, price manipulation, international dealings, and information through which property changed form and large concentrations of wealth changed hands (Walder, 2003: 904; McFaul, 1995). Almost two-thirds of the private business elite in 1993 who had acquired majority shares in two-thirds of privatized and privatizing firms were former members of the Communist Party (Hanley, Yershova, and Anderson, 1995: 654-62; McFaul, 1995: 210) and a small number of wealthy oligarchs assumed control of certain key sectors of the economy in large, capital intensive firms, such as extensive oil reserves and mineral deposits that require large capital investments to develop (often from abroad), and many of these former state firms entered contracts with foreign companies (McFaul, 1995: 210; Hanley, Yershova, and Anderson, 1995: 654-62; Goldman, 2003: 98-122).

Russian immigrants who were able to establish connections with regime insiders or wealthy oligarchs during the transition were more likely to establish successful transnational businesses in Russia. They were more likely to convert their political capital into economic capital in Russia, which they then transferred to Toronto.[3]

Circulation of Elites Theory

The *Circulation of Elites theory* (*Changing Elite thesis*) posits that individuals or their children who lost power with the rise of communism may have regained power after the fall of communism; the impact of Communist Party membership would be insignificant or even negative. In contrast to the elite reproduction theory, the circulation of elites theory suggests that the main beneficiaries of the transition are those who were in less privileged positions when the transition began. The transition results in a major change in the economic elite and creates a new class of entrepreneurs.

Two arguments have been proposed to explain elite circulation. First, Szelenyi's interrupted embourgeoisement theory predicts the emergence of a new economic elite from below. The interrupted embourgeoisement theory suggests that people that grew up during the Soviet command-style economy who were illegally involved in the black market economy where they learned skills in entrepreneurship were more likely to re-emerge as legal entrepreneurs when the transition occurred. Second, Nee's theory of structural compensation maintains that reforms in the direction of marketization create new avenues for mobility and provide an alternative to bureaucratic advancement (1989: 666-67). Szelenyi's (1988) interrupted embourgeoisement theory and Nee's (1989, 1991) theory of structural compensation both suggest that cadres will not be the new entrepreneurs (Rona-Tas, 1994: 46).

Szelenyi and Nee also suggest that higher education will prove more critical for business success abroad than connections to the communist party for immigrants coming from transition economies, meaning that more highly educated Russian immigrants may make more effective entrepreneurs in Toronto.

Russian Transition Economy Promotes Double Entrepreneurship

In a transition economy such as Russia, entrepreneurship incorporates two dimensions, a double entrepreneurship. The first is economic: an entrepreneur has to be innovative in identifying or creating a promising market. The second is sociopolitical: a successful entrepreneur must be talented in making use of institutional rules, such as government regulations, and manipulating the rules. Thus, double entrepreneurship refers to the interaction of institutional effects and entrepreneurial creativity (Yang, 2002: 134).

According to the double entrepreneurship perspective, people who became successful entrepreneurs during the transition to a market economy were both innovative and creative, identifying and creating new markets for goods manufactured in the state-run economy before the transition and discovering what goods could be imported from the West to Russia. They also had to make use of and manipulate institutional rules; when the government introduced new laws to promote the establishment of private enterprises, the people who had connections within the government and/or knew how to manipulate the laws were more likely to succeed.

Entrepreneurship in communist command economies has a high level of legitimacy but suffers from a lack of autonomy in exploiting rules. Command economies survive by demanding strict conformity. Having strict regulations, however, does not mean that there is no room for entrepreneurship. Entrepreneurs in the former USSR were highly innovative in carrying out state plans of building an industry and launching out new enterprises. In fact, some have argued that socialist states were dependent upon such entrepreneurship to maintain their political dominance (Yang, 2002: 139).

The traditional economic role of the state under socialism changed during the transition. Companies have been liberated from state direction and are free agents in free markets (Hill, Martin, and Vidinova, 1997: 236). In contrast, in well-established market economies, institutional boundaries for economic activities are so well established that, although entrepreneurs could extract maximum profits from rule exploitation, in most situations they play within legitimate fields (Yang, 2002: 139). In this sense, transforming a socialist economy into a market economy is a process of turning double entrepreneurship into legal entrepreneurship. In transitional economies, double entrepreneurship is about simultaneously getting maximum economic rewards and taking minimum sociopolitical risks in a time of changing institutions. Entrepreneurs seek promising economic niches from outside current institutional boundaries, but they also must acquire political and administrative protection from within previous and current institutional boundaries. Successful entrepreneurs in Russia were able to connect business opportunities in the market to gaps between institutional rules so that opportunities could be seized without provoking political, administrative, or public-relations problems (Yang, 2002: 140).[4]

The double entrepreneurship perspective suggests that in Russia's transition economy, access to sociopolitical capital for Russian immigrant entrepreneurs leads to higher chances of successfully establishing transnational businesses in Russia. By extension, the likelihood of entrepreneurial success for both cohorts of immigrants from the former Soviet Union should depend to some extent on the alliances forged at the beginning of the transition process between these immigrants and (a) state elites; (b) financial sector elites; (c) entrepreneurs; and (d) foreign firms.

Transitional Economy Approach: Suggestions for Russian Immigrant Entrepreneurs

Education plays an important role in status allocation in socialist systems; therefore, Russian immigrants come to Toronto with a great deal of human capital. There are greater incentives for individual effort in market transactions in Toronto than in the socialist system, which will result in higher returns on education, so well educated immigrants will have an advantage as entrepreneurs. Furthermore, if they were part of the new propertied and corporate elite and established successful businesses in Russia, they are likely to have brought financial capital with them. As a result, they do not need to depend on ethnic resources or ethnic-based cooperation because they will have the necessary class-based endowments of skill, education, and capital. A note of caution: this applies mostly to the second cohort, as the first left during the communist regime and is less likely to have amassed financial resources. However, immigrant entrepreneurs who grew up during the Soviet command-style economy who were illegally involved in the black market economy learned skills in entrepreneurship, such as making use of and manipulating institutional rules, and are more likely to re-emerge as legal entrepreneurs in Toronto.

The structural changes that followed the dismantling of the command economy created opportunities and incentives for entrepreneurial activity for both cohorts. Entrepreneurs from the first cohort who returned to Russia during the transition or immigrants from the second cohort who lived in Russia at that time obtained cultural capital, in the form of skills, knowledge, attitudes, and values.[5]

Limitation of Transitional Economy Approach

A limitation of the transitional economy approach is that it only focuses on how structures shape the interests of economic actors and how institutions determine the strategies of economic actors (Yang, 2002: 141). It does not address the role of ethnic and class resources, such as ethnic networks and social, financial, human and cultural capital, in starting and running a business. Therefore, I will now turn to the ethnic and class dimensions of entrepreneurship approach to demonstrate how entrepreneurs use ethnic and class resources to start a business.

2. Ethnic and Class Dimensions of Entrepreneurship Approach

Factors that have been conventionally identified as directing immigrants towards entrepreneurship, such as ethnic and class resources, are relevant in shaping business success. Economic sociologists have focused on group resources derived from particular ethnic and class embeddedness (Light, 1972, 1984, in Ley, 2006: 744). According to Light (1984) and Waldinger, Aldrich and Ward (1990), the inclination toward business and the relative success of entrepreneurial efforts by immigrants is a balance of class and ethnic resources (Light, 1984; Waldinger et al., 1990). An emphasis on ethnic resources expands the work on social capital to focus on supportive elements of trust, networking and mutual aid available within homogenous minorities, a significant factor, for example, in the development of enterprise among the Cuban population in Miami (Portes and Bach, 1985; Portes and Sensenbrener, 1993, in Ley, 2006: 744).[6] All groups possess class resources, which include financial, human, and cultural capital and ethnic resources, but the balance varies from group to group.

Ethnic Resources: Ethnic Social Networks and Social Capital

Ethnic resources are socio-cultural features of a group which co-ethnic entrepreneurs actively utilize in business or from which their business passively benefits. Typical ethnic resources include relationships of trust, ethnic-derived social capital, native language fluency, a middleman heritage, entrepreneurial values and attitudes, rotating credit associations, multiplex social networks, sojourning orientation, social networks and other characteristics based in group tradition and experience that connect the entire group (Light and Gold, 2000: 102-105). Ethnic resources contribute to economic survival and achievement among groups lacking class-based endowments of skill, education, or capital (Light and Gold, 2000: 106). Ethnic-based cooperation delivers resources to persons without the financial or educational means otherwise required for their acquisition (Light and Gold, 2000: 108). Collective resources, including trust and cooperation, help group members overcome the disadvantages of outsider status and maximize the value of their human and financial capital to achieve economic stability or betterment.[7] Research has shown that ethnic resources, such as enforceable trust and multiple social networks, encourage and support the founding of new business firms (Light and Rosenstein, 1995a: 202).

It is clear from the literature that new businesses arise from social networks. Social networks are the social context of businesses and can be activated according to need (Granovetter, 1985; Burt, 1992). Ethnic resources include social networks, and these help to start, develop and run businesses, and further entrepreneurship (Salaff, Greve, and Wong, 2001: 12). Schumpeter's conception of the entrepreneur states that "the function of the entrepreneur is to reform or revolutionize the pattern of production by exploiting an invention or ... by opening up a new source of supply of materials or a new outlet for products, by reorganizing an industry" (Schumpeter, 1975: 132). Placing Schumpeter's individual entrepreneur in a network of social connections permits specification of the sorts of structural environments in which innovative and creative entrepreneurs are more likely to succeed.

Entrepreneurs require information, capital, skills, labour and distribution channels to start business activities. While they hold some of these resources themselves, they often complement their resources by accessing their contacts (Aldrich and Zimmer, 1986; Cooper, Folta, and Woo, 1995; Hansen, 1995), seeking information, advice, social support and financial capital (Batjargal, 2003: 535-6; Aldrich and Zimmer, 1986; Shane and Cable, 2002; Uzzi, 1999). Newcomers intending to do business can draw on social networks for advice, information about business opportunities, access to credit, and customers, which are central to entrepreneurship during pre-start (motivation and idea development) and start-up (planning and organizing the founding of a firm) (Aldrich, 1999; Light, 1972, 1992, in Salaff et al., 2007: 102).

Ethnic networks include ethnic business associations, informal and formal credit groups, co-ethnic clientele, and co-ethnic workers. Such networks are important resources in the establishment and operation of firms (Light, 1972; Light and Gold, 2000; Waldinger et al., 1990). They provide what Granovetter (1985) has called "embeddedness', that is, networks of social relations that engender mutual trust and enforcement of norms. As Granovetter explains, embeddedness becomes especially powerful in conducting business (Marger, 2001: 441). Much of the success of immigrant entrepreneurs is attributed to their ability to utilize ethnic resources not available to non-ethnic business owners (Marger, 2001: 444). For example, research on Korean retailers in the United States (Min, 1988) shows that linkages to co-ethnic suppliers is advantageous because transactions are made in the ethnic language, and co-ethnic wholesalers are more flexible on credit (Aldrich and Waldinger, 1990: 129).

Three sorts of ethnic social networks play an important role in business startup. First, entrepreneurship runs in the family in many countries (Hamilton, 1991, Hsiung, 1996, in Salaff et al., 2007: 100). Those with relatives and friends who are entrepreneurs are more likely to become entrepreneurs (Djankov et al., 2005: 588). Second, co-ethnic colleagues can give even more useful help than family for those who sell professional goods and services (Birley, 1985; Marger, 1992; Westhead, 1995, in Salaff et al., 2007: 100). Co-ethnic colleagues from the community, school, or earlier jobs can provide a large social base for information, assistance, and favours of many kinds (Stark, 1986; Borocz, 1993, in Rona-Tas and Lengyel, 1997: 12). They also provide new business entrants with expertise, lines of credit, and links to suppliers and customers (Leonard and Tibrewal, 1993; Waldinger, 1986, in Salaff et al., 2007), and share specialized knowledge (Salaff et al., 2007: 100). Third, the most salient feature of early business efforts by immigrant groups is their dependence on an ethnic community (Chu, 1996; Portes, 1998). Without these supportive networks within the ethnic community, immigrant entrepreneurs have a narrow scope which limits their business (Salaff et al., 2007: 99).[8]

Established migrants become social resources. An immigrant community creates demand for ethnic products (Aldrich and Zimmer, 1986, in Salaff et al., 2007: 101). In the ethnic community, employers can find new employees, and customers can find the ethnic products they seek (Bonacich, 1973; Light, 1992;

Sanders and Nee, 1996; Waldinger, 1994; Zhou, 1992, in Salaff et al., 2007: 101).

The relationship between immigrant employers and workers and the ability to hire workers in the ethnic community has long been noted as an asset to ethnic business owners (Glazer and Moynihan, 1963; Bailey and Waldinger, 1991; Waldinger, 1985). The supporting ethnic community can also draw together resources for investment. Portes and Sensenbrenner (1993) argue that social closure within immigrant communities gives individuals greater access to financial resources. Immigrant entrepreneurs are thus able to finance projects via ethnic-based cohesive ties (Aldrich and Kim, 2007: 158). Information about permits, laws, management practices, sources of capital or potential investors, reliable suppliers, potential markets for goods and services and promising business lines is typically obtained through owners' personal networks that are specifically linked to their ethnic communities (Aldrich and Waldinger, 1990: 128; Aldrich and Zimmer, 1986: 17). According to Aldrich and Waldinger (1990), the ethnic community constitutes the first source of support and business opportunities encountered by immigrant entrepreneurs. Support comes from the large network of ethnic institutions, including other businesses, in the form of capital (Aldrich and Zimmer, 1986: 14-15). Some research has shown that immigrant entrepreneurs make little use of government networks and support services or of the host society's business associations; more commonly, they turn to their communities, friends, relatives or family members for assistance, such as loans (Filion et al., 2004: 298-99).

In short, the ethnic community offers advantages, including access to a pool of potential investors, experienced entrepreneurs, low-priced manpower, social and emotional support, and the possibility of operating in the entrepreneur's native language and in a familiar social and cultural environment (Filion et al, 2004: 300). Menzies and associates (2003) found that the use of co-ethnic employees and family members as workers, the use of co-ethnic markets as customers and suppliers and the use of family members and co-ethnics as primary sources of financing are common. Sizeable personal networks of entrepreneurs within the ethnic community increases the likelihood of locating clients and suppliers and purchasing raw materials and other production inputs at lower prices, allowing entrepreneurs to convert these social bonds into revenue growth (Aldrich and Waldinger, 1990: 128).

Ethnic networks can generate *social capital* within the ethnic community (Filion et al., 2004: 300). Social capital is a resource embedded in social networks and groups, and people can create opportunities by obtaining resources from their contacts (Burt, 1992; Mouw, 2006: 79; Coleman, 1988; Lin, 2001). Portes defines social capital as the ability of actors to secure benefits by virtue of their membership in social networks or other social structures, stressing that whereas economic capital is in people's bank accounts and human capital is inside their heads, social capital inheres in the structure of their relationships (1998: 7). Social capital refers to the social connections people can use to obtain resources they would otherwise acquire through expending their human or financial capital (Aldrich and Kim, 2005: 41).

Using their social ties skillfully, entrepreneurs can reap substantial returns on their social capital and boost their chances of commercial success (Aldrich and Kim, 2005: 5). Burt (1992) asserts that having the right connections constitutes a form of social capital and determines entrepreneurs' chances of success. Put otherwise, social capital is the set of connections that help people establish and run businesses (Bourdieu, 1986). It refers to norms of trust, obligation, and reciprocity established through membership in social networks (Coleman, 1988; Light and Gold, 2000; Portes, 1995; Portes and Sensenbrenner, 1993). Social capital facilitates job and status attainment (Lin et al., 1981; Marsden and Hurlbert, 1988), has positive effects on a firm's performance (Baker, 1990), enhances individuals' power (Krackhardt, 1990) and career mobility (Podolny and Baron, 1997), and impacts CEO compensation (Belliveau et al., 1996), revenue and managerial performance (Galunic and Moran 1999).

Entrepreneurs make extensive and important use of ethnic social networks when starting and running a business. Social capital constitutes their ability to mobilize those resources on demand (Portes, 1995). In the literature on minority entrepreneurship, social capital is illustrated by the use of co-ethnic employees, markets, suppliers, community sources of capital, advice and information, as well as membership in ethnic and/or community organizations. An ethnic community's social capital results in extended credit (Portes and Sensenbrenner, 1993, in

Fong and Luk, 2007b: 149), pooled financial resources (such as the credit rotation associations suggested by Light (1972) (Fong and Luk, 2007b: 149), and lower labour costs (Sanders and Nee, 1987, in Fong and Luk, 2007b: 149) for entrepreneurs.[9] Ethnic groups regularly provide their members with financial capital through personal loans, relying on reputation and enduring relationships as collateral. Within ethnic settings, actors rely on social capital created by common membership to reach economic ends (Light and Gold, 2000: 110).

Ethnic Resources: Social Networks and Social Capital - Homophily Principle

Social scientists have extensively documented the generalization that "birds of a feather flock together" (Almack, 1922; Bott, 1928; Wellman, 1926). *Homophily* is the central principle behind these consistent findings. The large literature on the principle of social homophily (see McPherson et al., 2001 for a review) suggests many dimensions along which individuals with similar characteristics socialize with each other (Mouw, 2006: 81). Studies range from research on friendships (Moffitt, 2001; Manski, 2000) and teams (Ruef, Aldrich, and Carter, 2003) to cultural and voluntary associations (Emerson and Smith, 2000; McPherson and Smith-Lovin, 1986) and business organizations (Ibarra, 1995; Kanter, 1977).

Homophily occurs when people with similar characteristics are attracted and when the structures of the social world make it difficult for people with dissimilar characteristics to associate (Blau, 1977; McPherson, Smith-Lovin, and Cook, 2001). For example, highly educated individuals are likely to have social networks consisting of others with high education (Nakao, 2004: 90, 96).[10]

A fundamental claim of the social capital literature is that the characteristics and resources of friends, contacts, and groups affect individual outcomes. However, because, for the most part, individuals choose their friends and groups, some of the positive correlation may simply be because similar people tend to associate with one another (Mouw, 2006: 81). Using data from the Panel Study of Entrepreneurial Dynamics (PSED), a representative national survey of 830 people who reported they were in the process of trying to start a new business in 1999-2000, Ruef et al. (2003) showed that two principles dominated team formation: homophily and familiarity. In the PSED, teams were extremely homogenous with respect to occupation. The principle of familiarity asserts that people who associate with one another are more likely to continue the association in other circumstances. Research shows that people rarely establish relationships with those they meet by chance (Grossetti, 2005). In the PSED, 51 percent of teams were based on colleagues whom they know and trust, the self-reinforcing pattern of homophily in social relations (Aldrich and Kim, 2007: 158-160).

The characteristics that bring people together can be ascribed and thus not easily changed by individual choice, such as demographic background (age, ethnicity, and sex), or achieved and thus potentially open to change. In practice, relationships are formed through combinations of ascribed and achieved characteristics (Aldrich and Kim, 2005: 10). Individuals fall short of maximizing potential gains from their social networks because of their propensity to associate with similar people and their difficulties in managing diverse networks (Aldrich and Kim, 2005: 43). Individuals' networks often lack significant diversity (Blau, 1977; McPherson, Smith-Lovin, and Cook, 2001)[11] and homogeneity emerges naturally in locally dense networks (Aldrich and Kim, 2005: 42). In the language of social networks, the friends of our friends are already our friends, rather than strangers (Aldrich and Kim, 2005: 5).

New people wishing to join an existing local network face potential barriers when they do not share common experiences and interests with current members (Aldrich and Kim, 2007: 153). People face an issue of trust when they go beyond relationships with those already known to them (Aldrich and Kim, 2005: 6). Family members, friends, work colleagues, and other close acquaintances constitute the most trusted social relations (Aldrich and Kim, 2005: 17). Network closure has some benefits for entrepreneurs: people share knowledge and feel secure. But the benefits of social capital fall mainly to entrepreneurs who are able to develop a broader, more diverse network (Aldrich and Kim, 2005: 7, 42). Successful entrepreneurs could avoid network closure by cultivating and maintaining indirect and weak ties, building a hybrid portfolio of ties varying in strength (Aldrich and Kim, 2005: 43).

Class Resources: Financial Capital

Light (1984) defines *class resources* as private property in the form of production and distribution, human capital, money to invest, and bourgeois values, attitudes, knowledge, and skills transmitted intergenerationally. Multiple social networks among the upper class permit individual members to connect with business partners through mutual friends and acquaintances. Class resources have become increasingly important with the rise in the international migration of skilled workers, professionals and business people. Successful immigrant entrepreneurialism needs an entrance into non-ethnic and non-local markets in growth sectors of the economy, and this requires class rather than ethnic resources (Ley, 2006: 747). Many authors have noted the importance of class resources in immigrant entrepreneurialism (Marger, 2001; Wong, 2002). In a study of Indo-Canadian entrepreneurs, Marger (1989) determined that class resources were integral to the formation of business, and Li (1992) reached the same conclusion with Chinese immigrant entrepreneurs. The class resources include financial capital, human capital and professional or entrepreneurial experience (Ley, 2006: 745).

Capital is any store of value that assists production and productivity. The classic form of capital is *financial capital*, an important aspect of class resources. Money and wealth are the two main forms (Light and Gold, 2000: 84-5). Motivated entrepreneurs need access to capital to take advantage of perceived opportunities (Aldrich and Zimmer, 1986: 3).

Class Resources: Human Capital

Human capital, another component of class resources, refers to an individual's investment in personal productivity. Education and work experience are its basic forms. Human capital as measured by education and work experience aids business startups (Borjas, 1986, 1990; Sanders and Nee, 1996). High levels of human capital create favourable conditions for long-term business success (Marger, 2001: 450) and play a role in immigrant business success (Portes et al., 2002: 288). Evidence shows that among all ethno-racial groups and categories, human capital increases rates of entrepreneurship (Light and Gold, 2000: 87). People with higher educational levels have higher self-employment rates than those with lower average educational levels. Even among business owners, additional human capital increases the likelihood of owning a bigger business (Light and Gold, 2000: 88).

Portes and Zhou (1999) show that human capital does not explain the superior entrepreneurship of four national origin groups (Chinese, Japanese, Koreans, and Cubans). Human and financial capital do not guarantee optimal entrepreneurship. Nor do money and human capital explain intergroup differences in entrepreneurial responsiveness. Therefore, it is necessary to look at the internal characteristics of groups to explain persistent intergroup differences. Some of these differences are cultural; others are not.

Class Resources: Class-Specific Cultural Capital

Different classes have different forms of capital. Some have financial capital, others have human capital, and still others have both. Some classes have financial and human capital, but do not know how to use them. The business class, especially entrepreneurs, have class-specific cultural capital – the knowledge of how to use their resources to establish and run successful businesses.

In addition to money, which confers the ability to buy human capital, affluent people have a class culture that encourages them to want human capital. This class-specific cultural capital furnishes an outlook that broadly supports educational attainment. Pierre Bourdieu (1989) calls this a *habitus*. A class culture's encouragement of education extends to the habitus and to financial means (Light and Gold, 2000: 90).

Cultural capital is a class resource often defined as competence. Bourdieu (1986), the developer of the concept of cultural capital, defines it "as competence in a society's high status culture". In Bourdieu's formulation, people acquire cultural capital in the family and formal schooling. Education can help people to accumulate human capital, and cultural capital, so education has two different functions. Cultural capital is converted to income in several ways, of which the principal means is educational certification. Human capital increases its owner's productivity, a competence which employers reward with wages. In contrast, cultural capital conveys prestige recognition on the strength of which people get desirable jobs and make business contacts (Light and Gold, 2000: 91). What Brigitte Berger (1991) has called "the culture of entrepreneurship" is an occupational culture; the skills, knowledge, attitudes, and values required by bourgeoisies to run the market economy are transmitted in the course of socialization at home and in school. Entrepreneurship is the occupational culture of bourgeoisies (Light and Gold, 2000: 92).

Interaction of Class and Ethnic Resources

As Light and Gold (2000: 106) explain, however, class and ethnic resources are commonly intertwined, and various forms of capital are both class- and ethnic-derived. All ethnic ownership economies depend upon mixed class and ethnic resources (Light and Gold, 2000: 103). Development of ethnic resources is often linked to one's class position. For example, those lacking money will be limited in their ability to fully develop ethnic membership and to access the ethnic resources with which it is associated (Light and Gold, 2000: 106).

Ethnic and Class Dimensions of Entrepreneurship Approach: Suggestions for Russian Immigrant Entrepreneurs

The ethnic and class approach to entrepreneurship suggests that the success of entrepreneurial efforts by immigrants from the former Soviet Union will be influenced by the interaction of class (financial, human, and cultural capital) and ethnic resources (ethnic social networks and social capital).

Family networks play an important role in business start-ups, especially since entrepreneurship often runs in the family, and friends and relatives play significant roles in establishing business networks and businesses. Some of the Russian immigrant entrepreneurs may have worked in occupations similar to their parents and some may have started businesses in the same occupational fields as their parents. An established community of earlier immigrants from the former Soviet Union, a form of social capital in the host country (in this case, Canada) may send signals to newcomers, indirectly promoting entrepreneurship by providing information regarding the business climate and feasible enterprises.

This approach suggests that entrepreneurs from the former Soviet Union with personal networks in Russia or Toronto composed of resource-rich and powerful members will have higher rates of return for themselves and their firms because they will have access to a wider range of information about potential markets for goods and services, as well as access to capital or potential investors, labour, clients, and suppliers. Russian immigrants with more social capital, in the form of contacts and connections with other entrepreneurs and firms in Toronto and Russia should attain higher status, enhance their power, and increase their financial compensation in their businesses.

This approach also suggests that the immigrant entrepreneurs will need access to financial capital to take advantage of opportunities in Toronto. Russian immigrants unable to obtain loans from the bank or government may turn to the ethnic community for loans, relying on reputation and enduring relationships as collateral. If they cannot obtain financial capital from social networks, such as family, friends, colleagues and the ethnic community or from banks and the government, they cannot take advantage of opportunities to start businesses. Immigrant entrepreneurship success for the second cohort of immigrant entrepreneurs will likely be partly determined by the amount of financial/material resources that they have brought with them; arguably, they accumulated a significant amount of financial capital during the transition in Russia. These immigrant entrepreneurs will be less likely than those in the first cohort to turn to the ethnic community for seed capital.

Some entrepreneurs from both cohorts may draw on social networks, including friends, former colleagues, and the Russian community for advice about planning and organizing their business and resources, including the acquisition of financial capital and links to suppliers and customers. The ethnic and class dimensions of entrepreneurship perspective suggests that the Russian ethnic community offers Russian immigrants several advantages, including access to a pool of potential investors, experienced entrepreneurs, a co-ethnic clientele, low-priced co-ethnic workers, social and emotional support, and the possibility of operating in the entrepreneur's native language and in a familiar social and cultural environment.

Class resources, including financial capital, human capital (education and professional or entrepreneurial experience) and cultural capital (skills, knowledge, attitudes, and values obtained from the education system in Toronto or Russia, experience in the Toronto labour market and/or in the black market economy in Russia or the market transition) will be necessary to establish a business in Toronto. Immigrants from the former Soviet Union who came with more human capital or who obtained more human capital in Toronto, in the form of years of education, work experience and high occupational skills will likely be in an advantageous position.

Limitation of Ethnic and Class Dimensions of Entrepreneurship Approach

The ethnic and class dimensions of entrepreneurship approach focuses on how local social networks impact entrepreneurship and business development and does not fully address the role of transnationalism. Some networks cross borders and draw on business communities back in their home country (Salaff et al., 2001: 13). In recent decades, studies documenting the importance of the direct and indirect impact of transnational linkages on ethnic business operation have shown how products, clients, and employees are recruited from either the sending countries or the receiving countries (Kyle, 1999; Landolt, 2001, in Fong and Luk, 2007a: 11). Growing numbers of migrants are participating in the political, social, and economic lives of their countries of origin, even as they put down roots in their host countries (Levitt, 2001). Such processes are likely to give rise to new structures and forces that determine ethnic entrepreneurship (Zhou, 2004: 1054). Therefore, I will turn to the transnationalism approach to demonstrate how immigrants draw on business communities from their home country and from the receiving country – transnational networks – to become successful entrepreneurs in their new host country.

3. Transnationalism Approach

The emerging transnationalism perspective stimulates new ways of thinking about how contexts of exit and reception intertwine to affect the probability of self-employment; what constitutes the structure of and access to opportunities; what enables individuals of diverse socioeconomic backgrounds from the same national origin or ethnic group to engage in transnational business; how transnational entrepreneurship affects or is affected by the immigrant's past and present experience in the middleman minority situation, ethnic enclaves, or ethnic niches in the host country (Zhou, 2004: 1066). Transnationals have different cultural histories, and these cultural histories affect the type of occupation and business that transnational entrepreneurs will enter abroad.

One important form of immigrant economic adaptation used by immigrant entrepreneurs is the practice of transnationalism as manifest in their engagement in transnational business practices (Wong, 2004: 143). Immigrants can join together previously unconnected direct and indirect ties in their countries of origin and destination (Landolt, 2001, in Salaff et al., 2007: 102). In the past, diasporic communities routinely exploited the opportunities for international business that their dispersion afforded (Weber, 1927; Cohen, 1971; Light et al., 1993: 38-43; Laguerre, 1998 in Light, 2007: 90).

Economic linkages with other countries have long been a feature of national economies. However, these linkages have accelerated and intensified since World War II, due to technological developments, the decreasing cost of transportation, and the emergence of international trade organizations (Chass-Dunn et al., 2000; Held et al., 1999, in Fong and Luk, 2007a: 7). In the middle of the 1980s, the term "globalization" came into popular use to represent these economic linkages (Held et al., 1999). Globalization has expanded the share of immigrants who notice and exploit international trading opportunities, making use of international social capital (Levitt, 2001: 62; Cohen, 1997: 176; Massey et al., 1993: 446 in Light, 2007: 90). What is new about contemporary transnationalism is that the scale, diversity, density, and regularity of such movements and their socioeconomic consequences are unmatched by the phenomena of the past, as a result of jet flights, long-distance telephone and fax services, the Internet, and other high-tech means of communication and transportation, and most importantly, the restructuring of the world economy along with the globalization of capital and labor.

To understand these various types of transnational economic activities we need a perspective that goes beyond centering on the host country (Levitt and Glick Schiller, 2003). *Transnationalism* is generally defined as "the processes by which immigrants forge and sustain multi-stranded social relations that link together their societies of origin and settlement" (Basch et al, 1994: 6). Portes and associates (1999) define it as occupations and activities that require regular and sustained social contacts over time across national borders for their implementation. Immigrants are increasingly leading dual lives, participating in two polities, and finding new paths of economic mobility on the basis of cross-border social networks (Levitt, 2001; Poros, 2001).

Many migrants to Canada are now engaged in transnationalism and transnational social spaces. Drawing on transnational ties for social capital, immigrants bring together resources from many institutional fields. They make contacts from their past professional relations in their country of origin. Immigrants who are bilingual and who have international social networks have serious natural advantages in trade promotion (Collins, 1998: vol 2, 398-99; Lever-Tracy et al., 1991: xi, 113 in Light, 2007: 90). They more easily notice the business opportunities that cultural frontiers generate and have the international social capital that supports international business (Fukuyama, 1995; Walton-Roberts and Hiebert, 1997; Wong, 1998: 95 in Light, 2007:90).

The levels of economic development in the countries of origin also shape particular structures of opportunities unique to national-origin groups and determine who is engaged in what type of transnational activities. At more advanced stages of economic development in sending countries, formal and large-scale economic activities, such as import/export, transnational banking and investment in both knowledge-intensive and labor-intensive industries, are likely to dominate, as in the case of Taiwanese and Koreans (Min, 1987; Yoon, 1995; Li, 1997; Zhou and Tsang, 2001).

Transnational Linkages among Immigrant Entrepreneurs

Transnational linkages are common among immigrant entrepreneurs who conduct business between their home and receiving countries (Fong and Luk, 2007a: 10). The locational choices for such transnational business activities are obvious because these are the places with which they are most familiar. However, conducting transnational business between two countries requires the maintenance of stable linkages to sustain business networks, expand clientele, and follow local market trends (Chang and Tam, 2004, in Fong and Luk, 2007a: 10).

Immigrants often draw on business communities from their home country and the receiving country. These transnational networks are strengthened by the rapid development of telecommunications and business travel. Hong Kong Chinese immigrant entrepreneurs mobilize their Hong Kong-based enterprises to start businesses in British Colombia (Wong and Ng, 1998). Salvadoreans make use of their home ties to establish businesses in North America (Landolt, 2001). These transnational entrepreneurs reinvest in firms back home while remaining abroad. Other migrants may return to their original country, bringing with them new business connections (Salaff et al., 2007: 100).

If transnational business is to succeed, entrepreneurs' contacts must be embedded in a business environment (Granovetter, 1985). The challenge for immigrants is finding social resources to start a business in a new land. Some draw on the social networks they developed before emigration to connect the new business to transnational networks. Others combine resources in the new country with those of the home country to create a business that appeals to the local market. If they do not expand their networks, entrepreneurship is limited to the ethnic economy (Salaff, 2007: 102).

Transnational Entrepreneurship

In the United States, the emerging literature on the relationship between transnationalism and entrepreneurship has come primarily from ethnographic case studies (see Grasmuck and Pessar, 1991; Portes and Guarnizo, 1991; Mahler, 1995; Chin et al., 1996; Durand et al., 1996; Gold, 1997, 2001; Guarnizo, 1997; Li, 1997; Guarnizo and Smith, 1998; Itzigsohn et al., 1999; Kyle, 1999; Landolt et al., 1999; Landolt, 2001; Levitt, 2001; Light et al., 2002; Portes et al., 2002; Tseng, 1995, 1997; Yoon, 1995). These case studies cover a wide variety of transnational entrepreneurship. The first is related to financial services, including informal remittance handling agencies and investment banks. The second is related to the import/export of raw material, semi-processed products, manufactured durable and non-durable goods, and air, sea, and land shipping companies and trading firms. For example, by using business connections already in place before migration to Canada, Russian entrepreneurs engage in the transnational trading of goods. The third type of transnational entrepreneurship entails various cultural enterprises, such as ethnic language media and organizing tourist groups. The fourth includes manufacturing firms operating across national boundaries, such as a garment factory in China that belongs to the same owner in New York's Chinatown. The fifth are return migrant micro-enterprises, such as restaurants, auto sales and repairs, which are established in places of origin using migrant wages and personal savings acquired elsewhere (Landolt et al., 1999). Case studies show that many immigrants in the United States are building bases abroad rather than aiming at permanent return; they have bought real estate, opened bank accounts, and established business contacts from which they create new economic opportunities. They organize their transnational lives in both the sending and receiving countries by strengthening transnational networks that sustain regular back-and-forth movements (Zhou, 2004: 1055).

Transnational Networks

International trade requires that buyers and sellers trust one another, so international social networks will be influenced by social capital. For example, a Diaspora's people are generally multilingual which permits them to communicate in the customer's language when abroad, but in their own language when addressing co-ethnic merchants scattered around the globe (Head and Ries, 1998: 48 in Light, 2007: 90). Drawing on transnational networks which are based on transnational linkages to their country of origin, entrepreneurs can mobilize more resources for their enclave businesses than are available locally (Portes, Haller, and Guarnizo, 2001; Wong and Ng, 2002). For example, Min (1990) found that the modal occupation of Korean immigrant entrepreneurs in Los Angeles was importing from Korea.

Gould (1990) proposes that immigration increases foreign trade for several reasons. First, immigrants obtain cultural fluency in the country of destination, thus reducing transaction costs for international trade. Second, they import familiar consumer goods from their countries of origin. Gould (1990) found that in both Canada and the United States, the more and better skilled the immigrants from any country and the longer they reside abroad, the more the international trade that later develops between the home-land and the adoptive country (Light, 2001: 57). Immigrant transnational entrepreneurs promote bilateral foreign trade with their homelands, so their businesses are not limited to local markets of the host society (Light, 2001: 59; Levitt, 2001).

Individuals with more extensive and diverse social net-works will be in a better position to initiate and sustain transna-tional enterprise (Kyle, 1999; Poros, 2001). Networks play a cru-cial role in facilitating transnational entrepreneurship and promoting their growth (Guarnizo et al., 2003). Networks estab-lished through international transactions influence a firm's growth and expansion to other countries (Boojihawon, 2004: 220). Network connections are generally significant in interna-tional business relationships (for a review of relevant studies, see Coviello and McAuley, 1999).

Transnationalism Approach: Suggestions for Russian Immigrant Entrepreneurs

Russian businesses have been networking internationally since the breakdown of the former Soviet Union. Some of the new Russian businesses started by Russian immigrants in Toronto are propelled by globalization and oriented towards transnational net-working. These businesses differ from their predecessors in scale and structure. "Enclave" is no longer an appropriate word to describe these businesses because their success depends on transnational linkages.

The transnationalism approach suggests that Russian immigrants in Toronto are building bases abroad. They organize their transnational lives in both Russia and Canada, strengthening transnational networks that sustain regular back-and-forth move-ments.

Furthermore, the main types of transnational entrepre-neurship in which Russian immigrants are involved are most likely the following: 1) import/export of raw material, semi-processed products, manufactured durable and non-durable goods, and air, sea, and land shipping companies and trading firms; 2) manufacturing firms operating across national bound-aries; and 3) return migrant enterprises, such as clothing stores and furniture companies established in Russia with personal savings accumulated in Toronto.

The transnationalism perspective suggests that immigrants who experienced the transition to a market economy in Russia or who returned to Russia at that time are more likely to participate in the Russian political, social, and economic environment while their families live in Toronto. They are likely to import/export raw material, semi-processed products, manufactured durable and non-durable goods, to act as intermediaries between potential buyers in North America and suppliers in the former Soviet Union, or to set up transnational manufacturing firms with production based in the republics of the former Soviet Union and distribution in North America.

These immigrants are also more likely to have extensive and diverse social networks in the former Soviet Union that help them to initiate and sustain transnational enterprise. They are likely to engage in the transnational trading of goods by using business connections from past professional relations.

The transnationalism perspective suggests that some highly educated immigrants, especially from the second cohort who lived in Russia during the transition or immigrants from the first cohort who returned to Russia during the transition, will quit their well-paying salaried jobs to pursue entrepreneurship because they can better utilize their skills, bicultural literacy, and transnational networks to reap material gains. Many use transnational entrepreneurship as an effective means of maximizing human capital returns and expanding middle-class status to become part of the elite in their communities.

The Russian immigrant entrepreneurs actively look for opportunities and market niches beyond the national boundaries of Canada, utilizing their bicultural skills and binational ethnic networks. Many of their transnational businesses will likely be based in Toronto with links to Russia.

Paths to Entrepreneurship

I will conclude this chapter by discussing several theories that explain why people with varied amounts of class and ethnic resources take diverse paths to entrepreneurship.

1. Structural or Disadvantage Theory

The structural model emphasizes the constraints and opportunities available to immigrants. It suggests that immigrants are pushed to self-employment as a result of discrimination that blocks other alternatives, or as a result of limited language skills that make it more difficult to enter the mainstream labor market (Brettell and Alstatt, 2007: 383). Structural theories postulate that the emergence of ethnic enterprise in North America has been linked historically with institutional discrimination, resulting in a lack of employment opportunities for minority groups (Li, 1976, 1979). Min and Bozorgmehr (2003) formulate this as the "disadvantage hypothesis" (see also Bonacich, 1993; Kim, 1981; Mata and Pendakur, 1999; Tsukashimi, 1991).

Disadvantage theory asserts that certain immigrant groups go into business because they are disadvantaged in the general labour market due to poor English, inferior education, lack of host country credentials and licenses and discrimination (Kim, 1981; Min, 1988). Some studies stress blocked mobility as the antecedent factor accounting for the emergence of immigrant entrepreneurship (Aldrich et al., 1989; Blalock, 1967; Li, 1998; Min, 1984). The blocked mobility thesis or disadvantage thesis, a structural level theory, proposes that labour market arrangements create barriers to the mobility of certain groups (Beaujot, Maxim, and Zhao, 1994: 82). According to the labor market disadvantage interpretation, discrimination and host society antagonism keep immigrants from all but the least desirable jobs in the majority-controlled economy (Anwar, 1979; Bonacich and Modell, 1980; Ladhury, 1984; Light, 1979). Due to these obstacles, minority group members seek opportunities in self-employment.

Immigrants experience various kinds of disadvantages in the labour market in North America (see Light, 1979; Satzewich and Li, 1987). Many suffer from unfamiliarity with the social, economic, and legal structures of the host society, difficulties with languages, non-recognition of credentials and discrimination. They may have difficulty finding jobs in the core sectors of the economy, especially if they do not have additional education or training in the host country (Kim et al., 1989; Min, 1984). Exclusion from job opportunities or dim prospects in the labour market leads many immigrants to seek out business opportunities and self-employment as an alternative (Aldrich and Waldinger, 1990: 116; Chan and Cheung, 1985: 143). Some immigrant groups have not been able to turn their previous education and experience into positions comparable to those they held prior to migrating because they have language problems or lack proper credentials. When these immigrants find that their way into well-paying jobs are blocked, they sometimes turn to entrepreneurship (Min, 1988). They earn higher returns on their human capital in self-employment than in wage and salary employment (Light, 1979; Min, 1984, 1988: Ch.5).[12] For example, Light and Bonacich (1988: Ch.8) found that Korean wage earners in Los Angeles County received only 76% of the return on their education that non-Koreans received. But Korean entrepreneurs received 93% of the return on education that non-Korean entrepreneurs received. Therefore, Koreans had a greater financial incentive to undertake self-employment (Light and Rosenstein, 1995b: 19).

Before they can practice, professionals need to validate their credentials. This sometimes requires additional training, a process that may take years (Cobas, 1986: 105). Markus and Schwartz (1984: 85) found that the professional training Russian émigrés received in the Soviet Union is frequently not recognized in North America, and licensing is denied until Western professional standards are met. Beaujot, Maxim, and Zhao (1994: 90-2) found that immigrants with higher educational credentials but no Canadian education have higher propensities towards self-employment because of blocked mobility, or specifically the non-recognition of education credentials; self employment represents real economic opportunities for these immigrants.

Gold (1988) found that disadvantage does play a major role in motivating Soviet Jews to enter business, but he found little evidence to indicate that self-employment was a direct alternative to unemployment (Light, 1972, Min, 1984). Few individuals, including Soviet Jews can move from a status of unemployment to that of successful business owner because running a business requires a great deal of capital, knowledge and commitment (Gold, 1995a: 57-8; Gold, 1988: 418). Business is more often an alternative to underemployment or the low quality of employment, specifically among Soviet Jews (Gold, 1995a: 58; Gold, 1988: 419). Initial jobs provide Soviet Jews with cultural socialization, English language proficiency and investment capital (Gold, 1995a: 58). But Chan and Cheung (1985: 147) found that close to three quarters of their Chinese Canadian respondents admitted they had never personally experienced racial discrimination; none had experienced it in relation to employment or promotional opportunities. They did not find an overwhelming feeling of inequality or disadvantage among the Chinese who become business entrepreneurs or self-employed professionals in Toronto. Thus, disadvantage does not explain the engagement of Chinese in business entrepreneurship (Chan and Cheung, 1985: 147). Chan and Cheung (1985: 152) conclude that institutional discrimination is no longer a satisfactory explanation for the continued interest of some ethnic groups in self-employment.

The disadvantage theory suggests that the Russian immigrants are more likely to enter self-employment and establish businesses if the professional training they received in the former Soviet Union is not recognized in North America, if licensing is denied until Western professional standards are met, and if it is difficult to find jobs in the main sector of the economy.

By emphasizing the agency of individual Russian entrepreneurs, my analysis goes beyond the "disadvantage hypothesis" that has characterized much of the previous explanations of why immigrants turn to entrepreneurship.

2. Cultural Theories

Cultural theory claims that certain groups, such as Jews, Chinese and Japanese (Bonacich, 1973: 583) possess certain cultural attributes which encourage and facilitate their participation in business activities (Gold, 1995a: 56; Gold, 1988: 415-16). Self-employment is a means by which immigrant Jews have traditionally supported themselves and their families, from German Jews of the 1850s and Eastern Europeans of the 1880-1920 era to contemporary Israelis (Goldscheider and Zuckerman, 1984; Howe, 1976; Glazer and Moynihan, 1963). Data from the 1990 Census in the US indicate that a sizeable proportion of Soviet Jews are self-employed: 15% in New York and one fourth (25%) in Los Angeles, which is among the highest rates of self-employment for ethnic groups (Gold, 1995a: 55). These groups are said to have access to cultural institutions for raising capital, controlling family labour and insuring economic cooperation (Ward, 1986). Such groups see small business ownership as a prestigious and worthwhile activity (Light, 1985).

The cultural model emphasizes imported or transplanted culture in terms of values and beliefs that are retrieved and reproduced to start or to maintain a business (Brettell and Alstatt, 2007: 383). Related to this model is a body of literature that draws attention to ethnic resources, including rotating credit associations, a co-ethnic labor force, and an enclave economy, as factors that facilitate self-employment (Borjas, 1986; Marger and Hoffman, 1992; Min and Bozorgmehr, 2000; Yoon, 1991). Light's (1980) cultural theory of entrepreneurship takes into account both (a) truly "cultural" qualities in groups which endow or incline their members towards business enterprise, or the *orthodox* version of cultural theory, and (b) ethnic resources such as mutual-aid institutions, group network and group solidarity which facilitate and motivate group members toward entrepreneurship, or the *reactive* version of cultural theory. In the absence of cultural resources, Light argues, mere disadvantage does not necessarily lead to a propensity to engage in business (Chan and Cheung, 1985: 144). Cultural explanations for the preponderance of certain immigrant groups in business follow two different forms: orthodox and reactive (Light, 1980).

Orthodox Cultural Theory: Orthodox cultural theories claim that certain groups such as Jews and Chinese are, by nature, business oriented (Gold, 1988: 416). The orthodox interpretation of cultural entrepreneurship (Light, 1980) assumes that different ethnic groups have been endowed with unique cultural and psychological qualities which account for success or propensity to engage in business enterprise. For example, Asians are said to be hard-working and ambitious, and these cultural attributes are taken to be responsible for their success.

The sojourner hypothesis, an aspect of the orthodox cultural theory, asserts (Bonacich, 1973) that some immigrant groups have a high proportion of members who do not intend to settle permanently in the host society but plan to return to the homeland. Their reason for migrating is to make money, which is why they turn to self-employment. Cobas (1986: 115) claims that Bonacich's interpretation explains self-employment among groups such as Chinese in Southeast Asia but not among others, such as the Cuban exiles he interviewed. As Bonacich points out, Chinese immigrants left not so much because they wanted out of their homeland but because they wanted to amass fortunes overseas. As a rule, they left their families behind, a clear indication of the intended transitory nature of their migration. Cuban exiles, on the other hand, emigrated because they were unable to maintain the kind of life they preferred in their homeland, so they emigrated with the entire nuclear family (Cobas, 1986: 115).

The orthodox cultural theory suggests that since most of the Russian immigrants were Jews, they are more likely to enter self-employment because Jews have been endowed with cultural and psychological qualities which account for their success or propensity to engage in business enterprise. The sojourner hypothesis suggests that they have a high proportion of members who do not intend to settle permanently in Toronto but plan to return to Russia; they migrated to make money and therefore turned to self-employment.

Reactive Cultural Theory: Reactive cultural theories claim that being a minority encourages business ownership (Light, 1980: 34). The notion of reactive entrepreneurship is embedded in the concepts of the middleman minority (Bonacich, 1973) and pariah capitalism (Weber, 1927: 360). Light's (1980) reactive interpretation of cultural entrepreneurship stresses the collective nature of the response to structural disadvantage. Reactive cultural theories argue that cultural traits become important in encouraging business activity when other factors in the social environment make business enterprises an appealing and viable prospect (Gold, 1995a: 56). Light (1984: 208) hypothesizes that the use of community-based economic resources is greatest among the disadvantaged lower class immigrant entrepreneurs who lack other resources. Upper class immigrant tradesmen who possess resources of education and money are more individualistic and less collective (Gold, 1988: 424). Young (1971: 142) and Hagen (1962) also argue that entrepreneurship rises when newly subordinated groups react against real or threatened loss of status.

Reactive theories are context-based, so they combine disadvantage and cultural approaches (Gold, 1988: 416). They explain why immigrants such as Soviet Jews with no prior business experience became employed in business in the US in large numbers (Min, 1984: 17). Cultural theory applies most directly to the experience of Soviet Jews who open businesses out of choice, despite opportunities for employment in the larger economy; this includes engineers who found high paying employment in their field but preferred to work in business instead (Gold, 1995a: 57; Gold, 1988: 416). The cultural attributes of Russian Jews that could contribute to self-employment include flexibility, a goal-directed, future-time orientation; experience in finding personal ties and manipulating bureaucracies, an ability to get along with various social groups, a desire to function independently, literacy, mathematical competence, and a tradition of self-employment (Gold, 1995a: 56).

The reactive cultural theory suggests that the Russian immigrants came with many experiences and cultural attributes that could contribute to self-employment. If they experience disadvantages in the labour market, then according to this theory, they will use their experiences and cultural attributes and their ethnic resources to help start a business.

3. Opportunity Theory

Opportunity theory claims that potential entrepreneurs can only work with the resources made available to them by their environments, and the structure of opportunities is constantly changing (Aldrich and Waldinger, 1990: 114). The organization for which the entrepreneur has previously worked influences the likelihood that s/he may decide to open a spinoff company (Cooper, 1986: 156). So when immigrants are working in salaried jobs and an opportunity appears to start a business, they may decide to leave their salaried position. Opportunity theory suggests that if they find that after looking at the number of businesses already in the field, technological requirements, capital requirements, that there is an opportunity to serve the unfulfilled demands of the market, and they have the resources to do it, then they may start their own business.

4. Ethnic Economy Theory

Ethnic economy theory claims that participation in the ethnic subeconomy promotes self-employment in at least two ways. First, a small, though not insignificant, proportion of immigrants go into business soon after arrival by pooling resources with relatives (Answar, 1979) or by becoming solo entrepreneurs with the assistance of other co-ethnics. Most manage to stay in the entrepreneurial class (Portes and Bach, 1985: 215) because they are able to cut labour costs by hiring co-ethnics, who are cheap and loyal, and they are able to get assistance from friends and relatives in the form of loans, contacts, and business tips (Werbner, 1984). For those unable to go into business shortly after arrival, the ethnic sub-economy allows them to take jobs in a firm owned by a co-ethnic. In return for loyalty and hard work, the owner will aid his or her employees in times of emergency and provide opportunities for advancement, such as helping them start a business (Bonacich and Modell, 1980; Lovell-Troy, 1980; Portes and Bach, 1985; Wilson and Portes, 1980). Thus dutiful ethnic economy employees turn into entrepreneurs (Cobas, 1986: 104).

The ethnic economy theory suggests that some Russian immigrants will go into business soon after arrival, pooling resources with relatives or other co-ethnics, hiring co-ethnics, and getting help from friends and family. Others will become employed by co-ethnics who may help them start a business in the future.

5. Business Background Theory

Several studies (Light, 1984; Bonacich, 1973) have argued that business experience obtained outside North America helps immigrant businesses compete successfully in the North America economy. This interpretation (Light, 1984; Portes and Bach, 1985; Steinberg, 1981; Woodrum et al., 1980) asserts that the penchant for self-employment shown by certain immigrant groups is due to a concentration within these groups of individuals with business backgrounds in the country of origin. Self-employment in the country of destination, then, results from the ability to transfer business know-how acquired in the country of origin.

The business background theory suggests that Russian immigrants from the first cohort who obtained entrepreneurial experience in the command administrative economy and in the black market economy and the immigrants from the second cohort who obtained entrepreneurial experience by setting up business after the transition to a market economy will be more likely to become self-employed and set up businesses in Toronto.

Synthesizing Different Explanations for Paths to Entrepreneurship Using the Three Theoretical Perspectives

Cobas (1986: 109) argues that self-employment is associated with several paths, including business background, low education, perception of hostility, and prior self-employment, but not with sojourning. Entry into the ethnic economy is the most effective predictor of probability of self-employment, followed by business background; perception of hostility and low education are minimally consequential.

Whatever their differences, disadvantage explanations, cultural explanations, business background explanations, ethnic economy explanations, and opportunity explanations all revolve around and attest to the unequal propensity of groups to embrace entrepreneurship. In an attempt at synthesis, the *ethnic and class dimensions of entrepreneurship approach* reduces these approaches to ethnic and class resources (Young, 1971: 142; Light, 1984; Light and Karageorgis, 1994; Model, 1985: 79). The demographic, sociocultural, or socioeconomic features of a group that encourage its entrepreneurship represent entrepreneurial resources. These resources operate singly or jointly (Light, 1984). Both class and ethnic resources contribute to entrepreneurship, but the influences usually are not equal. Ethnic resources may be more important at the initial stage of business development, while at a more advanced stage, class resources may become more significant (Light and Rosenstein, 1995b: 22).

Ethnic resources, as mentioned previously, are socio-cultural and demographic features of the whole group that co-ethnic entrepreneurs actively utilize in business or from which their business passively benefits (Light, 1984; Kim and Hurh, 1985; Light and Bonacich, 1988: Ch.7).

Ethnic resources characterize a group, not isolated members. Typical ethnic resources include entrepreneurial heritages, entrepreneurial values and attitudes, social capital, multiplex social networks, and co-ethnic networks (Young, 1971: 142; Werbner, 1984: 167; Foner, 1985: 717). If one observes, for example, that Chinese work long hours, save more of their income than outsiders, help one another to acquire business skills and information, follow one another into the same trades, deploy multiplex social networks to economic advantage, then ethnic resources seem to promote Chinese entrepreneurship (Basu, 1991; Wong, 1987; Bailey, 1987: Ch. 3).

In contrast, class resources include private property in the means of production and distribution, human capital, and money to invest (Bates, 1985). Class-specific cultural capital includes occupationally relevant and supportive values, attitudes, knowledge, and skills transmitted in the course of socialization. Therefore, if one observes that ethnic or immigrant entrepreneurs had entrepreneurial parents, previous business experience in their homeland, large sums of money available for investment when they arrived, and graduate degrees, these resources define a class explanation of entrepreneurship (Light and Rosenstein, 1995b: 23).

Ethnic and immigrant entrepreneurship always draws on both class and ethnic resources although the balance can vary (Light, 1984: 202).

The first path to entrepreneurship asserts that immigrant groups go into business because they are disadvantaged in the general labour market due to poor English, inferior education, lack of host country credentials and licenses and discrimination (Kim, 1981).

The second path to entrepreneurship states that immigrants opt for entrepreneurship because they identify closely with and are socially and culturally attached to their ethnic group, living and interacting with that group (Light, 1980), or because they want to make enough money in the host country to return to the origin country (Bonacich, 1973), or as a collective response to structural disadvantage (Light, 1980).

The third path to entrepreneurship posits that when immigrants are working in salaried jobs and they have an opportunity to start a business, they may do so. This path is consistent with the ethnic and class dimensions of entrepreneurship approach (Light, 1984; Waldinger et al., 1990) and with the transnationalism approach (Lever-Tracy et al., 1991: xi, 113 in Light, 2007: 90; Wong, 1998: 95 in Light, 2007: 90).

The fourth path to entrepreneurship argues that participation in the ethnic sub-economy promotes self-employment because entrepreneurs receive assistance from other co-ethnics

(Portes and Bach, 1985) who may help them get a job in their co-ethnic firm and then help them start a business (Bonacich and Modell, 1980). The first, second, and fourth paths to entrepreneurship are consistent with the ethnic and class dimensions of entrepreneurship approach (Light, 1984; Waldinger et al., 1990).

The fifth path to entrepreneurship asserts that immigrant groups choose self-employment because they have business backgrounds in their country of origin (Light, 1984; Portes and Bach, 1985). This path is consistent with the transitional economy approach (Pontusson, 1995: 119; Nee, 1991: 267).

In the empirical section which follows, I demonstrate how human capital, social capital, financial capital, and home country experience influenced the path taken to entrepreneurship. These paths represent opportunity structures linked to the structural problems faced by all new immigrants, including these particular immigrants from the former Soviet Union.

NOTES

[1]   Such studies de-emphasize the differential levels of entrepreneurship between minorities of different national origins (Light, 1972, 1984, in Ley, 2006: 744).

[2]   The primary beneficiary of marketization is the old elite (Stark, 1990: 389; Staniszkis, 1991: 38-52; Burawoy and Krotov, 1992: 34). Szelenyi calls attention to the socialist cadres' ability to adapt to market institutions (Szelenyi, 1986-87; Rona-Tas, 1994: 44). According to the elite reproduction theory, privatization in the former Soviet Union permitted selected managers, the majority of whom were former communist party members to directly assume personal ownership of large concentrations of new privatized public assets and to amass large concentration of private wealth. Communist-era elites had an advantage in converting to entrepreneurs because privatization was rapid and poorly regulated, so they had a greater ability to seize assets (Walder, 2003: 900).

[3]   Two arguments explain the survival of the old elite. 1) **Technocratic continuity** contends that socialism developed a technocratic cadre that could maintain its position through its acquired expertise (Szalai, 1990: 182). This elite was also instrumental in bringing about the transition. Education plays an important role in status allocation in both socialist and market systems (Haller, Kolosi, and Robert, 1990; Blau and Ruan, 1990; Treiman and Ganzeboom, 1990). Under socialism, by the 1980s cadreship

was strongly tied to education (Szelenyi, 1987; Wasilewski, 1990; Li and White, 1990). There is a common meritocratic-technocratic character of both party and entrepreneurial recruitment that is the main source of continuity. As a whole, people with more education will do better in the newly forming market sector than those with less, and thus cadres will be in an advantageous position (Rona-Tas, 1994: 45). The technocratic continuity approach would suggest that people who were part of or had connections to the technocratic cadre who became the new economic elite in the transitional economies in former socialist countries were more likely to start a business and be successful in running a business when they immigrated to North America. 2) The **power conversion thesis** argues that power accumulated during state socialism is converted into assets of high value in a market economy. Stanizkis puts forth the concept of "political capitalism" to describe the direct conversion of communist political power into economic might (1991: 46). She argues that, in the process of the transition to a market economy, strategically located cadres can take advantage of their positions in acquiring state property. Through informal channels, exploiting the uncertainties of the transition, cadres can turn their limited control of state property into quasi or real ownership. According to this argument, cadres are at an advantage not just in setting up but also in operating companies, because they can use their personal networks to get access to valuable business information and credit. The importance of personal ties in socialist economies, both within and outside the state sector is amply documented (Walder, 1986: 181; Rona-Tas, 1990: 117-20; Major, 1992: 83; Borocz, 1993a), but they assume a special importance during the transition (Borocz, 1993b; Hankiss, 1990: 255; Prybyla, 1991: 16). Both horizontal and vertical ties are important in post-communist economies (Rona-Tas, 1994: 45). In the developing market, information about prices, demand, or the availability of goods is still carried through horizontal channels of personal connections during the transition (Oi, 1989: 213; Wank, 1992; Rona-Tas, 1991). Cadres obtained a wide network of connections through the party organization, and these connections survive even after the party formally ceased to exist. Having connections in the state apparatus or local administration can provide early knowledge of new laws and regulations. Starting and subsequently successfully operating an import-export business or a manufacturing plant requires connections in high places, which cadres are more likely to have. In Russia, a large number of the individuals occupying nomenklatura positions within the state bureaucracy maintained their elite status by jumping into top administrative positions within economic enterprises

(Hanley, Yershova, and Anderson, 1995: 640). Membership in party networks provides benefits in emergent markets, as almost two-thirds of the private business elite in 1993 consisted of former party members (Hanley, Yershova, and Anderson, 1995: 656). The current management of state enterprises is overwhelmingly made up of individuals with experience in administering state firms during the Communist period. Directors of state firms during the Communist period have managed to retain control of state enterprises (Hanley, Yershova, and Anderson, 1995: 659). The power conversion thesis would suggest that Russian immigrants will need to have connections with former party members or former managers of state enterprises in order to develop successful transnational businesses in Russia. This theory would suggest that people who immigrated from transition economies who had connections in the state apparatus or local administration who provided them with early knowledge of new laws and regulations during the transition were more likely to use these connections to establish successful transnational businesses with links to Russia.

[4] People with high access to sociopolitical capital in Russia enjoyed higher chances of creating viable businesses because they could obtain political and administrative favours and protections (Yang, 2002: 143).

[5] Entrepreneurs who were successful during the transition period were innovative in identifying and creating new markets to export the goods manufactured in the state-run economy before the transition and discovering what goods were in demand and therefore should be imported from the West to Russia. They also had to be talented in making use of and manipulating institutional rules, such as government regulations because the government introduced several new laws to promote the establishment of private enterprises, so the entrepreneurs who had connections within the government and/or knew how to manipulate the new laws will be more likely to become successful entrepreneurs. In Russia's transition economy, access to sociopolitical capital for Russian immigrant entrepreneurs will likely lead to higher chances of successfully establishing transnational businesses in Russia because they can obtain political and administrative favours and protections. The entrepreneurs who immigrated from the transition economy in Russia or who returned to Russia during the transition who had connections in the state apparatus who provided them with early knowledge of new laws and regulations during the transition will be more likely to use these connections to establish successful transnational businesses with links to Russia.

[6] Light and Gold (2000: 94) claim that ethnic networks provide sources of business inputs, including labour (Ng, 1999; Park, 1997, in Ley, 2006: 744).

[7]   In many cases, ethnic-based trust offers definite advantages over the impersonal and legalistic forms of cooperation that underlie modern economic exchange (Light and Gold, 2000: 110). For example, Gold (1995b) claims that Israelis' greater earnings may be attributed to their ethnic resources. These ethnic resources include a long tradition of middleman entrepreneurship, being accustomed to minority group status, being socialized in a country that emphasizes ethnic collectivism and cooperation, access to a sizable community of native-born co-ethnics (American Jews), and familiarity with Western-style social norms.

[8]   In their study of Chinese in San Francisco and Cubans in Miami, Sanders and Nee (1987) found that the ethnic economies are only of benefit to entrepreneurs (Fong and Lee, 2007: 149).

[9]   The economic returns correspond closely to those people working in the broader economy. According to Fong and Lee, this has been documented in the case of Cubans in Miami (Portes and Bach, 1985; Portes and Jensen, 1989); and Chinese in New York (Zhou and Lagan, 1989).

[10]   Mouw's (2006) study of the effect of social capital in the labour market suggests that often used measures of labour market social capital, such as the average education or job prestige of contacts, have a spurious, rather than causal, effect on wages. As a result, it is quite possible that much of the estimated effect of social capital simply reflects selection effect based on the myriad of nonrandom ways in which people become friends (Mouw, 2006: 80).

[11]   A socio-cultural constraint limiting access to social capital is that individuals with similar backgrounds and interests tend to associate with one another rather than with people having dissimilar backgrounds, thus generating social networks characterized by low diversity (Aldrich and Kim, 2005: 41).

[12]   Entrepreneurs may be motivated to start their firms because of negative "pushes" within their incubator organizations, such as being frustrated in previous jobs or being laid off (Cooper, 1986: 159).

CHAPTER 4

The Influence of the Historical, Economic, and Political Environment of the Former Soviet Union on Entrepreneurship

Introduction

I t is important to explore the history of entrepreneurial recruitment and inclinations in the former Soviet Union to understand immigrant entrepreneurial practices in Toronto. I explore three distinct phases in the evolution of economic enterprises: the Soviet period (before the 1980s), the first years of the transition (1980s-early 1990s), and the present (1990s-2000). I begin in the 1920s, before private business was officially recognized and proceed to the 1980s, when its future development was shaped. In the three historical periods I focus on: (1) how entrepreneurs developed in the official and unofficial economies; (2) how the regulative capacity of the state affected the emergence of entrepreneurs; and (3) the entrepreneurial strategies used to function in the Soviet command-style economy and strategies used during the transition.

1. Command-Administrative Economy in the Soviet Union (beginning in late 1920s)

A command-administrative economy took shape in the Soviet Union during the late 1920s and 1930s. It featured a centralized plan, suppression of private business, and limited engagement with the global economy (Bonnell and Gold, 2002: xiii-xxii). To achieve maximum equality, the Soviet state abolished property ownership in combination with tight economic regulation of wages and prices. The policy made it difficult for anyone to reach a significantly higher standard of living by increasing their work performance within the official economy. It was not possible to live outside the second economy, not only in terms of income, but in terms of social mobility and integration in society.

Nevertheless, many people were doing something similar to entrepreneurship, engaged in self-employed activity in the black market economy while also working as salaried employees of the state (Kurkchiyan, 1999: 84). The two levels of the economy had different functions. The official level, operating through the payment of salaries, secured a basic standard of living for the majority. The second economy complemented this, ensuring a principal source of income and providing a reasonable lifestyle. The two socio-economic structures were linked and interdependent. By taking part in the second economy, people grew accustomed to the practice of informal problem-solving. They cultivated a tradition of bypassing officialdom (Kurkchiyan, 1999: 84-88). The skills learned in the two levels of the economy allowed them to carry out projects, achieve goals and earn symbolic profits by conducting procedures, organizing people, relating to institutions, and these skills were unique because of their setting vis-à-vis the state in a socialist context. These socialist entrepreneurial skills proved crucial for the development of private business in the first post-Soviet years (mid-1980s). Furthermore, those who left Russia, such as the Toronto entrepreneurs, obtained some of their *cultural capital* from their experience in the black market economy.

2. Soviet Union's Collapse (end of the 1980s) – Erosion of Socialist Economy

By the time the USSR had collapsed at the end of the 1980s, the second economy had become the dominant force in the allocation of goods and services. The state became increasingly poor as a result of the growing pressure from the second economy on the legal economy, shifting an ever-expanding proportion of the benefits of economic activity away from the state into private hands. Young entrepreneurs started from scratch in the late 1980s building their initial wealth during Gorbachev's partial reforms when co-existence of regulated and quasi-market prices created huge opportunities (Guriev and Rachinsky, 2005: 139).

The first economic step under *perestroika* was to legalize part of the second economy in 1988. "Cooperatives," small businesses offering consumer goods and services, became permissible in an effort to improve the availability of services and provide a competitive spark to the economy (Jones and Moskoff, 1991). But they faced tight restrictions on size, activities, and property arrangements. The law "On Individual Work Activity" (1986) was the first to attract some enthusiasts into non-state economic activities. But the real starting point was the 1988 law "On Cooperation in the USSR," which provided much stronger legal support for the development of new entrepreneurship. It was followed by "The Basis for USSR and Union Republic Legislation on Lease-Holding" (November 1989), which established another method for the gradual conversion of state resources. According to official statistics, the number of cooperative enterprises, the number of their workers and employees, and the total quarterly output of coops increased by 5, 8, and 13 times, respectively, during the first year after the law "On Cooperation."

A diversity of private enterprises was concealed behind the legal status of the coop as the only enterprise legitimized by the state authorities. The first coop activities turned towards the production of goods and construction. Economic conditions during the first stage favoured start-up enterprises. The disappearing state-run enterprises left behind many market niches in consumer goods production and services. Although imported supplies of consumer goods were limited, it was possible to obtain bank loans at reasonable interest rates.

Low wages in state-run enterprises attracted highly skilled workers to the non-state sector. The first group of coop entrepreneurs were a poorly paid group of "technical intelligentsia" (engineers and other professionals with technical backgrounds), and the most active among these new actors. By 1987-1988, so-called Youth Centers for Scientific and Technical Creativity (for example, the Young Komsomol League) showed the conversion of political capital into private ownership. After 1989 they were accompanied by the Communist Party Committees who expressed a particular affinity for joint ventures with foreign capital participation (Radaev, 1997: 16-21). This set in motion a gradual extension of the territory occupied by the second economy under the Soviet system. It was abruptly stopped when the rapid political changes of 1988-1989 culminated in the total collapse of the USSR.

According to Radaev (1997), low wages in state-run enterprises drew highly skilled workers and employees to the non-state sector. Therefore, the first and most active coop entrepreneurs in the late 1980s were poorly paid "technical intelli-

gentsia" (engineers and other professionals with technical backgrounds). It seems likely that some of the Toronto entrepreneurs
were part of the "technical intelligentsia." These immigrants
likely built their initial wealth during Gorbachev's partial reforms
when co-existence of regulated and quasi-market prices created
huge opportunities, and it became possible to obtain bank loans
at reasonable interest rates.

3. Transition to a Market Economy (early 1990's) - From State Sector Careers to a Market Economy

When the Soviet system collapsed,[1] reformers set up a market
economy with two dimensions: *internal* liberalization intended
to create a functioning domestic money economy; *external* liberalization to remove all obstacles – such as foreign trade monop-
olies and non-convertible currency – that separated Russian producers from world markets.

     During the transition, jobs were redistributed from the
state to the private sector, from manufacturing industries (especially defense and heavy industry) to services and finance, and
from large to small and medium-size enterprises (Gerber, 2002b:
631). Russia's market transition introduced institutional changes
with great potential to transform the labor market: the rise of a
private sector; the removal of state controls over wages, prices,
and other firm-level decisions; the growth of foreign competition
and loss of protected access to markets in other (former) Communist countries; the curtailing of subsidies; and the legalization
of self-employment and unemployment.

     From 1991, the last year of the Soviet era and the first
year of the market transition era, to 1998, the Russian economy
experienced price, exchange rate, and trade liberalization, mass
privatization, hyperinflation, steep negative growth rates, bur-
geoning unemployment, wage arrears, capital flight, several political crises, and a general deterioration of state institutions. The
early years of transition in all countries of the former Soviet
Union were marked by uncertainty about income, the operational
rules of the economy and of society, and what might happen from
one day to the next. Many Russians lost their savings in 1992
when state price controls were removed. Setting prices free
brought years of hyperinflation. Hyperinflation, in turn, caused

the gross devaluation of the salaries and pensions of state employees – who before 1989 made up virtually 100% of the population. Salaries generally became so small in comparison with prices that they lost their significance, even as a guarantee of social security. The rate of self-employment increased as the push factors associated with economic crises intensified and Soviet-era restrictions disappeared (Gerber, 2002a: 11).

The Russian government's sweeping market reforms explicitly sought to transform the labour market. One goal was flexibilty. Liberalization and privatization were intended to spur a massive reallocation of labour from inefficient to productive firms, branches, and sectors. Freed from centrally established wages, promotion schedules, and suppliers, but facing foreign competitors, dwindling state orders, and shrinking subsidies, managers now had the flexibility and incentives to restructure their product lines and work forces in response to market signals. Initially, unemployment rose sharply, as inefficient enterprises shut down and successful enterprises shed excess labour. But after the initial shock of liberalization, gains from foreign investment, market incentives, and increased productivity fueled growth (Gerber, 2002b: 632).

Russia's post-Soviet reformers view private enterprise as the key to revitalizing the economy, but reform policies focused on privatizing state enterprises rather than developing new private firms (Boyco, Shleifer, and Vishny, 1995). Russian privatization and redistribution of economic assets involved four main steps. The first was known as the covert privatization or "insider privatization" of 1988-1991, by which workers and management in 75% of all privatized enterprises were allowed to retain 51% of the shares, even before open sales began. Step two was the "voucher privatization" of 1992-1994, by which the remaining blocks of shares were offered to the public at special auctions. All Russian citizens had been given special investment vouchers, which became valuable assets in a number of insider trading schemes (Hedlund, 2001: 15-21). Share ownership in which employees and citizens were given equal shares of transferable stock or vouchers resulted in highly concentrated private assets in a short period of time. Ordinary individuals pressed for income sold these shares to managers or to private funds at depressed prices, and assets once held by the government were converted into large concentrations of private wealth relatively quickly (King, 2001; McFaul, 1995). Quickly formed voucher investment funds managed to snap up large volumes of vouchers from a population content to trade in their vouchers for a bottle of vodka.[2] In stage three, "money privatization", the government abandoned free distribution and began to insist that further privatization must raise money for the budget. "Loans for shares" auctions of 1995-1996 that transferred a number of large state-owned enterprises to a limited number of business groups in exchange for subsidizing the state budget were a scam by which the major banks succeeded in taking over many of the "crown jewels" of Russian industry at rock bottom prices. The final stage, following Yeltsin's reelection victory, was the "banker's war" where oligarchs entered into open struggle for remaining spoils.

Elite insiders in the former Soviet Union had almost exclusive access to the kinds of financial instruments, asset transactions, price manipulation, international dealings, and information through which property changed form and large concentrations of wealth changed hands (Walder, 2003: 904). The absence of a state willing, ready and able to shoulder its role as a legitimate guarantor of the basic rules pushed economic actors to exploit the opportunities for gain offered by the weak state (Hedlund, 2001: 15-21).

Former managers of public enterprises emerged as modern corporate executives; freed of the restraints of the command economy, they allocated to themselves vastly increased pay and benefits, including stock shares, typical of managerial practices in corporate capitalism (Walder, 2003: 903). Selected managers also directly assumed personal ownership of large concentrations of new privatized public assets. These managers moved into a newly privatized business oligarchy. By 1993, regime insiders (almost two-thirds of the private business elite in 1993 were former members of the Communist Party) acquired majority shares in two-thirds of privatized and privatizing firms (McFaul, 1995: 210; Hanley, Yershova, and Anderson, 1995: 654-62) and a small number of wealthy oligarchs assumed control of certain key sectors of the economy in large, capital intensive firms, such as extensive oil reserves and mineral deposits that require large capital investments to develop (often from abroad), and many state firms entered contracts with foreign companies (Goldman, 2003: 98-122; Hoffman, 2002; McFaul, 1995).

At the beginning of the 1990s entrepreneurship was characterized by two basic features. First, step-by-step political liberalization legitimized one new economic form after another, including joint ventures, individual private enterprises, closed joint-stock companies, and "small enterprises". Second, the economic conditions for new entrepreneurship became tougher. The entrepreneur was expected to pay heavy value-added tax (up to 28%) and profit tax of 35%, along with commercial bank interest rates of 50% or more. The erosion of administrative control over state-run enterprises led to a spontaneous price increase.

An acceleration of privatization rates occurred during this period as well. Any new production was considered unprofitable, while easy fortunes were made from wholesale trade (especially foreign transactions) and currency exchange. Numerous commercial banks and commodity markets appeared, and stock markets took their first steps. The spontaneous privatization of about 2,000 enterprises occurred before the official start of the privatization program and enabled groups of managers in the state-run sector to transfer state-owned assets into non-state ownership.

The USSR law "On the Main Guidelines for the Destatization and Privatization of Enterprises" and the Russian Federation law "On Privatization of State-Run and Municipal Enterprises" (July 3, 1991) became the principal legislative acts for privatization. The former established the initial framework for paid-off privatization, and the latter introduced privileges for working collectively. In mid-1992 the government attempted to implement the large-scale privatization program; to impose control over institutional change, the government announced a mass transformation of the state-run enterprises into joint-stock companies. Small enterprises were to be sold in their entirety through competitive bidding or lease buy-outs. SMEs [small and medium-sized enterprises] in retail trade, food service, and consumer service were subject to mandatory privatization through auctions and tenders organized by municipalities. Large-scale enterprises had to be transformed into joint-stock companies (Radaev, 1997: 16-21).

Legislation became more detailed and assumed more regulatory functions. The following Russian presidential decrees were signed: 1) On the Introduction of Privatization Checks in the Russian Federation (August 14, 1992); 2) On Measures of Stock-market Organization in the Process of Privatization of

State-Run and Municipal Enterprises (October 7, 1992); 3) On the Utilization of Privatization Checks for the Social Security of the Population (October 26, 1992); 4) On State Guarantees for the Right of Russian Citizens to Participate in Privatization (May 8, 1993); 5) On Additional Measures to Ensure the Right of Russian Citizens to Participate in Privatization (July 26, 1993). There was also a boom in the SME sector (especially the non-state sector). The number of small enterprises increased 2.0 and 1.5 times in 1992 and 1993, respectively. This expansion was encouraged by the introduction of tax privileges for SMEs engaged in priority fields of activity in 1991 (Radaev, 1997: 16-21). The government's package of "shock therapy" measures in January 1992 abruptly eliminated controls on wages, prices, trade, currency exchange, and ownership of productive assets, along with state planning agencies, and mandatory state orders (Aslund, 1995; Blasi et al., 1997). The Russian government's sweeping market reforms paved the way for self-employment to grow unimpeded in Russia for the first time (Gerber, 2002: 4).

The present state in Russia started with the Russian Federation government decree "On the Principal Statements of the State Program of Privatization of State-Run and Municipal Enterprises in the Russian Federation After July 1, 1994" (July 22, 1994), which declared the end of voucher privatization. The field was now open to large investors involved in the distribution of assets. The turning point in the state support of SMEs was reached in 1995 when a special State Committee for SME Support and Development was established. Two special federal laws were enacted: 1) On the State Support of Small Enterprise in the Russian Federation (June 14, 1995); 2) On the Abridged System of SME Taxation, Recording, and Reporting (December 29, 1995). At the same time, in 1994-1995 the growth of SME numbers stopped abruptly. The highest rates of enterprise conversion were observed in 1992, after which they declined considerably year after year. In the end almost 120,000 non-state enterprises appeared (Radaev, 1998: 16-21).

Official control was completely withdrawn, and people could now start private businesses and control the entire budget of their business. It was now entirely permissible to engage in private economic activities that were illegal under communism and, therefore, restricted to the second economy. Currency exchange, private services, speculative trading and entrepreneur-ship switched categories from the forbidden to the encouraged (Kurkchiyan, 1999: 93-97). New forms of economic behaviour and new social groups, became prevalent, partially or fully replacing the state planning system with decision-making by individuals or individual firms operating in a global context and responsive to market factors, thereby reshaping institutions, ide-ologies and patterns of collective behaviour. As entrepreneurs began to supplement or replace communist managers, operating with some form of private or state-owned assets, their survival depended on their ability to master the skills of entrepreneurial-ism (Bonnell and Gold, 2002: xv).

The combination of legalizing private business with con-tinued government regulation of prices, export, import and inter-nal trade licensing, opened up possibilities for arbitraging or rent-seeking. For example, a new private firm that could obtain a license to export Ukrainian beer at still-low Soviet prices in 1992 to Poland where prices had long ago moved towards European levels, stood to make a lot of money very quickly. When low prices are set by government, and the transaction is regulated, not all can participate. Obtaining the government privilege (not granted to everyone) of buying the beer and exporting it to Poland or anywhere that it fetched a higher price yielded a special kind of profit economists call 'rent'; influencing the license-giving agency is the activity of 'rent seeking' (Havyrylyshyn, 2006: 179). Some time elapsed between legalization of private activity and the elimination of government regulations, causing a gap between market prices and official prices and created opportuni-ties for new capitalists to maximize profits. The extent of the opportunities and the magnitude of potential rents were greater with longer delays and partial reforms. The delays allowed a con-tinuation for many years of fiscal and monetary instability, infla-tion and exchange rate crisis (Havrylyshyn, 2006: 179).

High inflation and low interest rates combined with privi-leged relations between government officials and owners of the co-operatives in the late Perestroika period allowed them to borrow at huge negative rates and sometimes not repay them at all. When the time came to repay after two or three years of hyperinflation, the amount was so low in real terms that it was often forgiven by the government (Havylyshyn, 2006: 180). In the first few years (1989-

1992) successor states rents were easy to generate, but limited because the economy was still largely state-owned, and the lack of early stabilization sharply reduced the economic base for these rents. But once small-scale privatization added to the real assets available for purchase and stabilization began to take hold, the rent potential took off. It continued to rise as large-scale privatization provided the new capitalist class an even greater base for profit-making (Havrylyshyn, 2006: 183).

The Toronto immigrants who lived in Russia during the transition or who returned during the transition likely set up useful transnational social networks in the form of connections with state enterprise directors and business groups who took over large formerly state-owned enterprises during the covert privatization of 1988-91, the massive swift voucher privatization of 1992-94, and the loans-for-shares auctions of 1995-96. The real winners in Russia's new economy were those with the best personal contacts.[3] Russian immigrants with good contacts could set up a joint firm with an entrepreneur in Russia, who could take advantage of the combination of legalization of private businesses with continued government regulation of prices, export, import and internal trade licensing. For example, an entrepreneur in Russia could start a firm with an entrepreneur in Toronto by obtaining a license from the government (not granted to everyone) to export steel at still-low Soviet prices to Canada and the US or anywhere else where it fetched a higher price and where they both stood to make a lot of money very quickly. Some time elapsed between legalization of private activity and the elimination of government regulations, creating a gap between market prices and official prices and setting up opportunities for the new capitalists in Russia and Toronto to maximize profits.

4. Socialist Entrepreneurial Skills Influencing Business Success Abroad for Immigrants from the Former Soviet Union

Most of the first private entrepreneurs of the last Soviet generation followed three possible trajectories from socialism to post-Soviet business: from Komsomol activism to business, from industry and science to business, and from the black market to business. The first two trajectories are particularly widespread: in 1996 almost 40% of all entrepreneurs came from leading positions in the Komsomol and another 40% came from the Soviet industry (Yurchak, 2002). Komsomol schools, teaching ideological, economic and cultural skills to the younger generation during late socialism (from the mid-1960s to mid-1980s), according to Yurchak (2002), provided a new pragmatic understanding of work, time, money, skills, professional relations and particular hybrid understandings of the official plans, rules, laws, and institutions of the party-state, which proved to be fertile ground for the future growth of private firms. According to Yurchak, many members of the last Soviet generation, especially men, learned in the 1970s-1980s that by applying what they learned in the Komsomol, they could organize and manage an efficient work process and achieve required goals despite the obstacles associated with the economy of shortage and its political regulations. In the late 1980s, the first post-Soviet years, many became involved in the process of inventing the newly legalized private business (Yurchak, 2002). Yurchak claims that a large number of the new capitalists were in the Komsomol, the party's training school, and connections in the Komsomol were critical to business success (Yurchak, 2002). Formal education was another communist legacy. Education over the years increasingly emphasized technical knowledge over Marxist ideology. In terms of entrepreneurial inclinations of the immigrants I studied, education is a good predictor (Rona-Tas and Lengyel, 1997: 12). The first cohort (born between 1945 and 1960), which I call the *last Soviet Generation* (see Yurchak, 2002), immigrated to Toronto in the 1970s and early 1980s; they were educated and reached adulthood during the Brezhnev period. Most graduated from university, many with MA and PhD degrees, and all were assigned to the state sector after graduation. The largest group of successful entrepreneurs belong to this generation, and they are in their 30s to early 40s (Yurchak, 2002).

To a large extent, entrepreneurship is a matter of a certain culture, a set of values, habits, skills, and expectations (Berger, 1991; Lavoie, 1991, in Rona-Tas and Lengyel, 1997: 9). It entails a preference for independence and self-reliance, and a willingness to take some risk. However, entrepreneurial culture cannot be reduced to the values of individuals. These values are learned and reinforced in a social environment. A portion of entrepreneurial culture or cultural capital has its roots in the pre-communist past (Szelenyi, 1988; Rona-Tas and Borocz, 1996, in Rona-Tas and Lengyel, 1997: 9-10). As noted, entrepreneurship was not entirely absent under state socialism; there was a private sector, a hidden or second economy, on the periphery of the socialist economy, which although banned was well known to the authorities (Havrylyshyn, 2006: 36).

When young professionals graduated from college, they were assigned to state-sector jobs, finished their apprenticeships, became certified, and moved up the organizational ladder. They enjoyed security and expected life-time employment. In an economy of full employment under socialism, most people participated in the second economy part-time, while holding on to a secure state-sector job. Others used their jobs as a starting point for a full-time private enterprise later, taking advantage of equipment, facilities, and materials from their state jobs.[4] The socialist private sector thus fostered values and habits that were partially compatible with capitalist private enterprise (Rona-Tas and Lengyel, 1997: 10-11).

In other words, Russian entrepreneurs acquired skills in the socialist system which they could adapt to both the post-socialist era (if they stayed or went back) and the new capitalist conditions in Toronto. For example, frequently and widely applied techniques of deferral of payment and the renegotiation of terms and conditions were beneficially reincarnated in the post-socialist environment. Careful selection of the labour force, flexible change of business partners, easy replacement of one given constituent of production with another were key abilities developed amidst conditions of shortage and the lack of calculability under the old rules; successfully reapplied in the insecure economic circumstances of the early transition period (Laki and Szalai, 2006: 328), these skills could easily be transferred elsewhere.

Bolcic differentiates between potential entrepreneurs and those with non-entrepreneurial inclinations by their experiences in the hidden economy. Respondents in his study who participated in the hidden economy were more entrepreneurially oriented than those who did not (Bolcic, 1997-98: 18). More specifically, individuals from occupations requiring contacts and communication with people in important social circles or networks (such as management, commerce, and finance) have greater entrepreneurial inclinations and are more likely to be entrepreneurs. Additionally, those with large social circles or networks have a number of advantages by being able to obtain important information, support, and favours from others. For entrepreneurship, these are all relevant (Bolcic, 1997-98: 20). While this demonstrates the importance of knowledge to the success of an entrepreneur, both potential and actual entrepreneurs stress the importance of good connections with "powerful people in government" as the second most important element of success (Bolcic, 1997-98: 26).

In the command-administrative economy, state enterprise managers needed to behave in entrepreneurial ways to acquire financial resources and materials for their firms in conditions of chronic shortage and stifling bureaucratism. They also required skill in dealing with party and state officials. As marketization proceeded, state enterprise managers had to demonstrate exceptional entrepreneurialism to keep their firms afloat. With state firms subjected to the same hard budget constraints as private firms, their managers had to become risk takers comparable to capitalists in private sector businesses (Bonnell and Gold, 2002: xix). The legacies of communal cultural traditions and the Soviet economic system, and the extreme economic chaos prevalent in contemporary Russia made flows of goods and services through personal networks a dominant mode of exchange among organizations and individuals (Berliner, 1957; Kryshtanovskaya and White, 1996; Ledeneva, 1998).[5]

The command-administrative economy combined with the notorious inefficiency of state-socialist economies in providing and distributing consumer goods fostered an entrepreneurial spirit of the opportunistic (rather than modern-rational) kind, forcing the use of "unofficial" (informal/extralegal) means to make everyday life possible and turning this behaviour into the social norm (Morawska, 1999: 360). Soviet-period price and supply distortions generated many underground capitalists (Havrylyshyn, 2006: 189-90), who in a market economy would probably have been legal traders. The allocative distortions of central planning produced the conditions for the predominantly part-time entrepreneurship of the second economies (Nelson and Winter, 1982).

Although many skills developed under the socialist economy were useful during the transition and afterwards, the only thing that really worked during the worst years of transition was self-reliance – individual, informal problem-solving. The tactics developed within the economy of collapse included simple trading to criminal activity, as official control was completely withdrawn. The period of collapse had a strong psychological impact. On the positive side, there was an explosive growth in self-reliance, but there was also widespread rejection of authority.

Since the mid-1990s, a new economy has emerged whereby the institution of ownership –land, capital, and property in general – and its political and economic rules have become accepted as normal (Kurkchiyan, 1999: 89-92).

The structural changes[6] that followed the dismantling of the command economy created opportunities and incentives for entrepreneurial activity. The move toward a market economy provided opportunities for elite enrichment and created a wealthy entrepreneurial class (Walder, 2003: 911), as shown in the high number of entrepreneurs developing in a short span of time (Rona-Tas and Lengyel, 1997: 5).

Recent changes in the economy of the former Soviet Union have made it possible for educated people working in the command-administrative economy to become entrepreneurs. But they were able to transfer their skills. At the managerial level, the task of meeting plan targets required a dense network of informal ties that cut across enterprises and local organizations, and the allocative distortions of central planning produced the conditions for the predominantly part-time entrepreneurship of the second economies. The persistence of routines and practices, organizational forms and social ties from the socialist period became assets, resources, and the basis for credible commitments and coordinated actions in the post-socialist period (Nelson and Winter, 1982). As marketization proceeded, state enterprise managers had to demonstrate exceptional entrepreneurialism to keep their firms afloat. With state firms subjected to the same hard budget constraints as private firms, their managers had to become risk takers comparable to capitalists in private sector businesses (Bonnell and Gold, 2002: xix).

Immigrants who grew up in the command-administrative economy in the Soviet Union were likely to use their socialist entrepreneurial skills after the collapse of the socialist era. Those who participated in the hidden or underground economy were entrepreneurially oriented and more likely to become entrepreneurs when restrictions on private accumulation were lifted in Russia or when they immigrated to Toronto.

Their contacts and relationships influenced their entrepreneurial opportunities. Russian immigrants who worked in occupations that required networks, such as management, commerce, and finance, for example, seem well-oriented towards becoming entrepreneurs in the transition economy and/or when they immigrated to Toronto.

Formal education was another communist legacy, and those coming from Russia were likely to have arrived with a good education, particularly in technical fields, such as engineering. It seems likely that they could covert this human capital to business success.

Soviet Jewish Immigrants: The Soviet Experience – A Brief History of Jews in the Soviet Union

Since most of the immigrants I interviewed were Jews, a brief discussion of the history of Jews in the former Soviet Union is in order. What Soviet Jews learned in the Soviet Union shaped their perceptions of the ethnic community in Toronto (Markus and Schwartz, 1984: 73). The experiences and changing status of Jews in the Soviet Union since 1917 have strongly influenced their attitudes towards their Jewishness and have implications for their pattern of adaptation in North America. This background may help to explain some of the difficulties Soviet Jewish émigrés have encountered in integrating into the Jewish community in Toronto and seeking help to start businesses.

While the Jews constitute a legally recognized nationality group in Russia, a number of experiences have weakened their group identity. In the first decade after the Revolution, the regime's policies towards Jews were aimed at restructuring Jewish identification so as to strengthen support for the values of the new regime by promoting allegedly universalistic secular norms. During Stalin's rule, the isolation of Soviet Jews from their cultural heritage and from international developments affecting Soviet Jews was reinforced through official policy aimed to undermine group cohesion by depriving Jews of the means of religious and cultural expression. The systematic destruction of older Jews elsewhere as part of the Holocaust deprived Soviet Jews of an important link with their heritage (Markus and Schwartz, 1984: 74).

After 1928, large numbers of Jews were willing to assimilate into the dominant culture by adopting the Russian language, moving into large urban centres, and pursuing higher and specialized education degrees. A large proportion became urbanized and highly educated, and socio-economic mobility encouraged identification with the dominant secular culture (Markus and Schwartz, 1984: 75). Most of today's middle-aged Soviet Jews grew up in an atheistic environment that encouraged their assimilation – and other ethnic and nationality groups – to mainstream Soviet/Russian culture (Gold, 1995a: 7).

Before the 1960s, the Soviet system offered Jews access to higher education because technical experts were required for the nation's military and industrial development (Gold, 1995a: 7). By the 1960s, Jews were the most highly educated and urbanized of all nationalities in the USSR (Gold, 1995a: 3). Jews provided a disproportionate number of the newly emerging professional and skilled work force while at the same time demonstrating patterns of assimilation into the Russian socialist culture. The Jews' high rates of communist membership (to maximize career opportunities) also fostered assimilation.

Official manifestations of anti-Semitism occurred under Krushchev and Brezhnev. Socio-economic mobility that had led to the rapid advancement of large numbers of Jews began to work against them. Access to higher education and career advancement was now hindered by their national identity, and reduced economic opportunity became linked with anti-Semitism (Markus and Schwartz, 1984: 75). In order to escape anti-Semitism (whether covert or official) and achieve success within Soviet society, many actively adopted Russian culture and identity, if they had not already done so.

Because the majority of Soviet Jews in the US and Canada are from the major cities in Russia and the Ukraine – Moscow, Leningrad (now Saint Petersburg), Odessa, Lvov and Kiev – they were subjected to a national culture designed by the Soviet government to unify the many ethnic, linguistic and nationality groups in the USSR. The overwhelming majority have few distinctly ethnic or cultural traditions (Gold, 1995a: 8).

For most Soviet Jews, especially those born under the Soviet regime, Jewish identity is an ascribed status and a hindrance. Those émigrés who retained a strong and positive Jewish self-identity were attracted to Israel. Those who possessed a weaker sense of Jewish identity opted for North America. Large numbers have immigrated to North America from the major cities listed above that have been under Soviet rule since 1917. They are second and third generation Soviet citizens who have grown up and been socialized in highly industrialized areas and steeped in the dominant Slavic culture. A large number are well educated and self-identify as professionals and skilled tradesmen. They have been socially and occupationally mobile and successfully adapted to the Soviet regime's dual requirements that self-identity be expressed in terms of a blend of Soviet socialist secular values and Russian cultural forms (Markus and Schwartz, 1984: 76).

Because of the lack of community solidarity, it is unlikely that Soviet Jews will establish strong links with the existing Jewish community in Toronto, let alone get any aid to start their businesses.

The pre-migration economic environment is a key to understanding the employment experience of Russian Jews – as with other Russian immigrants. In the former Soviet Union, there was officially no unemployment; job placement as well as the whole Soviet economy was centralized and government controlled. After completing his or her education, a worker was assigned a job, which could last a lifetime. Until recently, private enterprise was prohibited. Nevertheless, a surprisingly large percentage have, like earlier generations of Jewish immigrants, set up businesses in North America (Gold, 1995a: 48).

Conclusion

As this chapter shows, political and social circumstances in the former Soviet Union may have aided entrepreneurship in Toronto for both immigrant cohorts. Which strategies are pursued in Toronto depends to a significant extent on several factors: the legal-institutional structure in the former Soviet Union, the existing networks of political and financial power at the time of the transition, and the privatization policies adopted by the post-communist government. These factors are, in turn, affected by alliances forged before and during the transition process between entrepreneurs and (a) state elites, (b) financial sector elites, and (c) Russian entrepreneurs.

In the following chapters, I look at the influence of socialist entrepreneurial skills and institutional arrangements before and after the transition to a market economy in Russia, using the central postulates of each of the three theoretical approaches (transitional economy, ethnic and class dimensions of entrepreneurship, and transnationalism) to explain the factors that influenced business practice and success in Toronto for the Russian immigrants I interviewed. I will discuss these factors by looking at two phases of entrepreneurship and the founding of a business (see Wilken, 1979): (1) pre-start-up: motivation and idea development; and (2) start-up: planning and organizing the founding of a firm. I will compare how these two cohorts learned entrepreneurship skills; where they got ideas about business in Canada; where they learned about getting capital for their business, and how they established or took over existing firms.

NOTES

[1]   Russia has only recently emerged from 70 years of severe restrictions on self-employment and continues to have a hybrid cultural and institutional environment combining elements from the Soviet era with market institutions and practices (Gerber, 2002a: 31).

[2]   Three options of privatization were suggested. The majority (70%) of enterprises chose the option that gave enterprise insiders 56 percent of the assets (including 51%). The program gave popular vouchers, intended to involve all citizens in privatization activities. A total of 150 million vouchers with a nominal value of 10,000 rubles (US $50) each was distributed among the population. Lack of capital kept the vast majority of the population from participating in the public auctions designed for selling out thousands of small enterprises in Russia. The former state-run enterprise directors, backed by their compact teams of supporters, played the leading role in the formation of entrepreneurship (Radaev, 1997: 16-21).

[3]   These Russian immigrants would be the real winners in Russia's new economy because those able to establish successful businesses in Russia were most likely present during the transition and were more likely able to buy shares in companies or had connections to people who bought these shares. In their careers professionals develop networks that shape

their occupational or entrepreneurial opportunities. The contacts and relationships that people had before they migrate shape what they do abroad (Salaff, Greve, and Wong, 2001: 15).

4　However, because of political uncertainty and restrictions on private accumulation, private entrepreneurs had little incentive to make long-term plans or to reinvest into their businesses. Most of the money made was spent on consumption.

5　The legacies of communal cultural traditions and the Soviet economic system, and the economic chaos in contemporary Russia makes flows of goods and services through personal networks a dominant mode of exchange among organizations and individuals (Berliner, 1957; Kryshtanovskaya and White, 1996; Ledeneva, 1998). Social capital is an indigenous phenomenon that is deeply embedded in local cultural and historical traditions (Batjargal, 2003: 536). Like other groups, the cultural inclinations of Russians to rely on personal connections, rather than other economic and legal means, has made them more relationship oriented (Bunin, 1994; Ledeneva, 1998). Blat – the system of informal contacts – served as an alternative mechanism for overcoming the rigidities in Soviet factory production and supply practices (Berliner, 1957) and for obtaining consumer goods and services under the rationing system (Ledeneva, 1998). The legacy of the Soviet economy of deficits, such as personal bargaining and barter trading, are core features of Russian economic exchanges today, perpetuating the personalized nature of business dealings. In common with other transition economies, economic actors in Russia use personal relationships as safeguards against legal, institutional and environmental uncertainties (Batjargal, 2003: 541; Sedaitis, 1998; Stark, 1996; Xin and Pearce, 1996).

6　The likelihood of success for those who left the former Soviet Union was affected by various political processes in the transitional economy: the extent of regime change (the dismantling of single-party hierarchies along with the command economy) and the disposition of public assets (the rapid conversion of public property to new owners and the ability of incumbent elites to assume ownership or managerial control) (Walder, 2003: 899).

CHAPTER 5

Pre-Start-Up: Motivation and Idea Development

Introduction

In the first phase of entrepreneurship and the founding of a business someone is motivated to start a business. The business idea is developed and social support is sought through discussions with other people (Greve, 1995: 3). The main incentives for startups include: gaining a better economic position; preventing unemployment; attaining higher social status (Radaev, 1997: 33). In the pre-start-up stage, potential entrepreneurs look for advice, financial resources, and moral support from families, friends, and business associates, usually exploring possibilities within a small circle of close contacts. They contact others to test initial ideas, develop a business concept and get further support (Kamm and Nurick, 1993).

This chapter discusses the influence of class and ethnic resources, the socialist and transitional economy, and transnational linkages on the pre-start-up stage of an immigrant business in Toronto. It considers where entrepreneurs get motivation and ideas for a business. Unlike Western entrepreneurs for whom the inclination toward business and the relative success of entrepreneurial efforts is influenced mainly by class and ethnic resources within the city where they start their business, immigrant entrepreneurs look to their financial, human, social, and cultural capital acquired elsewhere, in this case, the former Soviet Union.

Class Resources: Human Capital in the Former Soviet Union

Education and work experience are the basic forms of human capital. For the case of the immigrants, I will separate this into Russian and Canadian education and work experience.

Education in the Former Soviet Union

Both cohorts came to Toronto with a high education and excellent skill sets. All had at least a bachelor's degree; 80% had technical and professional degrees, mostly in engineering and other science subjects.

Table 2: Education Attained by Immigrant Entrepreneurs in the Former Soviet Union

Type of Degree	Respondents (%)
Civil, Mechanical, Electrical, Electronic, Radio Engineering (Some received an MA in Engineering)	18 (56%)
MA – Material Sciences	1 (3%)
PhD – Physiology and Biomedical Engineering	1 (3%)
MD	1 (3%)
MA – Industrial Economics	1 (3%)
BA - Economics	2 (3%)
PhD - Radiology	1 (3%)
BA – Kinesiology	1 (3%)
Cinematography	1 (3%)
MA - Refrigeration	1 (3%)

Class Resources: Human Capital and Class-Specific Cultural Capital - Socialist Entrepreneurial Skills Developed in the Education System in the Former Soviet Union

As noted in the previous chapter, formal education was a communist legacy, and over the years, it increasingly emphasized technical knowledge over Marxist ideology. Also as noted, Soviet Jews took full advantage of the socialist education system. As a result, a large proportion of Soviet Jews were highly educated (Markus and Schwartz, 1984: 75). By the 1960s, Jews were the most highly educated of all nationalities in the USSR (Gold, 1995a: 3). All immigrants from the first cohort and 65% from the second cohort were Jews, and the tendency to have acquired a good education predominates among them.

Igor L. claims that he learned important skills in the education system in Russia, which later proved to be important in business in Toronto:

> When you have learned Marxist political economy, you are actually learning what Adam Smith developed. So, I understood what added value is and how profit is generated. I applied Marxist theory when I came here. I understood when I came here that a lot of people make money by other people working for them and by selling products for more than it costs to make the product. It is very basic and it is taught by Marx. In Toronto, you understand that the person who organizes the industry makes it possible to make a profit, which is denied in the Soviet Union. In the Soviet Union, when people figured out how to make money, they were put to death or put in jail for making money for themselves. When you ran an enterprise in the Soviet Union, you are a good manager if you make what you are told to do. Engineering skills are no different in Toronto. There was a lot of knowledge that I brought with me in economics and organization of production. In the Soviet Union, business was not run for profit; it was run to satisfy the plan developed by the state. You do what you are supposed to do; you are not responsible for generating profit; and you are responsible for total production. In Russia, generating profit was punished.

For Igor, the Soviet education system helped him adjust to the discourse of capitalism in Toronto, with its emphasis on self-centered action.

Work Experience in the Former Soviet Union

Work experience is another form of human capital. Since the majority of the immigrant entrepreneurs were Jews, the majority attained a great deal of work experience because, as noted previously, by the 1960s Jews provided a disproportionate number of the newly emerging professional and skilled work force (Gold, 1995a: 48). Soviet Jews were well-equipped for the task of adjusting to North American life – highly educated, with urban experience, and possessing the skills and resources needed to find jobs.

Table 3: Work Experience Attained by Immigrant Entrepreneurs in the Former Soviet Union

Cohort	Respondents < than 3 yrs work experience before coming to Toronto (%)	Respondents > than 3 yrs work experience before coming to Toronto (%)
1	18 (56%)	11 (48%)
2	1 (3%)	7 (78%)

Half the immigrants from the first cohort had more than three years of work experience in the former Soviet Union before coming to Toronto, and about half of these worked in the engineering field; the majority had kept their original jobs.

About 80% of the immigrants from the second cohort had more than three years of work experience in the former Soviet Union before coming to Toronto; about half of these worked in the engineering field. Over 40% kept the same job, while over half had two to three jobs in different fields. Some started to work in state-sector jobs in the communist system, but all were still living in the former Soviet Union during the transition to a market economy, and 40% left their state-sector jobs to work in other professional fields or to open up businesses. The immigrants from the second cohort who started businesses in the former Soviet Union averaged only one business before immigrating to Toronto.

An example of an entrepreneur who worked for a state-run company and then opened up a business is Victor G., an immigrant from the second cohort, who worked as an engineer on several construction sites for a state-run company during the communist system, and when the transition began, he opened a construction company and started building apartments and malls throughout Russia.

Since the immigrants from the second cohort were more likely than the immigrants from the first cohort to have jobs in more than one field and only the second cohort could leave state-sector jobs and start businesses after the transition, they became entrepreneurs in Toronto as a result of different work experiences. But even though there was a variation in their employment experience and their source of training, as will be shown in due course, both cohorts learned socialist entrepreneurial skills in the primary and secondary economy in Russia that helped them develop businesses in Toronto.

The immigrant entrepreneurs did not inherit businesses from their parents nor were their choices to start businesses influenced by their parents, but their parents did influence their career choices. All entrepreneurs from both cohorts who became engineers had fathers who were also engineers; 60% of the first cohort worked in the manufacturing sector like their fathers; half the entrepreneurs from both cohorts whose parents were teachers or professors took the same occupation; and half of the entrepreneurs from the first cohort whose parents worked in the science field also went into the same field. Clearly, immigrant entrepreneurs from both cohorts were influenced by their parents when choosing their occupation.

Only 20% of the immigrant entrepreneurs from the second cohort opened a business in the former Soviet Union after the transition. Boris worked as an engineer on a car plant after university and then became the professional manager of a soccer team in Moscow, much like his father, who was a hockey coach. During the transition he opened a furniture business; he had accumulated financial capital from working as a soccer team manager and he saw an opportunity after the transition. He knew that labour and raw materials were still cheap in Russia; he could manufacture furniture cheaply and sell it for a large profit in Europe and Israel. He also realized that the middle and upper classes would start growing in Russia and would need furniture. So he opened a furniture business, manufacturing the products in Russia and selling them in Russia, Europe and Israel. He also manufactured furniture in Europe, which he sold in the Russian market. When they opened the business, he says that

> on the first morning, there was a line up that stretched for blocks and we sold all the furniture that we had in stock by the evening. There were no furniture stores in Moscow at the time, and people were starving for anything.

Class Resources: Class-Specific Cultural Capital - Socialist Entrepreneurial Skills and Entrepreneurial Experience in the Primary and Secondary Economy in the Former Soviet Union

Some entrepreneurs from both cohorts, as mentioned above, inherited skills from their parents which influenced their career choices, but they got entrepreneurial experience from the primary and secondary economy in the former Soviet Union. They obtained a portion of their entrepreneurial culture or cultural capital from the communist past, specifically the black market economy.

The early experiences of the members of the last Soviet generation significantly affected how they understood, practiced, and shaped the activity of private business in the late-Soviet and early post-Soviet years. They learned to rely on the beat-the-system/bend-the-rules orientation and informal connections, and immediate consumption rather than deferred gratification/investment oriented capital accumulation.

As noted in the previous chapter, Yurchak (2002) contends that the Komsomol was a school of entrepreneurship, which taught ideological, economic and cultural skills to the younger generation during late socialism and provided a new pragmatic understanding of work, time, money, skills, professional relations and particular hybrid understandings of the official plans, rules, laws, and institutions of the party-state. This contention is not borne out by my sample

The majority of the first cohort and the second cohort were Komsomol members. A few were not because they were too young when they immigrated, but virtually all from the first cohort (17 of 23) and second cohort (8 of 9) who were of age and eligible to join the Komsomol did so. The majority were members of the Komsomol because it significantly affected their ability to get into schools and find jobs, not because they learned anything useful. Abe, an immigrant from the first cohort, and president of a construction and contracting company, Norcity Group, claims that in the 1960s, everyone was a member of the Komsomol when they were 14 and entered grade 8. However, he also notes that they didn't learn anything important:

> You're very proud to become a Komsomol member even though it doesn't give you any privilege, but it's a big dis-

advantage not to be one. We only learned about Komsomol history, the heroes of the Komsomol, and important dates and events in Communist history.

Igor L., an immigrant from the first cohort, concurs:

The Komsomol is not the organization that teaches you anything or requires you to learn much. It is just a membership, or belonging to the most massive organization in the country, much bigger than the Communist party. You just have to belong and that's it because if you are not a member of the Komsomol you are obviously hostile to the Soviet power and communist ideas, and it would be more difficult to get admittance to university.

Only one immigrant entrepreneur, Igor A., while acknowledging that it helped him in the education system, also says that the Komsomol taught some important skills:

If you apply for university, they looked at whether you were a member of the Komsomol. It was a good system. It makes you more disciplined in your future career and it makes you more responsible.

Instead of acquiring their business sense from the Komsomol, the entrepreneurs from both cohorts learned about the free market system by reading books from the West and listening to BBC, the Voice of America, and Freedom (a station whose head office was based in London) which transmitted in Russian. Irene, an immigrant from the first cohort, says the following:

Most of the households in the former Soviet Union had radios where some people would try to listen to the transmission from international radio stations, such as BBC and Voice of America. Most of the time, the Soviet government tried to block the transmission, but people could still catch most of the transmission. If we couldn't catch the transmission on a certain day, my friends would catch it, and then we would talk about what they heard on these radio stations. It was also dangerous to listen to these stations because neighbours could report you to the KGB if they heard that you were listening to these stations. It was considered illegal since you were listening to enemies of the state. You were supposed to listen only to the official news, which was of course the usual Soviet communist propaganda. Despite the difficulties of getting access to books from the West, some of us had connections to people who travelled outside the former Soviet Union who brought back copies of books to Russia, which they would then make copies of or somebody would retype the books on plain paper for us to read, so that nobody would catch us reading these books. My husband and I also learned about entrepreneurialism because we had contacts with people who traveled to other European countries, such as Poland, East Germany, and Czechoslovakia, which were economically much better off than the Ukraine.

Of the immigrant entrepreneurs from the first and second cohort who worked for a short period in the socialist economy, some learned important skills while working in these state-run companies that they later applied in Toronto. Abe claims that state-run companies had no interest in looking for more work because they were only interested in fulfilling their quota. But he adds:

> What they were doing was finishing whatever was sup-posed to be done in a month in one week and the rest of the 3 weeks they would send some of the employees to do private jobs, like in cooperatives, where they would be paid directly. Each cooperative or farm would sell some-thing to the government, like produce, and the money that they received from the government they would use to pay private people or universities who would send students to work there in the summers. The students were making three times more salary in the summer than any engineer.

These cooperatives taught skills, such as how to negotiate higher payments to do private jobs. These were important when the immigrants started businesses in Toronto.

The immigrant entrepreneurs who grew up during the Soviet command-style economy and who were illegally involved in the black market economy learned skills in entrepreneurship and re-emerged as legal entrepreneurs when the transition occurred. To be a successful entrepreneur in the second economy, one made good use of institutional rules, such as government regulations, and manipulated the rules (Yang, 2002: 134). Abe learned skills in negotiating that he later applied to entrepreneurial pursuits:

> Everybody was stealing. For private jobs, construction workers would go for half a day to work in cooperatives. They were paying crazy money. For example, the cooperative would pay me 50 rubles/day while the government paid me 100 rubles/month. The cooperatives would need 4 trucks to complete a job and they would pay me for 4 trucks but I would only need 2 trucks to complete the job, so I would keep the rest of the money. In the Soviet Union, you needed skills in stealing; bargaining and trading wouldn't help. It's called stealing in the Soviet Union, but in Canada it's called business. For example, in the Soviet Union if you bought something for $1 and sold it for $1.10, you go to jail, while in Canada, it is part of business.

Blat – the system of informal contacts – was an alternative mechanism for overcoming the rigidities in Soviet factory production and supply practices and for obtaining consumer goods and services under the rationing system (Ledeneva, 1998). As in other transition economies, economic actors in Russia used personal relationships as safeguards against legal, institutional and environmental uncertainties (Sedaitis, 1998). Igor L., an engineer from the first cohort, recited how, through adaptability and exchanging favours at work, he developed the *blat* (influence) and *sviazy* (connections) to succeed in the work world. He worked for 8 years as a mechanical engineer at a drafting board designing Ford trucks, taking apart Ford trucks and re-designing them using what was available in Russia. Nevertheless he also required bartering skills:

> Once I was asked to go on a business trip to several car plants in Russia to convince them to provide parts that we

would use in our design for our experimental models. These plants were resisting very heavily because we were a design bureau and if we were to work an engine into the design, they would become responsible for supplying that engine to our plant. So while I'm asking for 5 engines for experimental purposes, they understood that that really meant 10,000 engines per year for the next 15 years and they didn't want that to happen. Every company was concerned with avoiding the responsibility of being unable to produce enough. So if a plant was producing 600,000 engines, they were absolutely not interested in making an additional 50,000 engines because they would be asked why they didn't respond to state-approved plans. Not fulfilling the state plan was almost a crime. They didn't want to have anything to do with all these industries like Ford trucks. I had to figure out a way to convince them to produce these parts for us.

As Igor L. demonstrates, flexibility, personal bargaining and the ability to negotiate were critical in state-run companies to fulfill state plans for production during times of shortage.

When Mark, from the first cohort, worked as a doctor in Russia, he had to develop creative methods of getting drugs that were in short supply:

When I was working as a doctor our drugs were limited. In order to get drugs, if someone was sick we would pretend he had a brain tumor, for example, so that we could order drugs and they would send it to us through the Red Cross. Drugs would come from various organizations, it would only cost us 2 rubles. If I had a 70 ruble salary, I usually made $3000 a month selling drugs to patients.

For his part, Paul, the son of an immigrant from the first cohort, believes that the entrepreneurial minds were always there and were used in the underground economy. He believes that the underground economy was a training ground for entrepreneurs, like a "Harvard business school of hard-knocks." Paul's father had to use skills in bartering and trading to obtain the materials he needed for his textile company. Recalling his father's experience in the former Soviet Union, Paul says:

My father couldn't get the raw materials to produce the
textiles that the factory was supposed to produce, and he
couldn't get the bricks that were needed to build an
approved extension of the plant. He had a staff of smart,
well-educated engineers who were wheeling, dealing, and
bartering, trading bricks for metal pipes. There was an
underground economy, barter economy, where you were
trading goods without any sort of official sponsorship of
such activity.

In sum, those from the first cohort realized that it was not
possible to live outside the second economy. Before the 1980s,
members of both cohorts resorted to the black market to sustain
a living, despite the illegality.[1] In the preexisting command-
administrative economy, enterprise managers, such as Igor L. and
Paul's father, needed to behave in entrepreneurial ways; their
dense network of informal ties cut across enterprises and organizations, allowing them to acquire financial resources and materials to meet planned targets in conditions of chronic shortage
and stifling bureaucracy (Laki and Szalai, 2006). They learned
to renegotiate terms and conditions, replace one given constituent
of production with another, and to deal with party and state officials – all of which were readily adapted to the Toronto environment. Meanwhile, those who worked in the second economy cultivated a tradition of bypassing officialdom (Kurkchiyan, 1999:
84-88). They learned to rely on three basic resources of Soviet-
style entrepreneurship: (1) beat-the-system/bend-the-rules (rather
than legal-institutional) modes of operation; (2) reliance on informal networks (rather than on individual skills and formal infrastructure); and (3) consumption-oriented, rather than production-
oriented capital accumulation whereby immediate or short-term
rewards take priority over long-term deferred gratification
(Morawska, 1999: 360).

Migration History and Work Experience in Other Countries

I will now discuss why the entrepreneurs decided to emigrate
from the former Soviet Union, the paths taken before they arrived
in Toronto, and the jobs they held in other countries to determine
how their motivations for leaving, their job experiences and the

financial capital accumulated in other countries influenced their decision to start a business in Toronto.

Table 4: Reasons for Leaving the Former Soviet Union

Cohort	Respondents who left because no opportunities in field (%)	Respondents who left because experiencing discrimination (%)	Respondents who left because wanted to create better life for themselves and their children (%)	Respondents who left because didn't want to continue living in a communist system (%)
1	0	8 (35%)	9 (39%)	6 (26%)
2	1 (11%)	1 (11%)	6 (67%)	1 (11%)

Virtually none of the immigrant entrepreneurs had social networks in Canada before they left the former Soviet Union and as a result, virtually none had any direct social assistance or advice from relatives. The immigrant entrepreneurs knew very little about the country to which they were moving. Because of restrictions on information, this was especially true among the first wave of émigrés who came before the fall of the Soviet Union.

Soviet Jewish émigrés cite several reasons for settling in North America. They frequently refer to better educational and economic opportunities for themselves and their children rather than the Jewish State as their primary motivation (Brym, 1993; Simon, 1985; Orleck, 1987). Initially, socio-economic mobility led to the rapid advancement of large numbers of Jews, but in the 1960s, access to higher education and career advancement was hindered by Jews' national identity; reduced economic opportunity came to be linked with anti-Semitism (Markus and Schwartz, 1984: 75). Soviet émigrés came to Toronto expecting to improve their career prospects and those of their children and attain economic well-being. While many cite anti-Semitism as a motive for leaving, emigration was generally the result of a combination of "push" and "pull" factors.

Before the fall of communism, push factors included personal and institutional anti-Semitism, blocked mobility, a low standard of living, and a repressive political environment. After that time, economic collapse and fear of violence rank highly. Pulls include political and religious freedom and a high standard of living. The majority of Soviet Jews claim that their children's future not religious freedom was their primary reason for emigrating (Gold, 1995a: 17). The first cohort left the former Soviet Union for one of the following reasons: discrimination, unhappiness with the communist system, and wanting to create a better life for themselves and their children. The majority of the second cohort left because they wanted to create a better life for themselves and their children.

Established migrants can become newcomers' social resources in starting businesses by providing information before immigration regarding the business climate, the types of enterprises that seem feasible, and the regulatory processes (Light and Bonacich, 1988; Marger, 2001: 443). However, none of the entrepreneurs that I interviewed received any information about setting up businesses in Toronto and had little to no knowledge of the economic prospects in Canada before coming to Toronto. Virtually all came to Canada based on their human capital as landed immigrants.

Before 1988, when permission to go abroad was finally granted, émigrés took a train to Vienna, where they stayed for about a week while initial processing took place. From there a small percentage who had retained a strong and positive Jewish self-identity flew directly to Israel. A much larger group traveled to the outskirts of Rome, where they remained for two or three months while their settlement to the US or Canada was arranged (Gold, 1995a: 21). Those opting for North America have tended, as a rule, to possess a weaker sense of Jewish identity.

Large numbers have immigrated to North America from major cities under Soviet rule since 1917. They are, mainly, second and third generation Soviet citizens who have grown up and been socialized in highly industrialized areas. A large number are well educated and identify themselves as professionals and skilled tradesmen, who have been socially and occupationally mobile. They had successfully adapted to the Soviet regime's dual requirements that self-identity be expressed in terms of a blend of Soviet socialist secular values and Russian cultural forms (Markus and Schwartz, 1984: 76).

The majority of the first cohort immigrated to Toronto through Italy or other countries, such as Israel, while the majority of the second cohort immigrated directly to Toronto because after the transition it was now allowed.

Those immigrants who immigrated to Toronto through Italy or Israel were more likely to work in a variety of jobs and start businesses before coming to Toronto. Immigrants who worked in jobs in other countries were able to accumulate some financial capital, as will be later discussed, and those who set up businesses in other countries learned from these experiences to set up businesses in Toronto. Misha K., an immigrant from the second cohort says:

> I started by working as an engineer in the export department of a company called Etco, and after nine years, I became the company's general manager. When I left Nigeria I went to South Africa and was employed as a company director in an air conditioning refrigeration company that worked in black areas of South Africa until 1995. In 1985, I started my own company. It was contracting and servicing air conditioning, plumbing, electrical, elevators, communication. A year and a half later I opened another company that manufactured and sold architectural light fittings. A year later I opened another factory or company that manufactured electronic safes for hotels. Gradually we expanded to export all those products into Africa and I travelled a lot. In 1994 I left South Africa to go back to Israel and in 1995 I started [a] telecommunications company in New York together with some other people. I was still living in Israel, and in 1998 I left to New York to manage that company. In 1998 I moved to Toronto and opened a telecommunications company in 2001. I'm still a shareholder in the company in New York. I opened the telecommunication company here that provided international long distance services for mostly the Russian community.

Class Resources: Financial Capital

Immigrant entrepreneurship success is partly determined by the amount of financial/material resources that immigrants bring with them (Zhou, 2004: 1046).

Since the Soviet government limited the amount of money and goods that émigrés could take out of the country (only about $100 in Rubles was permitted) (Gold, 1995a: 22), the majority of the immigrants came to Toronto with virtually no financial resources. They had also earned low wages in rubles in the state-run economy. A few came with financial resources because they had worked overseas, or had earned money while immigrating through another country to Canada. For example, Abe said that he had the $5000 that he needed to invest in a construction business with a partner when he came to Canada because he had worked as a tour guide in Italy. Leon was allowed to work in Iran, where he was the manager of all construction sites for an Iranian construction company and was in charge of 5000 employees. He worked there from 1975 to 1978, making $10,000 a month; when he immigrated to Toronto in 1978, he had financial capital.

On the other hand, over 40% from the second cohort came with a significant amount of financial resources from businesses they ran in Russia after the transition. The relative absence of constraints on asset appropriation due to a period of regime instability and a privatization program that occurred rapidly and in an unregulated manner and no institutional framework created a new propertied and corporate elite with greater opportunities to maintain control of public assets as they were privatized or to obtain personal ownership of assets and enter the emerging market economy with large business advantages (Walder, 2003: 907-8). For example, Victor G., who is a property investor in Toronto, ran several businesses in Russia, and came to Toronto with millions that he made from property investment in Russia.

Both cohorts had considerable human capital, coming to Toronto with a high education and skill sets. The majority of both cohorts had more than three years of work experience in the former Soviet Union before coming to Toronto; about half of the second cohort left state-sector jobs to work in other professional fields or to open up businesses. Even though there was a variation in their employment experience and their source of training in the former Soviet Union as a result of historical changes, both cohorts learned socialist entrepreneurial skills in the primary and secondary economy in Russia. Those who worked in jobs in other countries before immigrating to Toronto accumulated financial capital and acquired valuable knowledge.

Class Resources: Human Capital in Toronto

Education in Toronto

Virtually all immigrant entrepreneurs relied on the education and the cultural capital that they brought with them. Virtually all received their education in the former Soviet Union, but what seemed to be more critical was the fact that they had technical and professional degrees and had graduated from university, many with higher degrees.

Work Experience in Toronto

Fewer than 20% of the immigrant entrepreneurs in each cohort started their businesses in Toronto in the same occupational fields as their parents. As mentioned previously, many went into the same professional fields as their parents, but they started businesses in different fields. A few entrepreneurs started businesses in the same occupational fields as their parents, such as Zinovi, whose father was a tool and die maker in Russia. Zinovi currently owns a tool and die business, Maziro, which manufactures parts for the automobile industry. But none indicated that their parents were influential in their choice to become an entrepreneur or their decision as to what kind of business to start.

Since the immigrant entrepreneurs in both cohorts were not influenced by their parents to become entrepreneurs, I will introduce the concept of paths, or institutional continuity, which posits that once a person is in an institutional structure, other opportunities open or close naturally (Hill, Martin, and Vidinova, 1997).

The following table illustrates the amount of work experience that the immigrant entrepreneurs acquired in Toronto.

Table 5: Work Experience Attained by Immigrant Entrepreneurs in Toronto

Cohort	Respondents < than 5 yrs work experience before starting business (%)	Respondents > than 5 yrs work experience before starting business (%)
1	6 (26%)	17 (74%)
2	5 (56%)	4 (44%)

Over 70% of the first cohort of entrepreneurs indicated that they had a vast amount of human capital, having accumulated on average 5 years of work experience in Toronto before starting a business. Over 40% of the second cohort of entrepreneurs also had substantial human capital; they too accumulated on average 5 years of work experience in Toronto before starting their business. Cohort 1 was more likely to have more than 5 years of work experience while cohort 2 was more likely to have less than 5 years of work experience. The difference between the two cohorts may be explained by the fact that the second cohort of immigrant entrepreneurs came to Toronto after the transition to a market economy in Russia. They were more likely to have gained entrepreneurship experience in the former Soviet Union; as a result, they were more likely to come with financial capital, as we shall later see, that allowed them to develop seed capital earlier, and more likely to have come to Canada knowing that they wanted to do business. Since the first cohort immigrated without any entrepreneurial experience in the former Soviet Union, most went to work in professional jobs; staying in these jobs for over 5 years was common (17 of 23 or 74%).

Over 80% of the immigrants from the first cohort were concentrated in the following fields before starting their businesses: engineering, science, finance, and retail. All immigrants from the second cohort were concentrated in one of the following four fields: engineering, manufacturing, retail, and arts. To start their entrepreneurial careers, more than half had left four main economic industries: engineering, manufacturing, science, finance, and retail. Initial jobs provided these immigrants with skills that they could later use to establish a business, such as English language proficiency, and some financial capital which they could invest in business.

I will now discuss the 5 different paths to entrepreneurship taken by the immigrants from both cohorts. Human capital, social capital, and opportunities were all relevant for each case, but they differed.

Five Paths to Entrepreneurship

Path 1: Immigrants who couldn't get their credentials accredited, or for whom the Canadian institutional structure of the field for their profession differed, decided to go into business. Path 1 is consistent with the disadvantage theory, which suggests that immigrants are pushed to self-employment as a result of disadvantages in the mainstream labour market and human capital handicaps, such as the inability to get well-paying jobs due to poor English, lack of host country education, credentials and licenses, and discrimination (Beaujot, Maxim, and Zhao, 1994: 82; Aldrich and Waldinger, 1990: 116; Chan and Cheung, 1985: 143; Cobas, 1986: 103). Disadvantaged entrepreneurs undertake self-employment because they earn higher returns on their human capital in self-employment than in salaried employment (Light, 1979; Min, 1988; Beaujot, Maxim, and Zhao, 1994: 84). Russian immigrants who took path 1 to entrepreneurship started a business because the professional training they received in the former Soviet Union was not recognized in North America and licensing was denied until Western professional standards were met; consequently, it was difficult to find jobs in the main sector of the economy.

Path 2: Immigrants who lost their job and couldn't find another job in their field or an allied field decided to start a business. Path 2 is consistent with some aspects of disadvantage theory and reactive cultural theory. Disadvantage theory suggests that entrepreneurs may be motivated to start their firms, in part, because of negative "pushes" within their incubator organizations, such as being frustrated in their previous jobs or being laid off (Cooper, 1986: 159). Reactive cultural theories suggest that immigrants who experience disadvantages in the labour market will use their experiences and cultural attributes from their origin country and ethnic resources within their community to help start a business (Light, 1980; Gold, 1995a: 56). Russian immigrants who took path 2 to entrepreneurship were frustrated in their previous jobs or were laid off; they used their experiences and socialist entrepreneurial skills and/or drew on ethnic resources within their community.

Path 3: Immigrants who found business opportunities within their field or an allied field left their salaried jobs to start a business. Path 3 is consistent with opportunity theory, which suggests that when immigrants are working in salary jobs and an opportunity comes up to start a business, they may decide to do so (Aldrich and Waldinger, 1990: 114, 116; Cooper, 1986: 156). Russian immigrants who took path 3 to entrepreneurship found opportunities within the organization where they were working and decided to open a business.

Path 4: While they were working for co-ethnics in salaried jobs that may or may not have been associated with their field, some immigrants talked to friends who told them about a business opportunity. They decided to leave their salaried jobs to start a business. Path 3 is consistent with some aspects of opportunity theory and ethnic economy theory. Opportunity theory suggests that potential entrepreneurs can only work with the resources made available to them by their environments, and the structure of opportunities is constantly changing (Aldrich and Waldinger, 1990: 114). Ethnic economy theory suggests that for those immigrants who are unable to go into business shortly after arrival, the ethnic sub-economy allows them to take jobs in firms owned by co-ethnics. In return for loyalty and hard work, the owner will aid his or her employees in times of emergency and provide opportunities for advancement, such as helping start a business (Bonacich and Modell, 1980; Portes and Bach, 1985; Wilson and Portes, 1980; Cobas, 1986: 104). Russian immigrants who took path 4 to entrepreneurship started by working for a firm owned by a co-ethnic or a Canadian firm; while working here, they found out about an opportunity to open up a business from their co-ethnic friends, and if they had the necessary resources and capital requirements, they decided to do so.

Path 5: These immigrants came to Canada with business experience and financial capital, already knowing that they were going
to start a business. Some thought they could avoid the dangers
of doing business in their origin country. These immigrants had
very little work experience in the host country. Path 5 is consistent with business background theory which suggests that immigrants who have business experience outside of North America
or in their country of origin are more likely to use their business
experience to establish businesses in their host country (Light,
1984; Bonacich, 1973; Portes and Bach, 1985). Russian immigrants from the first cohort who took path 5 obtained entrepreneurial experience in the socialist and black market economies;
immigrants from the second cohort obtained entrepreneurial
experience by setting up a business after the transition to a market
economy.

The first, second, and fourth paths to entrepreneurship
are consistent with the ethnic and class dimensions of entrepreneurship approach, which states that the inclination toward business and the relative success of entrepreneurial efforts on the part
of immigrants is based on a balance of class resources: financial,
human, and cultural capital and ethnic resources, which include
ethnic social networks and social capital (Light, 1984; Waldinger
et al., 1990).

The third path to entrepreneurship is consistent with the
ethnic and class dimensions of entrepreneurship approach, which
states that the inclination toward business and the relative success
of entrepreneurial efforts by immigrants is influenced by their class
resources: financial and human capital, specifically the money they
made and the experience that they accumulated in their previous
salaries jobs (Light, 1984; Waldinger et al., 1990). This path is also
consistent with the transnationalism approach; if they started
transnational businesses, they more easily notice the business
opportunities that cultural frontiers generate and have the international social capital, social networks and bilingual ability that support international business (Lever-Tracy et al., 1991: xi, 113 in
Light, 2007: 90; Wong, 1998: 95 in Light, 2007:90).

The fifth path to entrepreneurship is consistent with the
transitional economy approach (Pontusson, 1995: 119; Nee,
1991: 267), which states that the immigrants who were present
during the transition to a market economy are more likely to set

up businesses and come to Toronto with business experience and financial capital.

The following table illustrates why the immigrant entrepreneurs left their professional jobs or the paths that they took to entrepreneurship.

Table 6: Paths Taken by Immigrants to Entrepreneurship

Cohort	Path 1 (%)	Path 2 (%)	Path 3 (%)	Path 4 (%)	Path 5 (%)
1	9%	9%	52%	30%	0
2	0	0	44%	22%	33%

The majority of the immigrants from both cohorts worked in the field in which they obtained their degrees; the most prominent field for the immigrant entrepreneurs was engineering.

I will now discuss the findings from table 6 and provide examples of immigrants from both cohorts to illustrate the 5 paths to entrepreneurship.

Path 1: Only 2 (9%) of the immigrants from the first cohort and none of the immigrants from the second cohort couldn't get credentials (or the institutional structure of the field for their profession was different in Canada) and decided to go into business as a result.

Gold's study (1995) of Soviet Jews in New York found that about half of those who had held professional, technical and managerial occupations in the USSR found similar jobs in New York. Gold found that lack of job-related licenses and certifications, limited English language skills, and the incompatibility between certain Soviet and American occupations make it hard for many highly skilled émigrés to get the kinds of jobs they would like and are trained for (1995: 50). It is well known that immigrants have to reacquire credentials when they come to Canada, but none of my entrepreneurs went back to school.

Professionals who are frustrated in their ability to find work in their fields of expertise may turn to entrepreneurship.

Only 2 immigrants from the first cohort who came to Toronto with a lot of human capital, in the form of high education, seeking professional work were frustrated in their field of expertise or couldn't get a job in their profession, and turned to entrepreneurship. For example, Abe, an immigrant from the first cohort, claims that he couldn't get a job as an engineer, so he decided to open a construction company. Since coming to Toronto, he has started about 10 companies, all involved in the same business, building new homes, commercial and industrial construction and general contracting. Victor, an immigrant from the first cohort, also failed to find a job in his profession. He claims that in the 1982 recession in Toronto, most structural engineering firms were going bankrupt, and most of the engineers were fired, so he decided to start a window company; eventually he opened his current baked goods company, Uppercrust.

Path 2: Only 2 (9%) of the immigrants from the first cohort and none of the immigrants from the second cohort lost their job and were unable to find another job in their field or an allied field, and decided to start a business as a result. For example, when Triam decided to close their research development group in Canada, Jacob, an immigrant in the first cohort, declined to continue working for the company in the US because he didn't want to move there with his family. After looking for a job for about 8 months, he learned that he was overqualified for all the jobs he was applying for; this motivated him to start his own business. But he acquired all the skills required to open and run his business, Integrity Testing Laboratory, such as how to use the transmission electronic microscope and x-ray electro-microscope, by working at Triam. Triam also sold him all the machines they had been using in Canada for a very reasonable price.

Path 3: Over half the immigrants from the first cohort and nearly half from the second cohort found business opportunities within their field or an allied field. Zinovi, an immigrant from the second cohort, couldn't get a job in his profession. When he came to Toronto no one wanted to hire a mechanical engineer who couldn't speak English, so he ended up working in a warehouse. He lost his job, and when he heard about an opportunity in his field, he decided to start a business. Zinovi says:

After losing my job, I met Alex, who convinced me to open up a company, called Maziro Cars, that would produce parts for the automobile industry. Then we met our third partner who was working at that time with Magna, one of the biggest manufacturers of car parts in the world who introduced us to the company. It was just our luck. It was Christmas time and they had a job which had to be made during the Christmas time. The companies who were usually doing the job for them didn't want to do it because it was Christmas time. We used this opportunity, and as soon as we got that order, we started to develop our own company and when we finished this first order they found out that we weren't so bad so they started to use us more and more. In the first year we made $370,000 in revenue. I'm amazed at how it happened because we started our business by using our visas.

When Zinovi seized an opportunity, he became successful. As a result, human capital, in terms of his professional engineering degree, his experience in the Canadian labour market, and social capital came together in a successful venture.

Many other immigrants started a business because opportunities opened within their field of expertise; they could use the connections they developed in the company they were working for to open a business. For example, Igor L., an immigrant from the first cohort, learned the basics of business systems while working at Becton Dickinson, skills he later used when he joined SAP, the only big success story in the software industry outside the US, where he became a pre-sales engineer. Igor L. opted for entrepreneurialism when SAP decided to open up a channel (certain companies are allowed to resell the company's software) in Canada, and his team won the competition to take over the channel. His company became one of the most successful channels worldwide.

Vladimir, an immigrant from the second cohort, started a business because opportunities opened up within his field of expertise, He had been working in the automotive industry for six or seven years, so he had experience and connections. Because he knew what the automotive industry needed, he thought that if he opened his own company, AVN Automation, manufacturing automotive parts, he would make more money. Human capital and social capital, in terms of experience and connections in the automotive industry came together.

Jake, an immigrant in the first cohort, did the same thing. Jake developed sales experience, selling vacuum cleaners for three and a half years for a company called Filter Trim. He became one of the top Canadian salesmen out of 3,000 people. He left this company to become the sales manager for Rollag, eventually joining the board of directors, and working for the company from 1979 to 1984. But he ultimately set out on his own to manufacture the same products as Rollag. He says:

> When I started working for Rollag they were in the hole, $2 million dollars in debt. When I became the sales manager, we made half a million dollar profit in five to six years. This was an achievement and I understood that I could do more for this company. But at the same time I understood I could also do more for myself and my family. If I started slowly and took my time, I could do it myself, instead of working under a salary. I already had the business attitude, and a   couple of years before leaving Rollag, I had been talking to the owner of the company when he visited Canada from Germany and told him I didn't want to work on a salary, I wanted to work on a straight commission, and he told me that this was crazy because what would happen if there were no sales. I said I wanted to have very heavy commission from the sales of the company and what did   they have to lose? They put me on commission, and this was already like in a business because whatever you make is yours. That is how I understood that enough is enough and it was time to have my own. I left Rollag to start my own business, a company, called Rolltec, which would manufacture the same thing that Rollag did, windows, shutters and awnings. Having collected this kind of experience I thought it was time to do it on my own. I was buying the same product from them as if I was their dealer until I slowly decided I would start to manufacture my own and I started to buy parts from Europe and assembled it here. I assembled it to customer's specifications. Over time, my

company grew from 900 square feet to 25,000 square feet, and I started buying machines and slowly started manufacturing my own parts. By 2005 I already produced and designed our own awning system.

In this case, Jake had a well-paying job but left it to start a business which manufactures and sells the same thing; he believed this business would be an effective way to maximize his human capital returns and expand his middle-class status through higher earnings. Again, human capital in terms Canadian labour market experience and social capital came together.

Ilya, an immigrant from the first cohort, started a business because opportunities opened up within his field of expertise where he could use the connections developed in the company where he was working. Ilya had a well-paying salaried job working for Malco and Associates, which manufactures technologies for the defense industry. He left his high-paying job for the following reasons:

> I saw an opportunity to create a company that would manufacture technologies for our military and satellite industry because the company that used to produce these technologies, Advantech, was bought out by Hewlett Packard and they decided that it was no longer profitable enough for them to continue making these   technologies. So I basically built a company that Canada never had, serving a lot of niches that no other company can serve.

Ilya linked several networks and created opportunities by spanning structural holes between them (Burt, 1992). New entrepreneurs, such as Ilya, go between their networks to start up business (Greve and Salaff, 2003, in Salaff et al., 2007: 101). They get ideas from different contacts, bridging structural holes and combining resources in novel ways (Burt, 1992, in Salaff et al., 2007: 101). Ilya got the idea to create a company that would manufacture technologies for the Canadian military and satellite industry while working for Malco and associates. Working for Malco allowed him to gain experience in the military and satellite industry and generated a long list of contacts that proved instrumental to the success of his own business.

Alex started his own business because an opportunity opened up within a field closely related to his field of expertise after developing close connections with a businessman who had good connections in Russia sourcing steel. Alex, an immigrant from the first cohort, decided to quit the company that he was working for in Switzerland after he met someone from Belgium who was a steel trader, and he became his partner in the steel business, and they decided to form a company together in 1992 called Transstall. Alex decided to start the steel business with his friend because he believed that this transnational business would be an effective means of maximizing his human capital returns and expanding his middle-class status through higher earnings and would give him more economic independence. As a result, human capital, in terms of his experience in the labour market in Switzerland and Russia, and social capital came together in a successful venture. Some of the highly educated immigrants, such as Alex, quit their salaried jobs to pursue entrepreneurship because they thought they could better utilize their skills, bicultural literacy, and transnational networks to reap material gains.

Path 4: Thirty percent of the immigrants from the first cohort and about 20% of the immigrants from the second cohort talked to friends and were convinced by them to leave a salaried position and start a business. Some were employed in their area of specialization; others were not. Many of the latter, in fact, were overqualified in their present jobs, such as engineers working in construction. The point, however, is that they were employed when they decided to become entrepreneurs.

Igor A., an immigrant from the first cohort, couldn't get a job in his profession; he worked in several jobs not associated with his field until he met a friend who told him about a business opportunity:

> When I came to Edmonton, I realized I would not be able to work as a physical education or sports instructor, which is what I got my degree in the Ukraine. It didn't work out because sports in Canada is not as important as it was in Russia and it receives very little support from the Canadian government. If you don't have support from the government, then you have to look for other ways to put

money on the table. So I ended working at a steel company. Then a recession came in Edmonton, and I began to work for an Industrial tools company. I wasn't making enough money, so I went into the taxi business. After that I went into the food business and worked for two bakery companies, Interfoods, followed by Uppercrust. I wasn't making enough money at either of these companies, which is when I met the inventor of a new ice fishing rod, called the Wonder Strike Rod, and we opened Winter Wonders together.

In this case, as a result of a chance meeting with an inventor of a new fishing rod, who happened to also be from the Ukraine and who worked with him in the taxi business, Igor decided to open a business venture with the inventor. He was frustrated working in jobs unrelated to his field of expertise and inadequate pay. Although he knew nothing about the business, he thought that the combination of his business expertise and his friend's expertise (he was a professional fisherman), they could start a successful business. As a result, human capital and social capital came together in a successful venture.

Leon, an immigrant from the first cohort, talked to friends while he was working in a salaried job that was within his field of expertise. They mentioned a business opportunity, and he decided to leave his well-paying salaried job to start a business with them. Thus, his social capital was important. Leon, formerly chief engineer at a General Electric factory in Alberta, says:

I made $85,000 a year in wages, plus a car and benefits and allowances, and medical insurance. Then, I got an offer from two friends who told me that they were starting a shoe factory. I told them I didn't know anything about shoes. One of them said that he already worked for one year in a shoe factory, and he already knew the companies and he said that there is a shortage in the market for high fashion ladies shoes. He said bringing them from Europe is good business with a lot of opportunities. We started to send samples of our shoes to several companies in Toronto, and they said that they were interested and wanted to buy shoes from us. I brought some money from Iran that I made working as an engineer there and I put the money into the business. Our company, Luxan Shoes Manufacturing, lasted from1991 to 1997. We made Italian shoes for major shoe retail stores in Canada. Then we decided to open up factories in Russia and the Ukraine.

The chance encounter with friends from the Russian community who were in the process of opening up a business led Leon to leave his salaried position. Leon believed that this transnational business would be an effective means of maximizing his human capital returns and expanding his middle-class status through higher earnings and would give him more economic independence. Like Igor A., he drew upon both human capital, in terms of his experience in the Canadian labour market, and social capital.

In yet another case, Jack, an immigrant from the first cohort, quit a well-paying salaried job within his field of expertise to pursue entrepreneurship after talking to friends from the same Russian ethnic group who convinced him to join their business. He says:

> Two of my Russian friends who already had a business going, called Uppercrust, which was a small frozen dough production company, convinced me to become a partner with them. At the time, it was a small company but the proposition was interesting, so I left my job and joined that company. I made a lot of money there. I worked at Uppercrust for 7 years, from 1985 to 1991. During this period the company grew from a very small company, maybe half a million dollar a year of sales to about 4-5 million dollars. It grew almost 10 times in its size and sales.

Like Leon, Jack left a good job in his profession to open a business because of a chance encounter. Again like Leon, he believed this business would be an effective means of maximizing his human capital returns and expanding his middle-class status through higher earnings and would give him more economic independence. And again, an immigrant success story unites human capital with social capital.

Path 5: A unique path was also evident for cohort 2, where 3 out of the 9 immigrants came to Canada with both business experience and financial capital, already knowing that they were going to do business. Most thought that coming to Canada would give them the opportunity to start a business; some wanted to do business in Toronto, thinking they could avoid the dangers of doing business in their origin country. These immigrants had little work experience in Toronto before starting their business.

Misha K. came to Toronto in 1998, planning to continue in the telecommunications industry, where he had previous business experience, opening companies in several countries. His Toronto telecommunications company opened three years after his arrival; it provided international long distance services for mostly the Russian community:

> I decided to open up a business in Toronto because it's a simple succession of my path. Since 1985 I started to establish businesses. I became an independent entrepreneur. So I knew that if I was coming to Toronto, I would continue the same path by opening a company that was related to my past work. During my business entrepreneurship, I started many businesses related to the engineering field. It's just a matter of interest and opportunity. At the end of 2001, I came from New York with a background in telecommunications. It was natural that I would continue in the same way in Toronto, especially when I was still a shareholder in the company in New York. If one knows the nature of this business, then one knows that telecommunication is not really nailed to a place. Telecommunications is a universal service and you can do it from wherever you want. It is also a lot of partnerships, especially in the wholesale international telecommunications business, you buy and sell throughout the world. I buy termination in China to a telephone card provider in Toronto, or California or Vancouver. The routes are so flexible so you don't have to be tied up with a wire. It is the technology that brings you wherever you want.

In this case, Misha K. came to Canada with international business experience and financial capital, already knowing that he was going to do business. Although he had little work experience in Toronto, he drew upon his human capital, in terms of his expertise and experience in the international telecommunications industry, his social capital, in terms of his connections to providers around the world, and his financial capital.

Victor G., as mentioned previously, opened a construction company and started building apartments and malls throughout Russia after the transition; he had no work experience in Toronto before starting a similar business. Victor G. says:

> I was making millions doing various construction projects in Russia. It was very dangerous for businessmen like me in Russia who were making millions because I was approached by mafia groups who said that they would provide a 'krysha' (protection) for me if I would pay them protection money, meaning a percentage of my profits. While I was doing business in Russia, I of course complied, and in return for paying them a percentage of my profits they would ensure that all my customers paid me on time and they would ensure the safety of my business. But it was still dangerous to do business in this type of environment, and I did not want my kids to be exposed to this and be in any danger, so I decided to move to Toronto, where it would be safer to do business. In Toronto, I immediately became involved in the real estate and construction business, buying and selling real estate and building and leasing shopping malls.

Before immigrating, Boris, also mentioned above, opened a furniture business where he manufactured furniture cheaply and sold it for a large profit in Russia, Europe and Israel. When he moved to Toronto he continued to operate his furniture business in Russia. He had also opened a business in Brazil where he produced vodka and sold it to various countries; he also produced vodka in Russia. Boris came to Canada with business experience from Russia and financial capital from his businesses in Russia and Brazil.

Ethnic Resources: Ethnic Social Networks and Social Capital

To establish a business that can produce and market its products or services efficiently, entrepreneurs often draw upon ethnic resources, which typically include relationships of trust, ethnic-derived social capital and social networks (Light and Gold, 2000: 102-105). Many critics (Light and Gold, 2000: 110) argue that groups' collective resources, help them maximize the value of their human and financial capital to achieve economic stability or betterment. Ethnic resources, such as enforceable trust and multiple social networks encourage and support the founding of new business firms (Light and Rosenstein, 1995a: 202). Entrepreneurs use their social capital to access resources in each phase of the establishment process. Social contacts more than individual achievement prompt business entry. Brokers in a network, entrepreneurs pool resources to start their firms (Burt, 1992). That being said, the established community of earlier Russian immigrants in Toronto, a form of social capital in the host country, did not send signals to newcomers. Earlier Russian immigrants in Toronto did not provide any information to the immigrant entrepreneurs from either cohort regarding the business climate or the types of enterprises that would be feasible in Toronto.

In fact, only a few Russian entrepreneurs from either cohort spoke to friends from the Russian community about business related matters. For example, when Jacob, an immigrant from the first cohort, and a Lithuanian Jew, opened his company, Integrity Testing Laboratory, he received some help from Irene, an immigrant from the first cohort, and a Ukrainian Jew. She supplied leads for clients, and some of those leads became his clients. Jacob and Irene have similar scientific educational backgrounds and were close friends with similar interests. This could have resulted in social networks with low diversity, often called the homophily principle (Aldrich and Kim, 2005; McPherson, Smith-Lovin, and Cook 2001; Aldrich and Kim, 2007), but this did not happen. Instead, Irene introduced Jacob to a wide social network that helped him establish a diverse clientele for his business.

The Soviet Jewish immigrants did not turn to the established Jewish community for information about business opportunities, access to credit, and customers because for most Soviet Jews, especially those born under the Soviet regime, Jewish identity is a hindrance to educational and economic opportunities (Markus and Schwartz, 1984: 73, 76). It could be expected, therefore, that once in Canada they would repeat the adaptation pattern successfully applied in the Soviet Union and acculturate in the dominant secular patterns by learning English in a secular environment and working outside the Jewish community. As a result, Soviet Jews are not likely to join, participate in, or seek help from Jewish institutions in Toronto (Markus and Schwartz, 1984: 82). Soviet Jews have not developed large ethnic enclaves in the US or Canada like those that underpin the success of Cuban and Korean entrepreneurs (Gold, 1988: 427; Wilson and Martin, 1982; Min, 1986; Portes and Bach, 1985). They are unlike earlier immigrants who banded together to survive (Light, 1972; Glazer and Moynihan, 1963; Portes and Rumbaut, 1990).

While Soviet Jews are united by language, immigration experience, estrangement from North American Jews, and shared notions of ethnic identity, as a group, they are also segmented (Gold, 1995a: 90). Many émigrés are individualistic in nature and they tend to distance themselves from co-ethnics because of feelings of distrust. Consequently, they are unlikely to turn to their immediate ethnic community to get any aid to start their business. Regionalism is a further source of division because émigrés from Russia (especially Moscow and St. Petersburg) generally consider themselves to be above those from the Ukraine. The divisions and ambivalent feelings toward fellow immigrants help explain the small number of formal organizations among Soviet Jews (Gold, 1995a: 92). Moreover, Russian Jews who were under the pressure of communism are tired of being forced to join different organizations; in North America they want to be free from all organizations (Gold, 1995a: 93). Because they come from a country where the government, until recently, controlled all organizational life, Soviet Jews immediately regard any type of organization with cynicism, despite the potential benefits of collective action (Gold, 1995a: 119). In short, Soviet Jews have not merged with North American Jews nor have they set up strong, community-wide formal organizations. These new immigrants, who are skilled and educated, have fewer reasons for organizing their communities than did the immigrant Jews of an earlier generation who had few resources beyond their own organizations for satisfying basic needs.

Even so, some immigrant entrepreneurs drew upon their ethnic resources. For example, Alex, an immigrant from the first cohort, met his current partner, Edward, a fellow Russian, who was working as a head representative for a Hong Kong-based steel trading company. Edward knew all the general directors in Russia, and he knew the steel business inside out. Alex convinced Edward to become his partner, telling him he would be given freedom to operate and much more authority in their new company, Midland. Alex also offered to finance it. He took the capital that he needed from his old company, Transtall, which eventually stopped operating. In this case, Alex used his ethnic resources to enhance his business.

Victor, an immigrant from the first cohort formed a business relationship with an individual from the Russian community who had expertise in the wholesale frozen and baked goods industry, and provided him with information about business opportunities. Interaction among Soviet Jews is frequent in the Russian Jewish nightclubs where émigrés spend long evenings celebrating secular events (Gold, 1995a: 99). Most Soviet Jews prefer the company of fellow émigrés in an informal context that emphasizes Russian culture (Gold, 1995a: 116). This was the case for Victor, who met his partner at a Russian nightclub. Victor, who is the sole owner of Uppercrust, a company that bakes specialty breads, says,

> I met my former partner at a Russian nightclub and he was working for a company called Maple Leaf, which was a very small company at the time with two owners. He was working there making $3 an hour making dough and croissants. He expressed his desire to me to become partners to open up our own wholesale frozen and baked goods company, called Uppercrust, which would sell to supermarket chains. I thought it was a great idea and with his expertise in the field and my business acumen, I expected that we would be successful.

Another entrepreneur who got information about business opportunities from members of the Russian ethnic community is Leon, an immigrant from the first cohort. Leon says that two friends from the Russian community convinced him to become a partner in a shoe factory even though he didn't know anything about shoes. One partner had been working for a year in a shoe factory; he knew there was a shortage in the market for high fashion ladies shoes. He convinced Leon that bringing these shoes from Europe and selling them in Toronto would be a good business.

Conclusion

The three theoretical approaches reviewed in this chapter, including the ethnic and class dimensions of entrepreneurship, transitional economy, and transnationalism all figure in explaining the factors that influenced and shaped business practice and success in an immigrant community in Toronto.

Ethnic and Class Dimensions of Entrepreneurship Approach

Human capital as measured by education and work experience increases rates of entrepreneurship, aids business startups and plays a significant role in immigrant business success. In both cohorts, immigrant entrepreneurs who came with more human capital or who obtained more human capital in Toronto, in the form of education and occupational skills were in an advantageous position to start businesses.

Immigrant entrepreneurs also need access to financial capital. In the case of the second cohort, immigrant entrepreneurship success is partly determined by their accumulation of financial capital during the transition in Russia.

An established community of earlier immigrants, a form of social capital in the host country, may send signals to newcomers, indirectly promoting entrepreneurship. Some entrepreneurs from both cohorts drew on social networks, including friends, former colleagues, and the Russian community for advice.

The Transitional Economy Approach

Both cohorts of immigrant entrepreneurs came to Toronto with human capital, specifically technical and professional degrees. Because there are greater incentives for individual effort in market transactions in Toronto than in the socialist sector, which will result in higher returns on education, those immigrants from the first cohort who came to Toronto with a higher level of education were in an advantageous position to enter entrepreneurship.

Immigrants who were able to take advantage of the transition to a market economy in Russia in the late 1980s and early 1990s and establish successful businesses in Russia came to Toronto with a lot of financial capital. On the other hand, the majority of the immigrants from the first cohort arrived to Toronto with virtually no financial resources because they left during the communist system. In this case, they turned to their human capital.

Immigrant entrepreneurs from both cohorts, who grew up during the communist system, obtained entrepreneurial culture or cultural capital, in the form of skills, knowledge, attitudes, and values required to succeed in entrepreneurship from the primary and secondary economy in Russia. In an economy of full employment under socialism, most entrepreneurs participated in the second economy or black market economy part-time, while holding on to a secure state-sector job, where they learned important skills in entrepreneurship, such as making use of, and manipulating institutional, rules that they could then apply to becoming entrepreneurs in Toronto.

The Transnationalism Approach

Some highly educated immigrants, especially immigrants from the second cohort who lived in Russia during the transition or immigrants from the first cohort who returned to Russia during the transition, quit their well-paying salaried jobs to pursue entrepreneurship because they could better utilize their skills, bicultural literacy, and transnational networks to reap material gains. Many of their transnational businesses are based in Toronto, using transnational entrepreneurship as an effective means of maximizing their human capital returns and expanding their middle-class status.

Case Observations

Both cohorts of immigrant entrepreneurs embodied considerable human capital, coming to Toronto with a high education and excellent skill sets. All had graduated from university, many with higher degrees. The majority were Jews, the most highly educated of all nationalities in the former Soviet Union. Since the majority obtained professional degrees, it seems that those who have significant amounts of human capital may make more effective entrepreneurs.

Since the immigrants from the second cohort were more likely than the immigrants from the first cohort to possess jobs in more than one field in Russia, and only the second cohort could leave state-sector jobs and start businesses after the transition, they had different employment experiences in the former Soviet Union. But even though there was a variation in their employment experience and their source of training, both cohorts learned entrepreneurial skills in the primary and secondary socialist economy.

Immigrant entrepreneurs from both cohorts were influenced by their parents when choosing their occupation. Since none of the parents of immigrant entrepreneurs from either cohort were entrepreneurs in the former Soviet Union, neither cohort became entrepreneurs because that's what their parents did. Some entrepreneurs from both cohorts inherited skills from their parents which influenced their career choice, but they got their entrepreneurial experience from the primary and secondary economy in the former Soviet Union.

The majority of the first cohort and the second cohort were members of the Komsomol for reasons of survival. All entrepreneurs I interviewed claim that they didn't learn any important business skills when they were members of the Komsomol. Instead, they learned about the free market system during Soviet times by reading books from the West and listening to BBC, the Voice of America, and Freedom.

Immigrant entrepreneurs from both cohorts who worked for a short period in the socialist economy learned important skills that they could apply to becoming entrepreneurs in Toronto. Under state socialism, many were doing something similar to entrepreneurship in cooperatives (negotiating higher payments to do private jobs, for example). Prior to the 1980s, members of both cohorts also resorted to the black market to sustain a living, even though this entrepreneurial activity was not legal. By taking part in the second economy, they grew accustomed to the practice of informal problem-solving and cultivated a tradition of bypass-ing officialdom. By and large, they were more entrepreneurially oriented and were more likely to become entrepreneurs when restrictions on private accumulation were lifted in Russia and when they immigrated to Toronto.

Virtually none of the immigrant entrepreneurs had social networks in Canada before they left the former Soviet Union and as a result, virtually none had any direct social assistance or advice before they left from relatives. The first cohort left the former Soviet Union for reasons of discrimination, unhappiness with the communist system, and wanting to create a better life for themselves and their children; the majority of the second cohort left because they wanted to create a better life for them-selves and their children. This is consistent with past research that indicates that Soviet Jews almost universally seek to improve their career prospects and those of their children and attain eco-nomic well-being, not religious freedom.

None of the entrepreneurs received any information about setting up businesses in Toronto and had little to no knowledge of the economic prospects in Canada before coming to Toronto. Because of restrictions on information, this was especially true of the first wave of émigrés who came before the downfall of the Soviet Union. Virtually all came to Canada based on their human capital as landed immigrants.

The majority of the first cohort immigrated to Toronto through Italy or other countries, such as Israel, while the majority of the second cohort immigrated directly to Toronto because it was allowed after the transition. Very few entrepreneurs in either cohort held jobs in other countries, but those immigrants who immigrated to Toronto through Italy or Israel were more likely to work in a variety of jobs and start businesses before coming to Toronto. Those who set up businesses in other countries learned from their experiences.

The majority of the immigrants from the first cohort came to Toronto with virtually no financial resources; they left during the communist era where they earned low wages in rubles in the state-run economy, and the Soviet government limited the amount of money and goods that émigrés could take out of the country. There were a few exceptions; some members of the first cohort worked at various jobs and opened businesses in other countries, such as Italy and Israel, and earned money which they brought to Canada. Some of the second cohort brought money with them as a result of business activities after the transition in the former Soviet Union.

All members of the first cohort attained their education in the former Soviet Union; a small number of the second cohort received their university education in Toronto because they were too young when they left the former Soviet Union to have gone to university there. In short, virtually all of the immigrant entrepreneurs relied on the education and the cultural capital that they brought with them from the former Soviet Union to start businesses in Toronto. Even so, it didn't seem to matter for business development and success whether they received their education in the former Soviet Union or in Toronto. What seemed more critical was the fact that they had technical and professional degrees and had graduated from university.

None of the immigrant entrepreneurs' parents were entrepreneurs, as they all worked for state-run companies in the communist system. A few went into the same occupations as their fathers and started businesses in the same occupational fields as their parents. But none indicated that their parents were influential in their choice to become entrepreneurs or their decision about what type of business to start.

The human capital of the majority of the first cohort of entrepreneurs was vast. They had accumulated, on average, 5 years of work experience in Toronto before starting their business. Less than half of the second cohort accumulated that amount before starting their business. The difference between the two cohorts may be explained by the fact that the second cohort came to Toronto after the transition to a market economy in Russia; this means they were more likely to have come with entrepreneurship experience in the former Soviet Union as well as financial capital; they were also more likely to have come knowing that they wanted to do business. Since the first cohort immigrated without any entrepreneurial experience in the former Soviet Union, most went to work in professional jobs, and staying in these jobs for over 5 years was common.

To start their entrepreneurial careers, more than half of all respondents had left one of 4 main economic industries: engineering, manufacturing, science, finance, and retail. The majority of the immigrants from both cohorts worked in the same field that they graduated in and worked in the former Soviet Union; the most prominent field for the immigrant entrepreneurs was engineering. They used their high human capital to get jobs in their fields or allied fields. Initial jobs provided these immigrants with skills, English language proficiency and some financial capital.

Only two immigrants seeking professional work from the first cohort and none from the second cohort, who came to Toronto with a lot of human capital in the form of high education, were frustrated in their field of expertise or couldn't get a job in their profession because they couldn't get credentials or the institutional structure of the field for their profession was different in Canada. These two turned to entrepreneurship. It seems then, that the disadvantage theory and the ethnic and class dimensions of entrepreneurship approach, which help explain their decision, is of limited relevance.

Only two of the immigrants from the first cohort and none of the immigrants from the second cohort lost their job and couldn't find another job in their field or an allied field. These two decided to start a business. Disadvantage theory and reactive cultural theory and the ethnic and class dimensions of entrepreneurship help explain their decision, but again, this is only a very small percentage.

Over half of the immigrants from the first cohort and nearly half of the immigrants from the second cohort found business opportunities within their field or allied field, so they decided to leave their salary job within their field or allied field and start a business. Opportunity theory and the ethnic and class dimensions of entrepreneurship approach seem to have a much greater relevance in explaining entrepreneurial decisions.

NOTE

[1]   It was dangerous to work in the second or black market economy. Igor L. notes that Krushchev made economic crimes punishable by death in the criminal code: "There were many people in Lvov who committed economic crimes, and they were supplying everything, such as consumer goods and clothing for the rest of the Soviet Union. They had underground factories, and many people were put to death or sent to labour camps for running these underground factories." Despite the dangers, most immigrant entrepreneurs from the first cohort worked in the black market, obtaining much of their *cultural capital* from it.

CHAPTER 6

Start-Up - Planning and Organizing the Founding of a Firm

Introduction

In the second phase of entrepreneurship entrepreneurs start planning the business in detail; they work on financing the business, setting up business deals, agreements, and finding a property for their business (Greve, 1995: 3). In the start-up stage they establish their companies, reaching out to partners, staff, buyers, and suppliers. At this point, entrepreneurs need to mobilize a larger social network (Carter et al., 1996).

In this chapter, I will look at the influence of class and ethnic resources on the start-up stage of a business in the case of the Russian immigrants. The three theoretical approaches, the ethnic and class dimensions of entrepreneurship, transitional economy, and transnationalism, help explain how various factors, including financial, human, social, and cultural capital influenced the start-up.

I will ask how these new arrivals without a history of family firms that they could inherit in Russia and with little community support managed to procure the resources they needed to start businesses in Toronto. I maintain that while their class resources came into play, their ethnic resources were much less important.

Class Resources: Human Capital

Some studies of immigrant entrepreneurs assert that entrepreneurship is an alternative avenue of economic participation for members of a minority group who have little human capital, such as lower levels of education and English speaking ability, and that they participate in ethnic economies as an alternative means of achieving economic success (Portes and Jensen, 1989, in Fong and Lee, 2007: 162-3). In contrast, I argue that human capital as measured by education and work experience aids business start-ups (Sanders and Nee, 1996). This is seen in the entrepreneurs I studied who began with human capital they attained in the former

Soviet Union and accumulated even more experience and connections the longer they stayed in Canada.

Entrepreneurship was linked closely to technical knowledge. Graduates strong in engineering and professional expertise were most likely to start businesses within their professional fields. All the entrepreneurs that I interviewed had a high education, which they attained either in the former Soviet Union, in Israel, or in Toronto, depending on which cohort they belonged to. As mentioned previously, the majority of the immigrants from both cohorts worked in the same field that they graduated in and worked in the former Soviet Union, and the most prominent field for the immigrant entrepreneurs was engineering. They used their high human capital to get jobs in their fields or allied fields. The majority of the degrees that they attained corresponded to the business that they ended up establishing.

I will now discuss how human capital, social capital, and opportunities differed for the 5 different paths to entrepreneurship taken by the immigrants from both cohorts.[1]

Path 1: Russian immigrants who took path 1 to entrepreneurship started a business because the professional training that they received in the former Soviet Union was not recognized in North America, and licensing was denied until Western professional standards were met. This meant it was very difficult to find jobs in the main sector of the economy, and they opted for self-employment. But as mentioned previously, this applied to only 2 (9%) of the immigrants from the first cohort and none of the immigrants from the second cohort.

Abe, an immigrant from the first cohort, got a university degree in civil engineering in Russia and Israel. When he could not find a job as an engineer in Toronto, he went on to open up about 10 construction and contracting companies. All were in the same line of business, building new homes, commercial and industrial construction and general contracting; he has been operating his current company, Norcity Group, for 17 years.

Path 2: Russian immigrants who took path 2 to entrepreneurship came with human capital but were frustrated in their jobs or laid off. They used their experiences in the labour market to help them start a business. As mentioned previously, only 2 (9%) of the immigrants from the first cohort and none of the immigrants from the second cohort fit into this category.

Jacob, an immigrant from the first cohort, got a PhD in solid state physics in Russia. In Toronto, he was employed for 4 years by Triam, where he worked on semi-conductor materials to make lasers that would emit blue light used to send information from satellites. Triam closed its research development group in Canada, and after looking for employment for about 8 months, he used his educational and work-related skills to start his business, Integrity Testing Laboratory.

Path 3: Russian immigrants who took path 3 to entrepreneurship came with human capital and found opportunities within the organizations where they were working for a salary. After careful consideration, they decided there was an unfulfilled demand which they had the resources to meet, so they started a business. Over half of the immigrants in the first cohort and nearly half of the second cohort fit into this category.

Irene, an immigrant from the first cohort, got an MA in material sciences in Russia. While she was working towards her PhD at the University of Toronto, she worked as a lab technician for 5 years. After she received her doctorate, her position changed from lab technician to engineer, and she worked in the department of mechanical engineering for 5 years. Next, she worked at the Ontario Research Foundation for 5 years, where she started as the technical manager of electronic objects, before entering the environmental sciences department and becoming a consultant. Irene quit her job at Ontario Research Foundation to pursue entrepreneurship because opportunities opened up within her field of expertise where she could use the connections and experience that she developed at the research foundation. Her business, Environix Engineering, provides environmental services for governments, universities, boards of education, investigating buildings for the presence of hazardous materials, advising them of the presence of the materials, preparing technical documents, and then removing the materials. She says,

> Over there [at the Ontario Research Foundation] I already had a large group of technicians operating equipment and reporting to me, and I was signing reports and approving

technical conclusions. I gained experience for my business by just observing what was happening....I was providing services to the environmental consultants. All the analytic work was done by my technical group and I was supposed to invoice them, so I knew how much money they were spending on obtaining their analytical services....Now I have my own profit, I know everybody in the industry. I do not have to work so hard to make the same amount. So that was the reason behind starting my own business, I didn't want to push so hard and not to benefit as much. I realized that if I provide the services by myself and offer a better price I could keep all the clients and profit.

Irene believed that her business would be an effective means of maximizing her human capital returns.

Vladimir, an immigrant from the second cohort, also came with human capital. He received a PhD in mechanical engineering from the St. Petersburg Polytechnical Institute and started a business in Canada when opportunities opened up within his field of expertise where he could use his work-generated connections. He had been working for the automotive industry for almost seven years and had both experience and connections. Because he knew what the automotive industry needed, he thought that if he opened his own company, manufacturing automotive parts, he would make more money. He says,

The reason I decided to start my business is because I have a lot of skills and knowledge and I knew that I could do a better job than the people that were above me. I had been working for the automotive industry for almost six or seven years so I had a lot of experience and I knew what the automotive industry needed because the automotive industry is a closed club and I had all my old connections and networks from automotive companies that I worked for, such as Nucap, ABC, and PMP.

Path 4: Russian immigrants who took path 4 to entrepreneurship came with human capital. They began by working for a Canadian firm, and while working at these firms, they learned of an opportunity to open a business from co-ethnic friends. If they had the necessary resources and capital, they did so. About 30% of the immigrants in the first cohort and about 20% of the second cohort talked to friends who told them about a business opportunity.

Leon, an immigrant from the first cohort, got an engineering degree in the Ukraine, and then passed the exam to become a professional engineer in Toronto. For one year, he worked as an engineer at a division of General Electric in Etobicoke, before being promoted to chief engineer at the division in Edmonton, where he worked for another year. Leon quit his job to pursue entrepreneurship after talking to friends from the same Russian ethnic group who told him about a business opportunity (see Chapter 6 for details) in shoe manufacturing. Although he knew nothing about shoes, he was convinced to join them as a partner, adding the capital he had earned while working in Iran.

Zinovi, an immigrant from the second cohort, also came to Canada with human capital. He talked to friends from the same Russian ethnic group while he was working in a job associated with his field. When they told him about a business opportunity, he decided to leave his job to start a business. Zinovi received a degree in mechanical engineering from Lvov Polytechnical University in the Ukraine. Initially, he couldn't find a job in the engineering field because he couldn't speak English, so he found work in a company that sold carpets, called Alta and Carpet. He worked there for 3 years, earning about $10 per hour. Then he got a job in his field but was laid off after about 6 months. He next found a job as a designer and production manager for a company that manufactured machines for the automotive industry. He says everything changed when he met a fellow engineer from the Russian community who was working in the same company:

> I met a guy there named Alex with whom I started to talk
> about doing a business with....So we opened a company
> and we rented a small office for $200. We opened up a
> company called Maziro Cars. Then we met our third part-
> ner who was working at that time with Magna, who intro-
> duced us to the Magna company. It was just our luck, it
> was Christmas time and they had a job which had to be
> made during the Christmas time. The companies who
> were usually doing the job for them didn't want to do it

because it was Christmas time. We used this opportunity
100%, and as soon as we got that order I quit my job and
we started to work on our own company and when we finished this first order they found out that we weren't so
bad so they started to use us more and more. In the first
year we had to sell $370,000. I'm amazed at how it hap-
pened because we put into our business by taking from
our visas.

Zinovi initially had problems finding employment within
his field of expertise but eventually did so. Even so, after a
chance encounter with a fellow Russian engineer who told him
about a business opportunity, Zinovi decided to start a company
that manufactures machine parts.

Path 5: Russian immigrants from the second cohort who took
path 5 to entrepreneurship came with human capital. They had
obtained entrepreneurial experience by setting up business after
the transition to a market economy in Russia or by going to other
countries, and they used this experience to set up businesses in
Toronto. One-third of the immigrants from the second cohort
came to Canada with business experience and financial capital,
already knowing they were going to do business.

One such entrepreneur is Misha K. who has an MA in
electromechanical engineering from the Technical University in
Haifa, Israel. When he came to Toronto in 1998, he planned to
continue in the telecommunications industry, where he had business experience opening companies in several countries. He
opened a telecommunications company in Toronto three years
after arriving, with the intention of providing international long
distance services for mostly the Russian community.

Class Resources: Financial Capital

Entrepreneurs need to raise money, invest in technology, locate
materials, get training, hire workers, find markets, and shape their
products and services to fit their clients' needs so they can take
advantage of perceived opportunities (Greve and Salaff, 2003;
Light, Bernard, and Kim, 1999).

The choice of financing source shows that human capital, in the form of years of education, work experience and high occupational skills, was recognized by the banks and the government. As a result, the majority of the immigrants obtained financing from traditional sources of capital, such as banks, or from a combination of sources, such as banks and private investors to start businesses in Toronto. Some social scientists suggest that formal community organizations are required for effective funding for immigrant businesses (Gold, 1995a: 59). But none of these entrepreneurs received financing solely from ethnic community members.

Table 7: Sources of Financing

Cohort	Banks (%)	Ethnic community (%)	Private investors not part of their ethnic community (%)	Own financing (5)	Several sources (%)
1	5 (22%)	0	4 (17%)	6 (26%)	8 (35%)
2	2 (22%)	0	1 (11%)	1 (11%)	5 (56%)

The immigrants who took path 1 to entrepreneurship came to Canada with human capital. They had education and work experience from the former Soviet Union but couldn't get their credentials recognized in Canada. These immigrants were more likely to obtain financial capital from a variety of sources. Abe, an immigrant from the first cohort, started several businesses in construction and has been operating his current constructing and contracting company, Norcity Group, for 17 years. Abe discusses how he obtained his financing from a variety of sources, including his own financing, private investors, and banks:

> I paid $5000 to get in to the business. I had that money when I came to Canada. So, we didn't have to apply for a loan because we were getting paid for each building job by the customers. So that was the financing we were getting and that was it. Later when I was building new

houses and selling them I was getting mortgages. I was getting financing from banks. After my first business, I was mostly using banks, and relatives, friends, and private money. People who had private money were asking me if I would take their money because they were making good money and they had no problem investing the money with me. In 1987 and 1988 they were making 50% return on their investment with me in less than a year. Whoever invested $100,000 whether it be friends, acquaintances, would end up making $150,000 back. It wasn't a fixed amount that they requested in return and they were basically waiting for a percentage of the profits and the percentage was so high in 1987 that it sometimes ended up being 50% in 6 or 7 months....So the only time you needed the banks was to get a mortgage to purchase the land. The rest of the money was supplied by the customers. Financing was never a problem...

The immigrants who took path 2 to entrepreneurship came to Canada with human capital, then lost their jobs and couldn't find another job in their field or an allied field. These immigrants were more likely to obtain financial capital from banks to start their business. Jacob, an immigrant from the first cohort, got all his seed capital from the bank to start his business, Integrity Testing Laboratory, which manufactures and tests materials for the aerospace industry. To do so, he re-mortgaged his house.

The immigrants who took path 3 came to came to Canada with human capital, worked within their field or an allied field for a few years; then as a result of their social capital, they found business opportunities. They were more likely to obtain financial capital from banks, a combination of their own financing and the bank, or private investors and the government. Irene, an immigrant from the first cohort, got all her seed capital from her own financing, which she accumulated by working for the Ontario Research Foundation for 5 years. She says that she did not need any financing because all the equipment that she purchased was inexpensive and/or second-hand.

Paul, an immigrant from the first cohort, on the other hand, received all his education and work experience in Toronto and found entrepreneurial opportunities within his field. Eventually, he left his salaried job at IBM to open a software company. Paul became CEO of pVelocity, a software company after receiving a six and a half million dollar investment from a British Columbia venture capital company in Toronto, called Edgestone Capital. He also received capital for his software companies, PPT and pVelocity, from SRED, the Canadian Government Recognition of Research and Development Fund used for the technology industry. SRED gave him some money for research and development activities that he could claim every year. The potential financial returns of high-tech firms, such as pVelocity make such firms of particular interest to the financial community. One study estimated that 60 to 70 percent of investments by the leading venture capital firms were in technology-based firms (Cooper, 1986: 153).

Vladimir, an immigrant from the second cohort, obtained seed capital for his business, AVN Automation, from his own finances and the bank:

> I came with a lot of financial capital from Russia which I accumulated by working for the aerospace and defense industry from 1981 to 1986, teaching at the university from 1986-1999, and then working for the defense industry again from 1996-1998. In Toronto, I was able to accumulate financial capital by working at several automotive companies, such as Nucap, ABC, Anton, and PMP. So, I used my own financial resources, and then I obtained a government guaranteed loan from the bank to buy machines for my new business, AVN Automation and the bank also gave me a line of credit.

Path 4 immigrants came to Canada with human capital; they talked to friends while they were working in a salaried job and these friends told them about a business opportunity. Consequently, they decided to leave their jobs and start a business. These entrepreneurs were more likely to obtain financial capital from their own financing or from a variety of sources. Leon, an immigrant from the first cohort, used all of his own financial resources which he accumulated from his engineering jobs before immigrating to Toronto, to become a partner in Luxan Shoes Manufacturing. As the business grew, the partners began to get additional financing from the bank. Leon says:

I came to Canada with a lot of my own money. I was the
manager of all the construction sites for a huge company
in Iran, where I had 5000 employees working under me.
In 1974, I started making $1600 dollars a month, but by
1975, I was already making $10,000 a month, and I
worked for this company for 4 years. When I worked as
the chief engineer for the General Electric division in
Alberta, I was making $85,000 per year. From Iran I had
brought some money so I put it into our new business,
and I ordered the machines. I went to the wholesalers of
electrical stuff in Toronto and I bought for $5000 all the
necessary materials, and in two months I completely finished building the factory by myself and my two partners.
We started to work for major shoe retail stores in Canada.
Everybody was buying from us and we got the first loan
from the bank of Montreal to receive a $300,000 line of
credit for the business. Over time, when the company
grew, we had a $3 million dollar line of credit for our
business.

Zinovi, an immigrant from the second cohort, also took
path 4 to entrepreneurship. He obtained the seed capital for his
business, Maziro, from his own finances and a venture capital
company:

When I came to Toronto, I came with some of my own
financial capital because I had a very good position as a
supervisor at the Lvov Bus Assembly Plant in the Ukraine
from 1977-1994. When I went to Canada in 1994 I was
the chief mechanic and vice-director of the plant. I also
earned a good salary by working at several companies that
manufactured parts for the plastics, furniture, and automotive industries. When we opened our business, Maziro,
with my partner, we hardly put in any money into our
business…and we didn't need to get a loan. We accumulated orders from Magna for $370,000 in the first year.
Eventually we knew we had to buy our own equipment.
The first equipment we bought was for $20,000 for lease,
and then we found other machines that were more expen-
sive that we needed. So we met one wonderful guy from

CAT financial group who was willing to give us a loan. He trusted us and said I am pretty sure you are going to pay it, go ahead I will give you money. I needed a venture capital company like CAT financial group because the companies that give me contracts to make machines and parts for the automobile and aerospace industry, such as Magna and the Canadian government only pay me two to three months after the machines and parts are delivered, so CAT gives me enough capital to operate my company while I wait for payment. Seven years later I am still working with him. All the equipment that I have I buy only through him.

The immigrants who took path 5 came to Canada with human capital, business experience and financial capital. They arrived intending to open a business and had very little experience working in Canada before starting a business. These entrepreneurs obtained financial capital from their own financing and/or from a variety of sources. Misha K., an immigrant from the second cohort, had financial resources that he accumulated from several international telecommunications and project management companies that he opened in several countries. He used this to open a telecommunications and international project management business in the field of mechanical and electrical engineering, and he also got a loan from the bank.

Ethnic Resources: Ethnic Social Networks and Social Capital

Ethnic groups regularly provide their members with financial capital through personal loans, which rely on reputation and enduring relationships as collateral (what Light and Bonacich (1988) call ethnic facilitation), but this was not the case for my entrepreneurs. The Russian ethnic community did not provide the majority of the entrepreneurs with any business advantages. Possibly they had adequate financial means already, or they had social capital in terms of education to obtain resources in Toronto. At any rate, none of the immigrants knew anyone in Toronto before they arrived. As a result, the majority of the entrepreneurs turned to banks and private investors for seed capital.

None of the entrepreneurs turned to Jewish or Russian organizations for financial capital, and none belonged to Russian business organizations. They did not feel that there was any benefit for their business to join Russian business organizations. However, over half of the entrepreneurs in the first cohort and over 30% in the second became members of professional trade organizations before or as soon as they started their businesses, and these helped them develop business contacts.

Victor, an immigrant from the first cohort, owns Uppercrust, where he produces bread and other baked good products. He is a member of the American Institute of Baking and Retail Bakers of America. He says that joining these organizations put him into contact with all the suppliers and customers in his field; furthermore, if he had not joined, none of the big chain stores in the US would have started buying from him. Sam, an immigrant in the first cohort, owns Sunrock, which sells synthetic chemicals and rubber; he is a member of the North American Rubber Association. Joining this organization put him in contact with all the companies in Canada and the US that use synthetic chemicals and rubber in their production process. He got his largest customer, Airbus, which manufactures planes, by being a member of this organization, and now he is their main supplier of synthetic chemicals. Vladimir, who owns AVN Automation, and Zinovi, who owns Maziro, both immigrants from the second cohort, manufacture machines and parts for the automotive and aerospace industries; they are members of the Association of Professional Engineers of Ontario. In their field it is necessary to be a member of this association because it certifies that you are a legitimate company; other companies are then willing to give you contracts. They also found most of their suppliers and customers in the automotive and aerospace industry from this association.

These entrepreneurs began to network through mainstream and formal channels (i.e. professional associations and specific trade organizations), rather than joining ethnic associations or organizations.

They also developed network contacts for their business by attending trade shows and industry events. Paul, an immigrant from the first cohort, uses trade shows to develop network contacts and meet venture capitalists looking to invest in software companies. He also gets ideas for his company from these industry events:

I am part of an organization called AceTech, which you can only be a part of if you are the CEO of a software company, and the membership is comprised of thousands of CEOs of technology firms across Canada. As an organization we get together once a year, and we also hold smaller events throughout the year with regional chapters and groups. CEOs present their company's story and how they did what and what decisions they made, and who helped and who didn't and what succeeded and what didn't.

Irene, who owns Environix Engineering, which provides environmental services for the government, universities, boards of education, used to be a member of the American Society for Metals and American Society for Material Sciences and currently belongs to the Association of Professional Engineers. She developed network contacts by working at the Ontario Research Foundation (ORF) where she was providing services to the environmental consultants:

> I developed my contacts with environmental consultants while working at ORF....It was very helpful that I was on the board of directors of ORF because we were organizing conferences, so I was meeting people, and this is how I introduced what my company was doing. Then I developed contacts through the jobs that we completed for the school board, hospitals, and government organizations.

Irene no longer has to do any marketing because she now knows everybody in the industry, and people now contact her to see if her company wants to bid on the job.

Igor A., another immigrant from the first cohort, went to various fishing and hunting, sporting goods, and outdoor shows in the United States, Canada and Europe, such as ISPO where he found many of the distributors and chain stores that are now selling his fishing rods.

Even though all entrepreneurs from the first cohort were Soviet-Jews, fewer than 20% turned to Soviet Jewish friends, for seed capital or to invest in their business. They either came with their own financial capital or were able to obtain loans from banks. Leon said he came to Toronto with a lot of money from

his previous jobs in engineering in various countries, such as
Israel and Iran, and used all of his own money to open his factory.
Gabe worked in Moscow as an institutional equity salesman for
a U.S-Russian investment bank called UFG (United Financial
Group), and he made so much money in Moscow that he didn't
need to borrow any money when opening his investment company in Toronto. Sam used the money that he made working in
several jobs, such as national buyer and supplier for Mark's Work
Warehouse for 10 years, to open his current company. Michael
T. used the money that he made in construction jobs to open his
company; he has a branch in the Ukraine that manufactures
patented concrete reinforcers, and sells them to the construction
industry across North America.

Some entrepreneurs received some of their seed capital
from friends in the ethnic community and some had co-ethnic
friends who invested in their business. But the financial capital
they received from their friends was also accompanied by financing from other sources, such as private investors who were not
part of their ethnic community, and banks. There were only 4
entrepreneurs from the first cohort who got financial capital from
members of the Soviet Jewish community; for the most part, they
got financing from their friends because they did not have enough
money themselves and they did not get sufficient capital from
the bank. Therefore, they had to look elsewhere for financing.

Igor A. received a small business loan from BDC in the
amount of $100,000 to start his business, Winter Wonders. This
was not enough money because he needed to design and build
moulds to manufacture his fishing rods, and he needed to buy
many of the fishing rod components from the United States and
China. He approached his Ukrainian-Jewish friends to ask if they
were interested in investing in his business. His friends agreed to
invest $100,000, and in exchange they received a 30% stake in
the company. Victor received 50% of the capital to open his
bakery from a Russian friend whom he met in Italy before he
came to Canada, and who then worked with him in the construction business; in exchange he gave him 50% equity in the company. His finances and his friend's investment were not enough
to buy all the necessary machines, so they turned to the bank,
which gave them a small business loan and a line of credit. In
yet another case, Jacob got all the financing to start his business,

Integrity Testing Laboratory, by getting a second mortgage on his house; however, he got a small loan for his first microscope – a $5000 loan from a Jewish organization who gave him the loan interest-free.

Even though over 65% of the entrepreneurs from the second cohort were Soviet Jews, only one entrepreneur from this cohort turned to a Soviet Jewish friend for seed capital. When he was opening his gallery, Gregory invested 30% of his own money, borrowed 30% of the money from the bank, and borrowed 30% from a Ukrainian-Jewish friend. His friend received no equity in the gallery, but he promised to repay her within one year. Gregory was the only entrepreneur in the second cohort who turned to a Soviet Jewish friend for financing. The majority in this cohort came with a significant amount of money they had made in Russia after the transition. If they needed any extra capital, they turned to banks. In other words, they did not need to depend on ethnic resources because they had the necessary class-based endowments of skill, education, and capital.

Much of the success of immigrant entrepreneurs is commonly attributed to their ability to utilize social capital, especially ethnic resources, not available to non-ethnic business owners (Marger, 2001: 444). Information about permits, laws, management practices, reliable suppliers, and promising business lines is typically obtained through owners' personal networks that are specifically linked to their ethnic communities (Aldrich and Waldinger, 1990: 128). But the majority of the first cohort and the second cohort were not part of an enclave economy. Only 13% of the immigrants from the first cohort and 33% of the immigrants from the second cohort opened up businesses in an ethnically identifiable neighbourhood and targeted their businesses to customers from their ethnic group. Therefore, ethnic networks did not function as important resources in the establishment and operation of their firms. This was especially true for the first cohort of immigrants.

But the success of 13% of the entrepreneurs from the first cohort and 33% of the entrepreneurs from the second cohort was dependent upon their ability to utilize ethnic resources. These entrepreneurs targeted their businesses to the Russian ethnic community, hired co-ethnic employees, and used co-ethnic suppliers to buy their products.

Abe started his first construction company with the help of a fellow engineer who had immigrated to Toronto from Israel and spoke only Hebrew. Abe says,

> My partner took me in because he couldn't read English, and he needed help, he couldn't read drawings, couldn't estimate jobs, couldn't buy materials, he only spoke Hebrew, so he needed someone like me. He knew the way they build in Canada, which I didn't know. He taught me almost everything I needed to know about building in North America, which was completely different from all the countries that I had lived in before.

Abe initially built most of his homes for Russians, Jews, and Russian-Jews whom he knew from the Russian community. Eventually, Abe left ethnic enclave work and started to build homes all over Toronto in a variety of ethnic communities. He still works with some Russian sub-contractors because they offer him a lower price.

Another example is Paul, an immigrant from the first cohort. Paul knew nothing about the grocery business, but together with few people from his Russian ethnic group, he formed a food importing company called S&F Foods. Co-ethnics are an important source of customers for the goods and services of some businesses in the Russian community, such as food stores that cater to a Soviet-Jewish clientele. Paul and his partners imported food from Europe and Russia and sold about 70% of their products to an ethnic network of delicatessens across Toronto. The people who worked for the firm were also mostly Russian and Jewish. Paul says:

> I got invited to come into a food importing company that was owned by a couple of Russian guys that I sort of peripherally knew, and they made a lot of money with their business, and they wanted to professionalize their business a little bit, and they didn't know how. I mean one of them couldn't write in English, and so on. So, I joined them, which in retrospect was kind of a wild idea, it was a complete deviation from everything else I had done before and had an education for. Financially we did very well.

Although Alex, an immigrant from the first cohort, did not start a business within the enclave economy, his parents bought a European-style deli targeted to the Russian community shortly after they emigrated from Israel to Toronto. The father was too old and inexperienced to get a job as computer programmer; his mother, a dentist, did not speak English, so she could not easily acquire her credentials. Therefore, they bought a business. For Alex's parents, the Russian ethnic community offered a co-ethnic clientele, and the possibility of operating in their native language and in a familiar social and cultural environment. Their suppliers were from the former Soviet Union and all their customers were from the Russian community. As in the case of other immigrant groups, Alex's parents used co-ethnic employees and family members as workers; Alex even worked for his parents, helping to stock shelves and serve customers.

Shimon, an immigrant from the second cohort, who now owns a signs and engraving business, bought a Russian delicatessen with his wife in 1992. There was a recession in Canada and he was let go from an engraving company. Like Alex's parents, he drew upon co-ethnics as customers and suppliers.

Another immigrant from the second cohort, Valera, started the first Russian ethnic television channel in Toronto with his wife. The channel, called Russian Waves, is targeted exclusively to the Russian community. All journalists are Russian. This network combines reports on Russian immigrants in Toronto and programming from Russia, including news and entertainment.

Misha K. from the second cohort, already mentioned above, targeted his Toronto telecommunications company to his ethnic community, providing international long distance services for mostly the Russian community:

> When we started the telecommunications company in Toronto, I used Russian newspapers and television to target our products to the Russian community. We decided to focus on the Russian community because my partners were Russian-speaking so it was easier for them to target that community. They were much more recently out of Russia than myself, so they understood the Russian mentality better than anyone, and it was a good business sense. The reason we targeted the Russian community

was because of our ties to the Russian telecommunication market, so we were able to buy time cheaper than others, so it made sense that if we could buy those particular minutes from former Soviet Union telecommunications then we could compete better than others. Then we sold those minutes through calling plans to individual customers and businesses. We decided to initially focus on the Russian community because we had connections in Russia to buy cheaper calling time. If we were able to buy cheaper from India, then we would sell it to a service provider that was targeting the Indian community.

Zinovi, an immigrant from the second cohort, hires employees from the Russian ethnic community to manufacture machines and parts for the automobile and aerospace industry:

With the permanent employees 70% are Russian-Jews. The reason I hired mostly Russian Jews is because I live in a Russian-Jewish area and all the people who come to Canada from Russia are those with a high education. All my workers have a university education, so I didn't have to teach them anything - they are highly educated engineers.

Vladimir, another immigrant from the second cohort, has a similar reason for hiring Russia/Jewish employees for AVN Automation, which manufactures machines and parts for the automobile industry:

The reason I decided to hire all Russian employees is because they   are willing to work for a lower salary; they have more skills than Canadian employees; and I know what I can expect from them because I knows the education system in Russia and I know what they are capable of doing.

The majority of the immigrants from both cohorts did not target their businesses to the Russian enclave community or eventually expanded to other communities because they believed that they could make more money selling their products in a variety of different communities. This is consistent with studies in the

US which found that many successful Soviet Jewish entrepreneurs do not utilize the ethnic consumer market. Instead, they direct their operations towards the larger society or other ethnic groups. In so doing, they find that they have access to more customers and are able to charge higher prices (Gold, 1988: 427). Misha K. says that with time and experience they were able to buy cheaper time from other destinations for his telecommunications company, so it made business sense to re-sell the time that they bought to service providers from a variety of different ethnic communities in Toronto. Boris, from the second cohort, says that initially in the first year of sales all his clients for hardwood floors were from the Russian, Jewish, or Russian-Jewish community; he still has many clients who speak Russian, but now he works with builders from several different ethnic communities, such as Italians and Iranians, and as a result he makes much more money.

Arkady, an immigrant from the first cohort, says his company, Eurotrade, imports a variety of food products from Russia. Some of his salespeople are Russian, and they sell many products in Russian meat and deli stores, but over time he expanded to stores across Ontario:

> We started to integrate our business into the Canadian market. People are changing, and their eating habits are changing. My son is 46 and there is some kind of transformation now. He didn't want Russian food, and my grandchildren now don't want it either. We had to learn how to make a real packaged integrated business in the Canadian market. In order to grow the business we didn't want to just target the Russian ethnic delis, we wanted to expand. When we started expanding the business we started growing into the main food markets, targeting stores, such as Loblaws, Sobeys, and other big supermarket chains.

Other entrepreneurs have similar experiences. For example, Irene provides environmental services to Jewish schools but did not initially target these schools; her goal is to provide her company's services to as many schools and government buildings as possible. Jacob has a number of Jewish and Israeli clients who hire his firm, Integrity Testing Laboratory, to test materials for aerospace applications, but he did not intentionally target this group, and he has clients from a variety of countries all over the world, such as China and India.

The majority of the immigrants did not target their businesses to the Russian enclave community because they were concentrated in mechanical and technical fields where they manufactured and sold products to anyone in their field. For example, Zinovi, an immigrant from the second cohort, manufactures machines and parts for the automobile and aerospace industry, so he targets his business to huge corporations, such as Magna. Paul, an immigrant from the first cohort, owns a software company called pVelocity, which sells software to companies all over the world. Ilya, an immigrant from the first cohort, owns ITS Technology, which provides satellite communication technology for the military and satellite industry in Canada and other countries.

Other immigrants said that they did not like doing business with Russian co-ethnics and claimed that Soviet Jewish workers would challenge their authority in ways that others would not. Jack, an immigrant from the first cohort, says:

> The Russian people are the kind that think they know everything. Russian immigrants don't respect professional people. They don't respect professional knowledge, they think they know everything, and they don't like to follow orders.

David, an immigrant from the second cohort, agrees:

> I don't like the Russian mentality. Canadians ask me if I can fix this car and how much it costs. A Russian never asks me if I could fix the car or not, he will start negotiating the price as soon as I tell him what needs to be fixed.

In terms of hiring practices, the majority of the entrepreneurs said that they did not hire co-ethnic employees because they lacked the skills needed for their enterprise. They hired employees based on skills rather than simply because they were part of the same ethnic group. This backs up Gold (1995: 62) who found that Russian émigré business owners in New York, including some of the most successful, avoided employing co-ethnic work-ers because they lacked the skills and characteristics needed in their enterprises. High-technology firms, in particular, emphasize research and development, and as a result, employ people with technical training (Cooper, 1986: 154). Thus, Paul, an immigrant from the first cohort, only has 2 Russian programmers out of the 30 programmers working in his software company, pVelocity; he hires programmers based on their skills not their ethnicity.

Igor L., an immigrant from the first cohort, tried to hire Russian programmers by contacting Russian immigration con-sultants, who helped him find programmers immigrating to Toronto from Russia. This proved unsuccessful; he found that he could not rely on them and their stated motivations. Most merely wanted a letter stating his interest in their services; using this letter they could apply for independent immigration and receive more money for their services. As a result, not a single applicant worked out. Igor L. claims that his company has a pretty signif-icant Jewish contingent; however, they were selected not on the basis of their ethnicity[2], but on the basis of skills and abilities. He claims that in his field "ethnicity is very secondary".

Ilya, another immigrant from the first cohort, has a sim-ilar explanation for why he hires employees from a variety of ethnic groups to work at ITS Technology, a firm which provides satellite communication technology:

> I do have some employees who are Russian and Jewish. The rest are from all over. We do a very thorough selec-tion when we interview and hire people. Our company is extremely technology developed and we hire because of what people know and what they can do. They can be from anywhere, as long as they can fulfill the technology needs that we need and they must be fluent in English. If the Russians come in and start speaking in Russian, I say I can't help them because I don't work with them, people on the floor do, many of whom do not speak Russian.

Class Resources: Class-Specific Cultural Capital

Russian immigrants obtained cultural capital, in the form of skills, knowledge, attitudes, and values required to plan and organize the founding of their business in Toronto from the primary and secondary economy in the former Soviet Union, from the market transition economy in Russia, from the education system in Toronto, and from experience in the Toronto labour market.

Socialist Entrepreneurial Skills and Entrepreneurial Experience in the Primary and Secondary Economy in the Former Soviet Union that Helped Entrepreneurs Start Businesses in Toronto

Half the first-cohort immigrants had more than three years of work experience in the former Soviet Union before coming to Toronto; about half of these immigrants worked in the engineering field, and 70% of those started businesses in the engineering field or an allied field when they came to Toronto. Their prior work experience helped them start businesses in their field of expertise in Toronto.

For example, Abe got a degree in civil engineering from Vilnius, Lithuania, and worked there in various construction jobs. In Toronto he started several businesses related to his engineering experience. He says:

> In Toronto, I only opened up businesses related to my engineering experience. I've had several businesses, but it's always been in the same business with different companies, which is building and general contracting. So in all of these years in Toronto I had about 10 companies but all of these companies were doing the same thing, such as building new houses, construction work, building commercial, industrial which is all connected and similar to each other. I never established any other companies here which were doing anything different than construction.

Another example is Michael S., who has an engineering degree from the Institute of Precision/Fine Mechanics in St. Petersburg. He worked as an engineer for four years for a state-run company in Russia, and in Toronto, he worked as a senior engineer for eight years in the engineering department of a research organization. After that he opened up his own company, called RAM Machines, which manufactures metal components for a variety of industries.

About 80% of the immigrants from the second cohort had more than three years of work experience in the former Soviet Union before coming to Toronto; about half worked in the engineering field, and half of those working in engineering started businesses in the engineering field or an allied field when they came to Toronto. All were still living in the former Soviet Union when the transition to a market economy started; over 40% left their state-sector jobs to work in other professional fields or to open up businesses. The immigrants from the second cohort who started businesses in the former Soviet Union averaged only one business before immigrating to Toronto.

Victor G. got a degree in civil engineering from the University of Novosibirsk, and worked for several years as an engineer on construction sites for a state-run company during the communist system. During the transition, he opened a construction company, and started building apartments and malls throughout Russia. In Toronto, he opened a real estate and construction business, buying and selling real estate and building and leasing shopping malls.

Another example is Vladimir, who has a PhD in mechanical engineering from St. Petersburg Polytechnical Institute. He first worked as an engineer in a chemical plant and then as an engineer for the aerospace and defense industry for 5 years during the communist system. During the transition he became a professor of engineering and taught for 7 years. In Toronto, he worked as an engineer for several companies in mechanical design. Then he opened his own business, AVN Automation, which manufactures machines and parts for the automobile industry.

Even though both cohorts of immigrants had a lot of work experience in the former Soviet Union, especially in engineering, which helped them start businesses in Toronto in their field of expertise, only those from the second cohort could leave state-sector jobs and start businesses after the transition. But even though there was a variation in their employment experience and their source of training in the former Soviet Union, both cohorts learned socialist entrepreneurial skills in the primary and secondary economy in Russia that later helped them develop businesses in Toronto.

Those who worked in the socialist economy learned important skills that they could apply to start businesses in Toronto. The immigrant entrepreneurs who were illegally

involved in the black market economy also learned skills in entrepreneurship. Igor S., an immigrant from the first cohort, claims
that those who lived under the Soviet system learned that the only
way to succeed was to beat the system; people knew that if they
followed the rules, they would never be successful. Abe, an immigrant from the first cohort says:

> Everybody was stealing....In the Soviet Union, you needed
> skills in stealing; bargaining and trading wouldn't help. It's
> called stealing in the Soviet Union, but in Canada it's called
> business. For example, in the Soviet Union if you bought
> something for $1 and sold it for $1.10, you go to jail, while
> in Canada, it is part of business.

This "culture of adaptability" was retained by the immigrant entrepreneurs in Toronto.

Abe also talks about how he learned skills in negotiating
that he applied in Toronto, where he had to negotiate with individual customers and private companies to build private, commercial, and industrial buildings:

> When I worked for the cooperatives on various construc-
> tion projects, I learned skills, such as how to negotiate
> higher payments to do private jobs that I would later apply
> to negotiating prices with individual customers and pri-
> vate companies to build homes, stores, shopping malls,
> and hotels.

Another example from the first cohort is Igor L., who
worked for 8 years as a mechanical engineer at a drafting board
designing Ford trucks. Igor L. says flexibility, personal bargaining and the ability to negotiate were critical to maintain state-run
companies and fulfill state plans for production by sourcing
materials in a Soviet economy of shortage. Some of the skills he
learned were important in Toronto:

> Engineering is no different that it is here. There was a lot
> of knowledge that I brought with me in economics, organ-
> ization of production.

But he says many things are done completely differently in Canada:

> When I came to Toronto, I had to learn that business makes not what government tells you to make, but what can be sold for a profit. Whether you buy it or make it, you have to have a market. It was a big discovery when I started working with engineers from Toronto, that when they design they know how much it will cost to make. It was never a consideration in Russia, you designed it and sold it, and worked, it was never economical to make.... You start learning that everything costs dollars from scratch. That was a set of skills....I had to learn how to do product costing, I had to learn the basics of financial accounting, in all of that I was lucky enough to learn as I went through my work because I could not afford to go through school to learn it....Here you understand that the person who arranges everything really organizes the industry, and organizes and makes it possible to make that profit, which is denied in the Soviet Union. In the Soviet Union when people figured out how to make money, they were put to death or put in jail for making money for themselves. Basic Soviets were taught it was a negative thing. When you run an enterprise, you are a good enterprise manager if you make what you are told to do.

Skills and Knowledge Learned by Entrepreneurs who went through the Education System in Toronto that helped them to start Businesses in Toronto

Virtually all entrepreneurs relied on the education and cultural capital they brought with them from the former Soviet Union. The whole second cohort attained their education in the former Soviet Union; only 17% (4 of 23) of the first cohort were educated in Toronto: 2 received a BA in economics, 1 received a BA in Computer Science, and 1 received a PhD in Solid State Physics. These immigrants were educated in Toronto because they were very young when they left the former Soviet Union. However, the degrees that these 4 entrepreneurs attained in the education system in Toronto helped them get good positions in prominent firms which, in turn, helped them develop the skills, knowledge, experience, and contacts required to start a business.

For example, Paul got a BA in computer science from the University of Toronto and took several executive MBA classes at Harvard University. As a result of his education, he was hired by IBM Canada. The skills he learned in computer science, executive MBA classes, along with training courses and work experience at IBM helped him to eventually start a software company. Paul says:

> As a result of my degree in computer science from a prestigious university, I was able to get a job at IBM. After I worked at IBM for a while, I requested that I wanted to move to sales. But in order to be in sales at IBM you have to go through something that used to be called basic systems training, which at the time was sort of a 6 or 7 month training process. I learned a lot of things. In fact, I still look back at that time as the time when I picked up a lot of basic, fundamental knowledge that I needed to build my career on, not only as a successful sales person at IBM, but also as a successful entrepreneur when I opened my own software companies.

Another entrepreneur educated in Canada is Gabe. Gabe received his MBA from the Richard Ivy School of Business at the University of Western Ontario in London, Ontario; he also took a few professional development courses, including the Canadian Securities Course (CSC) at the Canadian Securities Institute. The Western MBA and the professional development courses helped him become a partner at an investment company in Russia, but he had to learn that an investment company in Russia operates completely differently from one in Canada:

> The education that I received at the Richard Ivey School of business was critical in developing the skills that I needed to work for an investment firm. A few years after graduating from Western University, I got a job as an institutional equity salesman for a US-Russian investment bank called UFG (United Financial Group). I worked there for a couple of years and I learned several skills that

helped me to eventually become a partner in the firm. I sold Russian stocks to portfolio managers and hedge funds in Europe, US, and other countries. After working there for a couple of years, I learned that there is a lot more regulation in Canada. There is a lot more transparency in Toronto. You have to report to a lot of people, everybody is watching trades to make sure nobody is getting screwed. In Russia everybody gets screwed, there is no transparency. It is very different, markets are still kind of developing so there is not as much liquidity, and there aren't as many players in the Russian market so people can take advantage of that....In Toronto the spreads are much tighter, and everybody sees exactly what you are making and the commissions are much smaller....So, there was less regulation, more opportunism in Russia. Things are certainly changing; I'm sure they have changed but they are still a long ways from Toronto.

Entrepreneurial Experience Developed in the Labour Market in Toronto or outside Toronto that Helped Entrepreneurs Start Businesses in Toronto

Since the first-cohort immigrants had limited access to relevant home country business experience because Soviet black market experience is different from business experience in Canada, Canadian business experience is vital to the success of their enterprises. However, entrepreneurs from both cohorts, regardless of their path to entrepreneurship, all said their experience in the labour market in Toronto helped them develop the skills, knowledge, experience, and contacts required to eventually start their own businesses.

Abe, an immigrant from the first cohort, took path 1 to entrepreneurship. He came to Canada with human capital, but couldn't get credentials to practice engineering in Canada. Abe says the jobs he had in construction gave him the skills, knowledge, experience, and contacts that he needed to start his own construction and contracting company, Norcity Group:

When I came to Canada I couldn't find a job as an engineer, so I started to work in several construction companies. I became a partner in one of the construction companies that I worked for that was doing renovation work. This partner...knew at the time completely the way they build in Canada which I didn't know. He taught me a lot. I learned from him almost everything. He showed me what a 2x4 is because at that time I didn't know that because in Lithuania, Israel, and Italy nobody knew what a 2x4 was; it was a completely different system. The way we build in North America is completely different from all those countries that I lived in before....As a result of what I learned from this partner and working for several construction companies, I ended up establishing 10 companies.

Jacob, an immigrant from the first cohort, took path 2 to entrepreneurship, arriving in Canada with a lot of human capital, but owes most of his company's success to his previous job. He got information, some supplies, and contacts while working for Triam:

Triam Canada was one of the big companies in the world. When I was working there they had about 75,000 employees around the world....They decided to close down our group in Canada, and offered us to go to the States. I refused to go, so for a year we as a group of five people tried to continue in the same field but without Triam, and we bought a lot of equipment for a very good price from Triam. That was the start, this opportunity to buy this equipment very cheap, plus my experience and everything gave me the idea to try to start my own business. At Triam, I learned how to use the transmission electronic-microscope, x-ray electro-microscope, so my skills in my private business were largely acquired during my work at Triam.

Ilya, an immigrant from the first cohort took path 3 to entrepreneurship, arriving with human capital and working in his field for a few years. Because of his social capital, he found a business opportunity within his field, and decided to leave his salaried job. Ilya says he gained experience to start his own company while working as a salaried employee. Ilya started his company, ITS Technology, after working for Malco and Associates in the United States and Canada for four years. At Malco he brought technologies purchased from Advancetech to Canada for the defense and satellite industry. While working at Malco, he realized that there were no longer any companies that were providing the services required by the military and satellite industry in Canada – in short, he discovered a niche:

> I worked at Malco and Associates for four years in US and Canada. They sent me to Arizona and I worked there and brought technologies to Canada for the defense industry. This type of company didn't exist in Canada. That job really started me and brought me to this level here. There were some market leaders who were bought and closed, or absorbed by larger companies, and there was nobody to serve the need and I decided I was going to do that....Basically we built a company that Canada never had, and we are serving a lot of niches that Advantech no longer served. Our business plan was based on Advantech. I basically wanted to build a Canadian Advantech....The business we are in is relatively small; it is only maybe 10-12 companies, so I decided to go into this market.

Another entrepreneur from the first cohort who took path 3 to entrepreneurship, but received all his education and job experience in Canada is Paul. He obtained training and experience at IBM and at a software company, Unitech, which he later used to start his own software company:

> I had a reasonably successful track record in sales with IBM Canada. Every year that I was in sales I was meeting my quota and exceeding my quota. In 1995, I was hired by a software company working out of Chicago called Unitech, which was maybe a $2 or $3 million company at the time. They were looking for some growth into Canada and they hired me because of my excellent sales record at IBM. So I joined forces with them and basically became in charge of their Canadian distribution. We built, in a couple of years, a nice business of about $5 or $6

million. They were also growing in the US. So I took responsibility for half of the US business. Then, when we decided to pursue international growth, so because I had the best sales record of all the executives, I was chosen to move to the Netherlands to take responsibility for the European part of business. During my 4-year period in the Netherlands, we basically built a $10 million business across Europe. We opened a subsidiary company in the UK, Germany, Sweden, Italy and Spain. So we had a pan-European business that was producing about $10 million in revenue for the company by the time we were done, which was in 2001. From there, I moved back to Chicago, and by that time we were a $35 million company....I learned a lot about how to build relationships, how to increase sales, and how to create a successful software company while working at IBM and Unitech. As a result, after a fairly short time I was able to build a successful software company.

Zinovi, an immigrant from the first cohort, took path 4 to entrepreneurship. He gained experience for his business, Maziro, which manufactures machines, equipment, and parts for a variety of industries, by working as an engineer at a couple of companies that were manufacturing parts for the automobile, furniture, and plastics industries:

In Canada, I worked a supervisor at one company that manufactured different kinds of machines for the plastic industry. I learned how to supervise a large staff and I also learned what goes into the process of finding customers, suppliers, and financing. Then I worked as an engineer at another company that manufactured machines and parts for the automobile industry. At this company, I learned what machines and parts the automobile industry needs and how to design and manufacture these parts. I also learned what type of machines a company that manufactures parts for the automobile industry requires, where to source these machines, and what these machines cost if they are new or used.

Second-cohort member Misha K. took path 5 to entrepreneurship. When he arrived in Toronto, he had human capital, business experience, and financial capital and knew he was going into business. He had gained work experience in international telecommunications and project management companies that he opened in several countries before coming to Toronto. His past experience helped him to open Lorotel, his telecommunications and international project management business in the field of mechanical and electrical engineering:

> Currently I am doing international project management. This came about when I was in Nigeria from 1976-1985 working for ETCO, where I eventually progressed to company general manager. In Nigeria one of my responsibilities was to build factories. The company that I worked for was a specialist sub-contractor for international companies that wanted to build factories in Nigeria. In that sense I developed an expertise in design and execution of various industrial projects, in many fields, such as car batteries and manufacturing, propane gas cylinders manufacturing, land rover and range rover manufacturing production lines. The factories themselves are not just manufacturing processes; in Nigeria and in most of Africa it comes with a lot of other things. They build their own power stations so you have to have the knowledge of how to build power stations, not just the production. If you look at the car batteries factory there are also a lot of chemical processes that go with it, you have to learn to do those too. I had opportunities to supply and install gas turbines for oil rigs. In 1985, I went to South Africa and started my own company, which was involved in contracting and servicing, air conditioning, plumbing, electrical, elevators, and communication. So, the knowledge and experience that I built up working in Africa was critical in helping me open my company in Toronto. In 1995, I opened a telecommunications company in New York. I came from New York to Toronto in 1998 with a background in telecommunications, so it was natural that I would continue in the same way in Toronto....I learned a lot about the telecommunications industry while running

the company in New York, and then in 2003....I sold my
shares, and opened Lorotel. Lorotel initially did services
in international and long distance, gradually it has
changed its direction to international project management
in the field of mechanical and electrical engineering,
which is what I am doing right now.

Entrepreneurial Skills and Transnational Ethnic Networks Developed During the Transition Economy in Russia that Helped Entrepreneurs Start Transnational Businesses Based in Toronto or Russia

An important form of immigrant economic adaptation is the practice of transnationalism.

The likelihood of establishing transnational businesses
for both cohorts of immigrants from the former Soviet Union
depended to some extent on the alliances forged at the beginning
of the transition process between these immigrants and (a) state
elites; (b) financial sector elites; and (c) Russian entrepreneurs.
It was important for these immigrants to have connections to
former managers of public enterprises who emerged as modern
corporate executives, freed of the restraints of the command
economy, as they acquired the majority of shares in most of the
privatized and privatizing firms and assumed control of capital
intensive firms. These firms required large capital investments
to develop (often from abroad); some immigrants took advantage
of this and established Toronto companies which entered into
contracts with these state firms and provided the capital investment
that they needed. About 35% of the immigrant entrepreneurs from the first cohort and the second cohort were able to
develop businesses in Toronto with links to Russia because they

Table 8
Paths to Entrepreneurship and
Establishing Transnational Businesses

Cohort	Path 1 (%)	Path 2 (%)	Path 3 (%)	Path 4 (%)	Path 5 (%)
1	1/2 (50%)	1/2 (50%)	3/12 (25%)	4/7 (57%)	0
2	0	0	0/4 (0%)	0/2 (50%)	3/3 (67%)

had connections to elite insiders in the former Soviet Union.

The immigrants who established transnational businesses took varied paths to entrepreneurship, as the following table illustrates.

Abe was the only immigrant from the first cohort who took path 1 to entrepreneurship and established a transnational business. Abe began to do business in the former Soviet Union during the transition because business was slow in Toronto:

> In the 1980s, the company was very successful. We were building a lot; 17 homes in one place, 6 homes in another, industrial buildings, etc, and we were making very good money. But in the 1990s, everything disappeared, prices were falling, and we lost a lot of money. I was going overseas in the 90s because there was nothing to do here.

In 1993, Abe began building overseas when he established connections with people who came to Toronto from the former Soviet republics. Opportunities started to emerge as a result of the changes going on in the former Soviet Union:

> When the Soviet Union fell apart, people from the Soviet Union were able to travel freely, and they started to come to Canada to look for materials and for Canadian experience on how to build. Before the Soviet Union became a free-market economy, we couldn't build there because everything was government operated. Once free enterprise and privatization began, people who became wealthy in Russia were interested in building homes, malls, industrial buildings. They didn't have the necessary supplies and knowledge about construction, so they began to look for connections with the Western world.

Abe's extensive and diverse social networks in Canada and Russia helped him to initiate and sustain transnational enterprise:

> From the Canadian side, it was Olympia-York, from the Russian side, it was the Chamber of Commerce of the Soviet Union. Before the Soviet Union collapsed, it was established in 1988 or 1989 and one of the top guys from

the Soviet Union was living in Toronto, and I was introduced to him in 1989 or 1990. We became good friends
and everyone that was coming from Russia, Ukraine, or
other republics, we'd go out for lunch together and they
would tell me what they need, and that's how I got to
know lots of people. As a result, in 1991, I was already
in Moscow. I continued to establish alliances with state
officials, bank officials, and owners of commercial businesses, malls, etc, and we were building for them.

Abe built commercial office buildings, shopping malls,
retail, and high rise residential buildings in Russia, Kazakhstan,
Ukraine, Lithuania, and Latvia. He was able to deal with government regulations because he spoke the language and could speak
directly to the people in the government when he needed building
and construction permits. He obtained supplies and construction
material from Canada because it was cheaper to bring the supplies from Canada or the US. For the most part, he was hired by
private companies and individuals. One of his biggest customers
was a Pension Fund company, New Century Holdings, based in
New York; this company was a big investor in the former Soviet
Union, and the money came from companies such as General
Motors, Kodak, etc. Then he got contracts in Almata, Kazakhstan,
and Riga, Latvia.

Jacob was the only immigrant from the first cohort who
took path 2 to entrepreneurship and did business transnationally.
He got involved in Russia and the Ukraine by organizing space
conferences. After developing contacts at these conferences he
decided to introduce his company, Integrity Testing Laboratory,
which tests and produces materials for aerospace applications, to
space researchers in the Ukraine and Russia. Jacob says that his
business opportunities emerged as a direct result of the market
transition:

> Before the transition happened, they didn't allow me to
> go to the Soviet Union to attend space conferences, which
> I was invited to, but couldn't attend because I was never
> given a visa to enter the country. The fact that you were
> now able to go and do business there is a direct conse-
> quence of the transition.

Igor S. is an immigrant from the first cohort who took path 3 to entrepreneurship and established a transnational business. He became successful by acting as an intermediary between a buyer in the Ukraine and a supplier in India. He established a trading company that supplied some medical goods that were in short supply in the Ukraine during the transition. He could do so because of his connections:

> It came through networking. A friend of mine was already doing business with Ukraine in construction materials. He told me that there are opportunities there; they still don't have a lot of medical supplies, and they can't afford the high-priced American goods. He had a relationship with someone high in the ministry of health, so it was very easy for us to follow all of the government regulations.

Alex, an immigrant from the first cohort, took path 3 to entrepreneurship and established a transnational business. Because of his connections, he was able to establish a company, Midland, which sourced steel from Russia and the Ukraine for low prices and sold it all over the world for large profits. Alex established his first connections in the former Soviet Union by working for companies doing business there. He moved with his family to Switzerland to work in a global steel trading company that was doing business in Russia. When he met a steel trader from Belgium, they decided to form a company together in 1992 called Transtall. They saw it as an opportunity since Alex had contacts in Russia and would be able to source the steel:

> He would tell me to go to such and such factory, we need to get such and such steel products. So I would go, or would ask my contacts to get as much as possible and we would sell it. Then we started getting leads to other factories. We had a company in the Ukraine and in Russia, and we had people that we hired that had contacts and were able to go and source steel products for the company.

Alex initially obtained steel by bartering and trading:

In order to feed their infrastructure, these steel companies would offer furniture, clothing, and other things to their workers in exchange for their work. They were willing to provide us metal if we could supply them with furniture and clothing in exchange for steel. We didn't need capital in the beginning because we could just exchange it for whatever goods we could find in the West.

Alex and his partner didn't need a lot of capital because these companies were willing to give up their steel based on trust:

They used to give us the steel before receiving anything in return. In the beginning you didn't require money; we made money with absolutely no money, just on trust.

Many foreign companies took advantage of this trust and made millions. But Alex and his partner decided not to break the relationship they had built up, and this gave them an advantage over other foreign companies:

A lot of foreign companies took advantage of these steel factories because these factories trusted them because they believed that there was no risk signing a contract with a foreign company. These foreign companies would take millions of dollars of steel and just disappear. We never did that because we figured we would make a lot more money in the future if we did straight business. A lot of these people would succeed initially, but then nobody would continue to work with them. If you are a foreigner you are a person of great respect. The general directors would not even ask us for money because we were doing them a favour by getting rid of all their steel.

Initially Alex and his Belgium partner made money by trading goods for steel (bartering). Later, they decided to concentrate only on selling steel:

We started to concentrate on steel because we realized that if we ship 20 million shipments of furniture it takes up a lot of time and storage, while we can sell more steel for a higher profit margin.

Alex and his partner had an advantage because the company directors had no knowledge of how to operate in a free market global economy:

> They were totally mismanaging their enterprises because they had no clue how to properly manage their enterprises because they were not in commerce. The general director was an engineer; he was not in business. The directors of these steel enterprises were used to getting all the raw materials and then they would get an order from the state in Moscow telling them where to ship all the steel. When Communism died, the general directors had no clue of what to do; they didn't know where to ship the material.

When the transition proceeded, the economic climate began to change and companies in the former Soviet Union were no longer willing to conduct business with foreign companies based only on trust; they now wanted prepayment for their products. Around 1993, the director of the steel mill in the Ukraine started requesting money upfront. Once again, Alex and his partner had an advantage over other foreign companies:

> Representatives of foreign companies were told by the steel factories that they wanted money upfront. The representatives would then offer them a letter of credit, and the general director didn't know what it was and said he needed money right away to pay his employees. We were able to get more steel because the other companies were not able to come up with the money.

Then the steel mills began to have problems with the companies producing the raw materials. For example, the coal mine would not release coal to the steel company because it already owed them too much money. The whole system collapsed; more specifically, the supply chain collapsed because of the large debts between the companies producing the raw materials and the steel mill. Transtall mended the supply chain and the payment orders. Because they had good connections with the companies producing the raw materials Alex and his partner had a new opportunity:

Now the general director tells me I need iron and coal, so if I get him the coal and iron, he will get me steel. So we bartered the raw materials for steel. This was even better for me because now I could make money on the coal because I would buy coal for maybe $30 per ton and sell it to him for $40 per ton. For me it was great, but for other foreign companies it was not because they had to take the risk on the coal mine, on the iron mine and the steel mine. Now we were controlling the source of raw materials, and were getting steel every month. Now there were three or four stages before we would get steel, and every stage we would make money.

In 1993, Alex met his current partner, Edward, who was working as a head representative for a Hong Kong based steel trading company. Edward had great contacts. He knew all the general directors in Russia and the Ukraine and he knew the steel business inside out. Alex and his new partner decided that to beat out all the foreign competition, they had to buy the largest steel mill in the Ukraine. Alex claims that they were successful in buying the steel mill because other foreign companies weren't willing to take the risk.

Alex's insider information and contacts in large scale state and private ventures bestowed credibility on his efforts. Drawing on transnational ties for social capital, Alex pieced together resources from many institutional fields. His networks bridged core industries in several countries. In network terms, he linked networks and created opportunities by spanning structural holes (Burt, 1992). He got ideas from different contacts and combined resources in novel ways, which is essential to starting profitable businesses (Burt, 1992, in Salaff et al., 2007: 101). Alex's ethnic background and Russian and Canadian networks legitimated him among the Russian players. His brokering role is atypical of enclave businesses, in that his role is more like any other importer or exporter of goods and services. But at the same time, his ethnic background enables his business ties. Like many other enclave and mainstream businesses he depends on transnational links, and his links were activated through his migration to Canada.

Sam is another immigrant from the first cohort who took path 3 to entrepreneurship and established a transnational business. He established contacts on a business trip to the Ukraine for his former employer during the transition in 1995; he met the manager of a plant that manufactures Carbon Black. He discovered there was a demand for Carbon Black in the rubber and tire industries in Canada and the US, so he formed a partnership with the director of the company and is now part owner of the company in the Ukraine. He established a company, Sunrock, which imports synthetic chemicals:

> On one of my business trips to Russia for my former employer, I accidentally met a manager of a factory that produces Carbon Black at a Russian restaurant. At the time, I didn't even know what Carbon Black was. He told me about the industries which use Carbon Black, and he asked me if I could help him export Carbon Black into the US and Canada. So, upon my return to Toronto, I did a lot of research, and I found out that there was a large demand for Carbon Black in Canada and the US, but at a much lower price than it was currently being sold at. I found a customer in Canada who bought a rubber plant and he was looking for suppliers of Carbon Black, so we made a business out of it, and he is now my main buyer. Then I found out about other companies that were also in the market for Carbon Black. In 1995, I went 10 times to the Ukraine and Russia before I started Carbon Black because first I had to prove that the product was good. I traveled to several plants in Russia and established connections with the plant managers. I agreed to buy it from them for a price that was considerably lower than the global market price and sell it in North America. They agreed to give me the exclusive rights to sell Carbon Black from their plants to North America. We started with Carbon Black; today we have synthetic rubber and chemicals.

Michael T. is another first-cohort immigrant who took path 3 to entrepreneurship and established a transnational business. He went to Russia and the Ukraine during the transition in 1990 to find material that he could manufacture in Russia or the Ukraine at a fairly low cost and then sell it to the construction industry in Toronto. He established contacts with local partners and directors of construction companies in the Ukraine and Russia, patented this construction equipment, and started exporting it from the Ukraine to Canada.

> After the collapse of the Soviet Union in the 1990s, I decided to go to the Ukraine and Russia to see if I could find the material that many people working the construction business, including myself believed was needed in the construction industry in Canada. At the time when I was travelling to the Ukraine and Russia I met up with managers of construction companies that were looking for construction materials from Canada, so I was able to supply it for them. And eventually that led to my current business, Performance Steel Specialties, where we manufacture the reinforcements for concrete and develop equipment for handling the product. I came across a manufacturing company in the Ukraine that could make the material that I needed. I set up production lines for construction equipment components out of Ukraine to Canada. It was one of the first deals that was made between Canada and those very well known manufacturing facilities. It was a newer technology at the time that was not available in Canada. I decided to manufacture it in the Ukraine because everything is cost-oriented. Manufacturing was set in very close proximity to the raw materials supply line. The labour force was cheap, but well-trained in the Ukraine, and it was also inexpensive to manufacture the material there. I had local partners in the Ukraine who were working there under the government and they knew what they needed to do in order to make sure that all the government regulations were followed and all the right people were paid off.

The enterprises established by immigrants like Sam, Alex, and Michael T. involved the production of goods at low prices which they could sell overseas for a large profit margin. Alex used his links in Russia and Ukraine to obtain a license from the government (not granted to everyone) to export steel at still-low Soviet prices to Canada and the US or anywhere else that it fetched a higher price, so he was able to make a lot of money very quickly. Some time elapsed between legalization of private activity and the elimination of government regulations, creating a gap between market prices and official prices and setting up opportunities for the new capitalists in Russia and Toronto, such as Alex, Sam, and Michael T., to maximize profits.

Leon is an immigrant from the first cohort who took path 4 to entrepreneurship and established a transnational business. Leon initially started Luxan Shoes with a few partners in 1980; they manufactured Italian shoes for major retail stores in Canada. Then they decided to expand to Moldova and the Ukraine in 1991. They were able to build successful shoe manufacturing plants in the former Soviet Union during the transition because he had good connections to former managers of state enterprises and to government officials:

> Americans and Canadians who went to Russia and the Ukraine to do business during the 1990s were not successful because they didn't know the language and they didn't have connections to anyone in the government or any of the enterprise directors. I went to Moldova because my brother who lived there and was the manager of a construction business had good connections with the general director at a metallurgical plant, who was interested in becoming our financial partner in a joint venture. In the Ukraine we knew of a manager of a chemical production factory that had 26,000 employees. I went there and I met this guy and brought him to Canada and showed him our factory here. He was very surprised that we were a big factory here and said let's build this factory in my place too, I will be a partner with you. So we became partners and built shoe factories in the Ukraine selling Italian shoes. They had special government rules in the factories and I went against the rules and said it was a capitalist venture and they had to work in accordance to my rules. I wanted to help the Ukrainian government understand that it is important not to lose the manufacturing sector during the transition. If you have a product inside the country, everything stays inside the country....I told the president that people were coming to work to make money, if the employee makes money then I make money,

the country makes money. The president of the Ukraine was very impressed at how I was able to build a capitalist enterprise in the Ukraine that exported Italian designed shoes all over the world. As a result, the president took care of all the government regulations. The president also introduced a new law that all joint ventures were free of any taxes and duties, so companies like mine were now free to manufacture the shoes in the Ukraine, and then sell them outside of the Ukraine without paying any duties for five years.

Leon had to close down the factories in Moldova and the Ukraine in 1997 because of legal changes and the dangers of doing business in the former Soviet Union:

In one year's time there was a new president which cut the law that stated that all joint ventures were free of any taxes and duties and put in a new one; you had to pay duty and taxes on the supplies that you brought into the country. It became impossible to work. It also became very dangerous to work because the Russian mafia would come to your business offering to be your cover (meaning that they would protect you against criminals, vandalism, theft, etc, and they would ensure that all your customers paid you on time) if you paid them 15% of your profits every month....So as a result of these mafia people coming in and threatening us, I closed down the business and told them to do whatever they wanted with the business. I no longer do any business with Russia or the Ukraine because today's "new Russians" are very close to the government and they stole everything. When we were there we built everything. Today the big businessmen are big crooks. They took from the government for $1 what was worth $100,000. For example, they bought a metallurgical company for 3 million dollars, which is now worth 3 billion dollars. The Russians no longer need us today. They needed us when they didn't know how to sell their products in the global market; now they know how.

Mark, who is currently the President of NEOS, an affiliate of E. H. Harms Company, is an immigrant from the first cohort who took path 4 to entrepreneurship and established a transnational business. He established contacts during his business trips to Russia during the transition in the 1990s, and because of his connections he was able to set up businesses in Russia:

> I established businesses in Kazakhstan and in other places in Russia when the Soviet Union collapsed in the early 1990s....We had several businesses in Kazakhstan, including managing an airline, an elevator company, and many others.

He talks about the need to know how to manipulate the system:

> In order to be successful in business you had to indirectly bribe government officials....After a while, it was a small group of people who were running the whole country, and if you had connections to some of these people, you could be successful in business.

Like the other entrepreneurs, he found that he had good profit margins doing transnational business – but again, this was based on his connections:

> It was the earlier people that were starting to bribe that are now in power. In my current business, we are still selling a lot of cars from Germany in Russia. I also currently have some companies in Russia manufacturing metals, so if it works I will sell it in the West. Russian steel companies and oil companies are good to develop because if you know how to bribe the right managers and officials, you will have the cheapest metal. If you ask what the difference is between the material bought here and made in Russia – i.e. a kilo made here in Canada costs $300, those from Russia cost $1.80. So, even though people say that products in Russia are now at the same price as anywhere in the world because now it has reached the global

market, they don't know what they're talking about.
People in Russia, like me, are still buying it for $1.80 and
selling it for $300. So there are still people in Russia who
know the right people, who know who to bribe and who
are still buying a variety of products for very little money
and selling them in the West for huge profits. This is how
people become billionaires. For example, the Boeing
company bought 90% of their steel from Russia. If you
go to Russia, the guy that sold them their steel is a bil-
lionaire. So as you can see, you don't have to be
extremely smart to become rich; you just have to have
good connections.

Only the immigrants from the second cohort who took
path 5 to entrepreneurship started transnational businesses. Boris
is one of these. He was able to set up a furniture manufacturing
plant and store in Russia that sold furniture in Russia, Europe,
and other markets in the world because he had connections and
because there was a large demand:

When I came back to Russia it was a new country and
everything started to grow. In 1995, I decided to open a
furniture business. My partner and I had connections to
the government to deal with logistics and people at the
border to let some of our parts arrive from Germany without having to pay high tariffs. We built our own factory
and we manufactured the furniture in Russia and Germany and sold it in Russia, Israel, Europe, and Canada.
When we opened our first shop, the next morning we sold
all our furniture exhibition. There was a huge line up all
day. There was nothing in Russia at all, so people were
starving for anything.

After a few years of successful sales, he decided that he
didn't want to spend most of the year in Russia watching over his
business while his family lived in Toronto, so he moved back to
Toronto and opened Sunca Hardwood, which imports hardwood
floors from a manufacturer in Russia and Brazil; he sells it to
individual customers and private contractors in Toronto. He also
exports hardwood from Brazil to Russia and Kazakhstan, and
from Brazil and Russia to Spain.

The people who became successful entrepreneurs in Russia during the transition to a market economy, such as Sam, Michael T., Mark, Abe, Leon, Igor S., and Alex, were double entrepreneurs (Yang, 2002). They were innovative and creative in identifying and creating new markets to export the goods that were manufactured in the state-run economy before the transition and discovering what goods were in demand and therefore should be imported from the West to Russia. They were talented in making use of and manipulating institutional rules, such as government regulations; this was valuable when the government introduced laws to promote the establishment of private enterprises. Because these entrepreneurs had connections with people who knew members of the government or had personal connections with members of the government, they could manipulate the new laws.

As transnational entrepreneurs, Sam, Michael T., Mark, Igor S., Abe, Leon, and Alex, are part of the elite in their communities; from their activities they make higher-than-average incomes.

Immigrant entrepreneurs do not merely react to structural disadvantages they face in their host countries but actively look for opportunities and market niches beyond the national boundaries of the receiving countries, utilizing their bicultural skills and binational ethnic networks. Drawing on transnational networks to their country of origin, some Russian immigrant entrepreneurs mobilized resources for their businesses that were not available locally. Those with extensive and diverse international social networks, such as Alex, Sam, Michael T., Mark, Igor S., Leon, and Abe, were in a good position to initiate and sustain transnational entrepreneurship. They better understood the cultural aspects of business practices, the government regulations in the former Soviet Union, and the language, and were able to link up easily with distributors and retailers in Toronto. This constituted a form of "insider advantage".

Some of the entrepreneurs made frequent trips to the former Soviet Union to conduct business while their families stayed in Toronto. These transnational entrepreneurs travel between their permanent homes in the West and their business in their country of origin. Abe would go to the former Soviet Union for months at a time for construction projects, and this continued for a period of 6 years. Paul constantly flew to various countries, such as the US, Sweden, France, the UK, and South America to sell his company's software products, while his family stayed in

Toronto. Alex travels every month to the Ukraine to his steel company to conduct business, while his family stays in Toronto.

Conclusion

The three theoretical approaches reviewed in this chapter, including the ethnic and class dimensions of entrepreneurship, transitional economy, and transnationalism all figure in explaining the factors that influenced and shaped the start-up stage of business development for the Russian-Jewish immigrant community in Toronto.

The Ethnic and Class Dimensions of Entrepreneurship Approach

Human capital as measured by education and work experience increases rates of entrepreneurship, aids business startups and plays a significant role in immigrant business success; immigrant entrepreneurs who came with more human capital or who obtained more human capital in Toronto, in the form of education and occupational skills will be in an advantageous position to start businesses.

All immigrant entrepreneurs will need access to financial capital to take advantage of perceived opportunities in Toronto. Entrepreneurship success for the second cohort of immigrant entrepreneurs will be partly determined by the amount of financial/material resources that they brought with them; most accumulated a significant amount of financial capital during the transition in Russia.

Immigrant entrepreneurs from both cohorts draw on social networks, including friends, former colleagues, and the Russian co-ethnic community for resources, such as financial capital, and links to suppliers and customers.

The Transitional Economy Approach

The structural changes that followed the dismantling of the command economy created opportunities and incentives for entrepreneurial activity for both cohorts of immigrant entrepreneurs.

Immigrant entrepreneurs from both cohorts who grew up during the communist system obtained entrepreneurial culture or cultural capital from the education system in Russia and from working in the state-run economy and the black market economy.

Entrepreneurs with experience of the transition economy in Russia (whether they were living there at the time or returned) and who had connections in the state apparatus who provided them with early knowledge of new laws and regulations during the transition were more likely to use these connections to establish successful transnational businesses with links to Russia.

The Russian immigrants who built their wealth by running businesses during the transition came to Toronto with enough financial capital to establish businesses in Toronto. They did not need to depend on ethnic resources or ethnic-based cooperation because they had the necessary class-based endowments of skill, education, and capital.

The Transnationalism Approach

Immigrant entrepreneurs do not merely react to structural disadvantages they face in their host countries but actively look for opportunities and market niches beyond the national boundaries of the receiving countries, utilizing their bicultural skills and binational ethnic networks. Entrepreneurs who obtain cheaper supplies through imports, export to global markets, and utilize international networks will be more successful in the global market.

Some immigrants from the second cohort who lived in Russia during the transition or those from the first cohort who returned during the transition will quit salaried jobs to pursue entrepreneurship to better utilize their skills, bicultural literacy, and transnational networks to reap material gains.

Case Observations

Graduates with engineering and professional expertise were most likely to start businesses within their professional fields. All the entrepreneurs whom I interviewed had a good education, which they attained in the former Soviet Union, Israel, or Toronto, depending on their cohort. They used their high human capital to get jobs in their fields or allied fields. The majority of their degrees corresponded to the business they established.

Disadvantage theory and the ethnic and class dimensions of entrepreneurship approach helps explain why Russian immigrants took path 1 to entrepreneurship, starting a business as a result of human capital handicaps, such as the inability to get good jobs due to lack of host country education, credentials and licenses. But only 2 of the immigrants from the first cohort and no immigrants from the second cohort who came to Toronto couldn't get credentials and therefore decided to go into business.

Disadvantage theory and the ethnic and class dimensions of entrepreneurship approach helps explain why some Russian immigrants took path 2 to entrepreneurship; this theory posits that those who came with human capital but were frustrated in their jobs or were laid off, used their experiences in the labour market to start a business. But only 2 of the immigrants from the first cohort and none from the second cohort fit into this category.

Opportunity theory and the ethnic and class dimensions of entrepreneurship approach help explain the Russian immigrants who took path 3 to entrepreneurship; they came with a lot of human capital, found opportunities within the organizations where they were working on a salary, and started a business. Over half of the immigrants from the first cohort and nearly half of the immigrants from the second cohort fit into this category, making it a more important explanation of entrepreneurialism.

The transnationalism approach helps explain why some Russian immigrants took path 3 to entrepreneurship. These immigrants noticed the business opportunities in Russia after the transition to a market economy and had the international social capital and social networks to support international business

About 30% of the immigrants from the first cohort and about 20% of the immigrants from the second cohort who came to Toronto with human capital talked to friends who told them about a business opportunity. Opportunity theory and ethnic economy theory and the ethnic and class dimensions of entrepreneurship approach helps explain why these immigrants took path 4 to entrepreneurship.

One-third of the immigrants from the second cohort came to Canada with human capital, business experience and financial capital, intending to do business. Business Background theory and the transitional economy approach help explain why these Russian immigrants took path 5 to entrepreneurship.

The choice of financing source shows that the immigrants' human capital, namely, years of education, work experience and occupational skills, were generally recognized by banks and the government; the majority obtained financing from banks or a combination of banks and private investors to start businesses in Toronto. The immigrants who took path 1 to entrepreneurship were more likely to obtain financial capital from a variety of sources to start their business. Path 2 immigrants were more likely to obtain financial capital from banks. Path 3 immigrants were more likely to obtain financial capital from banks, a combination of their own financing and the bank, or private investors and the government. Path 4 immigrants were more likely to obtain financial capital from their own financing or from a variety of sources. Path 5 entrepreneurs were more likely to obtain financial capital from their own financing or from a variety of sources.

None received financing solely from their ethnic community members, so ethnic ties on their own were not important for obtaining seed capital to start businesses. Possibly, the entrepreneurs had adequate financial or educational means to obtain resources when they came to Toronto, or they brought financial capital with them. In addition, none of the immigrants knew anyone in Toronto before they emigrated from the former Soviet Union. As a result, the majority turned to banks and private investors for seed capital to start their businesses.

None of the entrepreneurs from either cohort got aid in the form of seed capital solely from friends in the ethnic community, none turned to Jewish or Russian organizations for financial capital, and none were members of Russian business organizations. They did not feel that there was any benefit for their business to join Russian business organizations. However, over half of the entrepreneurs from the first cohort and over 30% of the second cohort became members of professional trade organizations before or as soon as they started their businesses. These entrepreneurs began to network through fairly mainstream and formal channels (i.e. professional associations and specific trade organizations), rather than joining ethnic associations or organizations.

Even though all of the entrepreneurs from the first cohort were Soviet-Jews, less than 20% turned to Soviet Jewish friends for seed capital or to invest in their business. They either came with their own financial capital or were able to obtain loans from banks.

Some entrepreneurs received some seed capital from their friends within the ethnic community and some whose co-ethnic friends invested in their business. But the financial capital they received from their friends was accompanied by financing from other sources, such as private investors who were not part of their ethnic community and banks. Only 4 entrepreneurs from the first cohort received financial capital from members of the Soviet Jewish community. They sought financing from friends because their personal finances were insufficient and/or they did not get sufficient capital from the bank.

Even though over 65% of the entrepreneurs from the second cohort were Soviet Jews, only 1 turned to a Soviet Jewish friend for seed capital for his business. As noted, for the most part, the second cohort came with a significant amount of financial resources, and if they needed extra capital, they turned to banks. They did not need to depend on ethnic resources.

The majority of the first cohort and the second cohort were not part of an enclave economy. Only 13% of the first cohort and 33% of the second cohort opened up their businesses within an ethnically identifiable neighbourhood and targeted their businesses to customers from their ethnic group. The majority from both cohorts didn't get investment capital, credit, access to customers, and information about permits, laws, reliable suppliers, and promising business lines from members of their ethnic community. Therefore, ethnic networks did not function as important resources in the establishment and operation of their firms. This was especially true for the first cohort.

But the success of 13% of the first cohort and 33% of the second cohort was dependent upon their ability to utilize ethnic resources. These entrepreneurs targeted their businesses to the Russian ethnic community, hired co-ethnic employees, and used co-ethnic suppliers.

The majority of the immigrants from both cohorts did not target their businesses to the Russian enclave community or eventually expanded to other ethnic communities because they believed that they could make more money selling their products in a variety of communities. Some provided services to a Russian/Jewish clientele, but they also targeted other ethnic groups.

The majority of the immigrants did not target their businesses to the Russian enclave community because they were concentrated in mechanical and technical fields where they manufactured and sold products to anyone in their field. Others said that they did not like doing business with Russian co-ethnics.

In terms of hiring practices, the majority of the entrepreneurs said that they did seek out co-ethnic employees; they hired employees based on skills. High-technology firms, in particular, emphasize research and development and employ people with technical training.

Immigrant entrepreneurs from both cohorts who were salaried employees of the state during the Soviet command-style economy learned important skills that they applied in Toronto. They also learned skills in entrepreneurship if they were illegally involved in the black market economy. This "culture of adaptability" was retained in Toronto.

Half of the immigrants from the first cohort had more than three years of work experience in the former Soviet Union before coming to Toronto, and about half of these worked in engineering; 70% of the immigrants who worked in engineering started businesses in the same field or an allied field in Toronto. Clearly, their prior work experience helped them to start businesses in their field of expertise.

About 80% of the immigrants from the second cohort had more than three years of work experience in the former Soviet Union before coming to Toronto; about half worked in the engineering field; and half of those who worked in engineering started businesses in the engineering field or an allied field in Toronto. All were still living in the former Soviet Union during the transition to a market economy; over 40% left state-sector jobs to work in other professional fields or to open up businesses.

Regardless of their experiences in the former Soviet Unions, Canadian business experience was vital to the success of immigrant enterprises. Entrepreneurs from both cohorts who took five different paths to entrepreneurship all discussed how their experience in the labour market in Toronto helped them develop the skills, knowledge, experience, and contacts required to eventually start their own businesses.

Those immigrants with experience of the transition economy were more likely to have transnational social networks that they used to help them become successful in business when they immigrated to Toronto. About 35% of the immigrant entrepreneurs from the first cohort and the second cohort were able to develop businesses in Toronto with links to Russia because they had connections to elite insiders in the former Soviet Union.

The immigrants who established transnational businesses came from varied paths to entrepreneurship, but only the immigrants from the second cohort who took path 5 to entrepreneurship started transnational businesses.

Some entrepreneurs made frequent trips to the former Soviet Union to conduct business while their families stayed in Toronto. They travel between their permanent homes in the West and their business in their country of origin in the former Soviet Union not merely to survive economically but to elevate their own and their families' socioeconomic status. In the case of the Russian immigrant entrepreneurs I interviewed, transnational entrepreneurship does not financially benefit the ethnic community, as these entrepreneurs seem to be only concerned with making millions for themselves. Even though these transnational Russian entrepreneurs may conduct routine activities across national borders, they weigh their future orientation and permanent settlement more on the host country, Canada, than on the sending country, Russia.

Russian businesses have been networking internationally since the breakdown of the former Soviet Union. Some of the new Russian businesses started by Russian immigrants in Toronto are propelled by globalization and oriented towards transnational networking. These businesses differ from their predecessors in scale and structure. "Enclave" is no longer an appropriate word to describe these Russian businesses because the success of these businesses depends on transnational linkages with Russia. Since these transnational entrepreneurs are economically successful, they may stimulate others to follow their example, thus expanding this mode of economic adaptation.

NOTES

[1] For an in depth discussion of the 5 paths, see the previous chapter.
[2] In this study, a common *ethnicity* will mean that members have some awareness of group membership and a common origin and culture, or that others think of them as having these attributes (Yinger, 1985).

CHAPTER 7

Conclusion: Elite Entrepreneurs from the Former Soviet Union
in Toronto - How the Transitional Economy, Ethnic and Class
Resources, and Transnationalism Influenced their Evolution

Introduction

The experience of Russian immigrants from the former
Soviet Union casts light on our understanding of contemporary immigrant entrepreneurship, reminding us that we
cannot glibly generalize about all immigrants – each case has its
own unique qualities. Since the collapse of the Soviet Union,
immigrants from the former Soviet republics have immigrated to
countries such as the United States and Canada, and settled in
metropolitan areas like Toronto. They have made millions establishing businesses in their new host countries. This research was
the first systematic study done in Canada to focus on these immigrant entrepreneurs.

The study was based on 32 interviews I conducted with
two cohorts of immigrants from the former Soviet Union, those
who immigrated to Toronto in the late 1970s and early 1980s and
those who arrived in the late 1980s and 1990s. The dates were
chosen in a bid to distinguish between those who learned their
business skills solely in the Soviet era and those with experience
of doing business during the post-Soviet transition to a market
economy.

To address how Russian immigrants established businesses
in Toronto, I examined how social capital, financial capital, human
capital, and home country experience, specifically experience in
the former Soviet communist economy and experience in the transitional economy affected Russian entrepreneurs at each stage of
business development in Toronto. I drew upon three bodies of literature: transitional economy, ethnic and class dimensions of entrepreneurship, and transnationalism. Using the central postulates of
each of the three approaches I considered how these four major
factors influenced and shaped business practice and success in
Toronto for the two cohorts. I focused the discussion on two phases
of entrepreneurship: pre-start-up and start-up.

Theoretical Implications and Contributions

1. Ethnic and Class Dimensions of Entrepreneurship Approach

This approach hypothesizes that the likelihood of immigrants, in this case the immigrants from the former Soviet Union, entering entrepreneurship is influenced by the interaction of class (financial, human, and cultural capital) and ethnic resources (ethnic social networks and social capital).

Human capital as measured by education and work experience increases rates of entrepreneurship, aids business startups and plays a significant role in immigrant business success; the immigrant entrepreneurs who came with more human capital or who obtained more human capital in Toronto, in the form of education and occupational skills were in an advantageous position to start businesses.

Immigrant entrepreneurs need access to financial capital to take advantage of opportunities. Immigrant entrepreneurship success for the second cohort was partly determined by the amount of financial/material resources they brought with them; members of this group were able to accumulate a significant amount of financial capital establishing businesses during the transition to a market economy. They were less likely than the first cohort to turn to the ethnic community for seed capital. However, Russian immigrants who weren't able to obtain loans for their businesses from the bank or the government, and who did not have enough of their own money, were more likely to turn to their ethnic community for loans.

Family networks play an important role in business start-ups, especially since entrepreneurship runs in the family in many countries, and friends and relatives help establish business networks and businesses. In this case, some immigrant entrepreneurs worked in occupations similar to their parents and some started businesses in the same occupational fields as their parents.

An established community of earlier immigrants, a form of social capital in the host country, may provide information regarding the business climate and the feasible enterprises. In fact, some entrepreneurs from both cohorts drew on social networks, including friends, former colleagues, and the Russian community for advice about business related matters, financial capital, and links to suppliers and customers. The Russian ethnic community offered Russian immigrants several advantages, including access to a pool of potential investors, experienced entrepreneurs, a co-ethnic clientele, low-priced co-ethnic workers, social and emotional support, and the possibility of operating in the entrepreneur's native language and in a familiar social and cultural environment. Immigrants with personal networks in Russia or Toronto composed of resource-rich and powerful ties were more likely to start businesses in Toronto; they had access to a wider range of information about potential markets for goods and services; access to capital or potential investors, labour, clients, and suppliers which would sell production inputs at lower prices.

My cases show that class resources, including financial capital, human capital, in the form of education and professional or entrepreneurial experience obtained in Russia or in Toronto, and cultural capital, in the form of skills, knowledge, attitudes, and values obtained from the education system in Toronto, from experience in the labour market in Toronto, or from the education system in Russia, or from the black market economy in Russia, or from the market transition in Russia all play a role in establishing a successful business in Toronto.

2. Transitional Economy Approach

During the transition to a market economy in Russia in the late 1980s and early 1990s, a privatization program occurred rapidly and in an unregulated manner. This created a new propertied and corporate elite with greater opportunities to maintain control of public assets as they were privatized or to obtain personal ownership of assets and enter the emerging market economy with large business advantages. Immigrants who were able to take advantage of this and establish successful businesses in Russia came to Toronto with a lot of financial capital. Some immigrants from the second cohort who built their wealth by running businesses during the transition came with enough money to establish businesses. They did not need to depend on ethnic resources or ethnic-based cooperation because they had the necessary class-based endowments of skill, education, and capital. However, the majority of the first cohort arrived with virtually no financial resources because they left during the communist system.

Immigrant entrepreneurs from both cohorts, who grew up during the communist system, obtained cultural capital from the education system in Russia. Most were highly educated, and since education in communist society increasingly emphasized technical knowledge over Marxist ideology, entrepreneurs from both cohorts learned skills (mostly in the engineering field) which proved important in Toronto. Furthermore, most of the immigrant entrepreneurs participated in the second economy part-time, while holding on to a secure state-sector job. If they were illegally involved in the black market economy, they learned skills in entrepreneurship, such as making use of and manipulating institutional rules, and were more likely to re-emerge as legal entrepreneurs in Toronto.

The structural changes that followed the dismantling of the command economy created opportunities and incentives for entrepreneurial activity. Entrepreneurs from the first cohort who returned to Russia during the transition or those from the second cohort who still lived there obtained some of their cultural capital at this time.

The likelihood of entrepreneurial success for both cohorts of immigrants depended to some extent on the alliances they forged at the beginning of the transition process with (a) state elites; (b) financial sector elites; and (c) Russian entrepreneurs. Immigrants with political capital in Russia or who had connections to the political elite were more likely to convert their political capital into economic capital in Russia, and transfer their economic capital to start a business in Toronto. Furthermore, in Russia's transition economy, access to sociopolitical capital (i.e., connections to the state apparatus and local administration) led to higher chances of successfully establishing a transnational business.

Those who became successful entrepreneurs during the transition to a market economy had to be innovative, identifying and creating new markets and discovering what goods were in demand – skills which were easily transferred to Canada.

3. Transnationalism Approach

Some of the highly educated immigrants, especially immigrants from the second cohort who lived in Russia during the transition and those in the first cohort who returned to Russia during the transition quit well-paying jobs to pursue transnational business, They used transnational entrepreneurship as an effective means of maximizing their human capital returns and expanding their middle-class status through high earnings, which gave them more economic independence and made them part of the elite in their communities.

The immigrants who were present during the transition in Russia or those who returned during the transition and started successful transnational businesses in Toronto were more likely to have more extensive and diverse social networks in the former Soviet Union. They drew upon these to set up and run their businesses.

Russian immigrants who engaged in transnational businesses became successful by importing/exporting raw material, semi-processed products, manufactured durable and non-durable goods; or by acting as intermediaries between potential buyers in North America and suppliers in the former Soviet Union; or by setting up transnational manufacturing firms, with production based in the republics of the former Soviet Union and distribution in North America.

Russian immigrants in Toronto bought real estate, opened bank accounts, and established business contacts in both the former Soviet Union and Toronto from which they created new economic opportunities. They organize their transnational lives in both Russia and Canada, strengthening transnational networks that sustain regular back-and-forth movements.

Immigrant entrepreneurs do not merely react to structural disadvantages they face in their host countries but actively look for opportunities and market niches beyond the national boundaries of the receiving countries, utilizing their bi-cultural skills and bi-national ethnic networks. Those who acquire cheap supplies through imports, export to global markets, and utilize international networks are successful in the global market.

Synthesizing Different Explanations for Paths to Entrepreneurship Using the Three Theoretical Perspectives

The paths to entrepreneurship represent opportunity structures linked to the structural problems that all new immigrants face in starting a business, in this case, two cohorts of immigrants from the former Soviet Union.

Whatever their differences, disadvantage explanations, cultural explanations, business background explanations, ethnic economy explanations, and opportunity explanations all revolve around and attest to the unequal propensity of groups to embrace entrepreneurship. In an attempt at synthesis, the *ethnic and class dimensions of entrepreneurship approach* reduces these approaches to ethnic and class resources of entrepreneurship (Young, 1971: 142; Light, 1984; Light and Karageorgis, 1994; Model, 1985: 79). Whatever demographic, sociocultural, or socioeconomic features of a group encourage its entrepreneurship represent an entrepreneurial resource. These resources operate singly or jointly (Light, 1984). Both class and ethnic resources contribute to entrepreneurship, but the influences usually are not equal. Ethnic resources may be more important at the initial stage of business development, while at a more advanced stage, class resources may become more significant (Light and Rosenstein, 1995b: 22).

The first path to entrepreneurship was explained using disadvantage theories of entrepreneurship; it asserts that immigrant groups go into business because they are disadvantaged in the general labour market due to poor English, inferior education, lack of host country accreditation and discrimination (Kim, 1981). The second path to entrepreneurship was explained using cultural theories of entrepreneurship; it states that immigrants become entrepreneurs because they identify closely with and are socially and culturally attached to their ethnic group, living and interacting on a regular basis with that group (Light, 1980), or they choose entrepreneurship because they want to make enough money in their host country to return to their origin country (Bonacich, 1973), or entrepreneurship is a response to structural disadvantage (Light, 1980). The fourth path to entrepreneurship was explained using ethnic economy theories of entrepreneurship; it says that participation in the ethnic sub-economy promotes self-employment because entrepreneurs receive assistance from other co-ethnics (Portes and Bach, 1985), who may help them get a job in their co-ethnic firm and then help them start a business (Bonacich and Modell, 1980). The first, second, and fourth paths to entrepreneurship are consistent with the ethnic and class dimensions of entrepreneurship approach, which argues that the inclination toward business and the relative success of entrepreneurial efforts by immigrants is based on a balance of class resources: financial, human, and cultural capital and ethnic resources, which include ethnic social networks and social capital (Light, 1984; Waldinger et al., 1990).

The third path to entrepreneurship was explained using opportunity theory; when immigrants are working in salaried jobs and they discover an opportunity to start business, they may decide to leave their jobs. This path is consistent with the ethnic and class dimensions of entrepreneurship approach, which states that the inclination toward business and the relative success of entrepreneurial efforts by immigrants is influenced by their class resources: financial and human capital, specifically the money they made and the experience they accumulated in their previous salaried positions (Light, 1984; Waldinger et al., 1990). This path is also consistent with the transnationalism approach, which posits that some immigrants start transnational businesses because they notice the business opportunities created by cultural frontiers, and they have the international social capital and social networks and bilingual ability to support international business (Lever-Tracy et al., 1991: xi, 113 in Light, 2007: 90; Wong, 1998: 95 in Light, 2007:90).

The fifth path to entrepreneurship was explained using business background theory; it asserts that immigrant groups choose self-employment because they have business backgrounds in their country of origin (Light, 1984; Portes and Back, 1985). This path is consistent with the transitional economy approach (Pontusson, 1995: 119; Nee, 1991: 267); immigrants present during the transition to a market economy are more likely to set up businesses in that economy and then migrate elsewhere (in this case, Toronto) with both business experience and financial capital.

Summary of Major Findings and Implications to our Understanding of Millionaire Immigrant Entrepreneurs from the Former Soviet Union

Both cohorts of immigrant entrepreneurs embodied considerable human capital, coming to Toronto with a good education and excellent skill sets. The majority were Jews, consistent with past research that found that Jews were the most highly educated of all nationalities in the former Soviet Union. They were able to use their human capital to develop ideas for business.

It didn't seem to matter for business development and success whether the immigrant entrepreneurs received their education in the former Soviet Union or Toronto. At any rate, this was difficult to determine, since virtually all of the immigrants I interviewed received their education in the former Soviet Union. What seemed more critical was the fact that they had technical and professional degrees and had graduated from university, many with higher degrees. This seems to indicate that those with significant amounts of human capital may make more effective entrepreneurs.

Graduates strong in engineering and professional expertise were most likely to start businesses within their professional fields. Overall, the degrees they attained corresponded to the business they established.

Since the immigrants from the second cohort were more likely than the immigrants from the first cohort to have had jobs in more than one field and only the second cohort could leave state-sector jobs and start businesses after the transition, the two cohorts became entrepreneurs in Toronto as a result of different sources of employment in the former Soviet Union. Nevertheless, both cohorts learned socialist entrepreneurial skills in the primary and secondary economy in Russia that later helped them develop businesses in Toronto.

Immigrant entrepreneurs from both cohorts were influenced by their parents when choosing their occupation. However, none of the parents had been entrepreneurs, as they all worked for state-run companies in the communist system. A few of the immigrant entrepreneurs not only went into the same occupations as their parents, but also started businesses in the same occupational fields as their parents. In other words, they followed a logical path, given their parents' fields, but none indicated that their parents were influential in their choice to become entrepreneurs or their choice about which business to start.

Immigrant entrepreneurs from the first and second cohort who worked in the socialist economy acquired socialist entrepreneurial skills, including the ability to negotiate and to deal with party and state officials. They also obtained some of their *cultural capital* from experience in the black market economy. Those who participated in the hidden or underground economy were more likely to become entrepreneurs when restrictions on private accumulation were lifted in Russia and when they immigrated to Toronto. They learned to rely on three basic resources of Soviet-style entrepreneurship: (1) beat-the-system/bend-the-rules (rather than legal-institutional behaviour); (2) reliance on informal networks (rather than on individual skills and formal infrastructure); and (3) consumption-oriented, rather than production-oriented capital accumulation whereby immediate or short-term rewards take priority over long-term deferred gratification. These three basic resources of Soviet-style entrepreneurship were taken by immigrants from both cohorts when they immigrated to Toronto and turned to careers in private business.

Countering generally accepted theories on immigrant entrepreneurialism, in this case, earlier Russian immigrants in Toronto did not provide any information to the immigrant entrepreneurs from either cohort regarding the business climate and the types of enterprises that would be feasible in Toronto. Because of restrictions on information, this was especially true among the first wave of émigrés who came before the downfall of the Soviet Union.

The majority of the immigrants from the first cohort came to Toronto with virtually no financial resources because they left during the communist system where they earned low wages; the Soviet government also limited the amount of money and goods they could take out of the country. There were a few exceptions; some first-cohort immigrant entrepreneurs accumulated financial resources and business experience in other countries before coming to Canada; they worked at various jobs or opened businesses in places like Italy and Israel. About half of the second cohort came with a significant amount of money they made in business after the transition.

The second cohort came to Toronto after the transition to a market economy in Russia; therefore, they were more likely to have entrepreneurship experience in the former Soviet Union and to come with enough financial capital to start a business. They were also more likely to arrive knowing that they wanted to do business. Since the first cohort immigrated without any entrepreneurial experience in the former Soviet Union, most found jobs where they worked for over 5 years before starting a business.

To start their entrepreneurial careers, more than half of all respondents had left one of four main economic industries: engineering, manufacturing, science, finance, and retail. The majority from both cohorts worked in the same field that they graduated in and worked in the former Soviet Union; the most prominent field was engineering.

Disadvantage theory and the ethnic and class dimensions of entrepreneurship approach helps explain the Russian immigrants who took path 1 to entrepreneurship, those who started a business because the professional training they received in the former Soviet Union was not recognized in North America; licensing was denied until Western professional standards were met, and they found it difficult to find jobs in the main sector of the economy.

Disadvantage theory and reactive cultural theory and the ethnic and class dimensions of entrepreneurship approach helps explain the Russian immigrants who took path 2 to entrepreneurship; they were frustrated in their Canadian jobs or were laid off, and therefore turned to business. They drew upon their experiences and socialist entrepreneurial skills from the former Soviet Union; some used ethnic resources within their community.

Opportunity theory and the ethnic and class dimensions of entrepreneurship approach helps explain the immigrants who took path 3 to entrepreneurship; they found opportunities within the organization where they were working on a salary. If they saw it as a good opportunity, and they had the resources to do it, they started a business. Path 3 can also be explained with the transnationalism approach if the immigrants started transnational businesses.

Opportunity theory and ethnic economy theory and the ethnic and class dimensions of entrepreneurship approach help explain the Russian immigrants who took path 4 to entrepreneurship; they started by working for a firm owned by a co-ethnic or a Canadian firm, and while working at these firms, they found out about an opportunity to open up a business from their co-ethnic friends, and if they had the necessary resources and capital requirements, they decided to start a business.

Business background theory and the transitional economy approach help explain the Russian immigrants from the second cohort who took path 5 to entrepreneurship; they obtained entrepreneurial experience by setting up a business after the transition to a market economy and transferred this expertise to Toronto.

Looking at Soviet Jews was informative, as these particular immigrants did not turn to the established Jewish community, arguably because for most Soviet Jews, especially those born under the Soviet regime, Jewish identity is a hindrance to economic opportunities. As a result, they may not feel comfortable joining or seeking help from Jewish organizations. There are also feelings of distrust and individualism within the Russian community generally, making it less likely that immigrants will turn to their ethnic community for assistance in starting a business.

Disadvantage theory and the ethnic and class dimensions of entrepreneurship approach help explain the Russian immigrants who took path 1 to entrepreneurship; they started a business as a result of human capital handicaps, such as the inability to get well-paying jobs due to lack of host country education, credentials and licenses. They could earn higher returns on their human capital in self-employment than in wage and salary employment.

Disadvantage theory and the ethnic and class dimensions of entrepreneurship approach help explain the Russian immigrants who took path 2 to entrepreneurship; they came with human capital, but were frustrated in their jobs or were laid off. However, they used their experiences in the labour market to start a business.

Opportunity theory and the ethnic and class dimensions of entrepreneurship approach help explain the Russian immigrants who took path 3 to entrepreneurship; they arrived with human capital and found opportunities within the organization where they were working and had the resources to start a business.

Opportunity theory and ethnic economy theory and the ethnic and class dimensions of entrepreneurship approach helps explain the immigrants who took path 4 to entrepreneurship; they arrived with human capital and started by working for a Canadian firm. While working there, they learned of an opportunity to open a business from co-ethnic friends. If they had the necessary resources and capital requirements, they did so.

Business background theory and the transitional economy approach helps explain the Russian immigrants who took path 5 to entrepreneurship; they came with human capital, and had obtained entrepreneurial experience by setting up a business after the transition to a market economy either in Russia or in other countries. They used this experience to set up businesses in Toronto.

The choice of financing source shows that the immigrants' human capital, in the form of years of education, work experience and occupational skills were usually recognized by the banks and the government; as a result, the majority obtained financing from banks or from a combination of sources, such as banks and private investors, to start businesses in Toronto.

None of the entrepreneurs received financing solely from ethnic community members, showing that ethnic ties on their own were not important for obtaining seed capital. Arguably, they did not turn to their ethnic community for financial capital because they arrived with adequate money or had the educational means to obtain resources in Toronto. None of the entrepreneurs from either cohort got seed capital solely from friends within the ethnic community, none turned to Jewish or Russian organizations for financial capital, and none were members of any Russian business organizations. They did not need to depend on ethnic resources because they had the necessary class-based endowments of skill, education, and capital.

Many of the entrepreneurs began to network through fairly mainstream and formal channels (i.e. professional associations and specific trade organizations), rather than joining ethnic associations or organizations. They also developed network contacts by working for established companies in their field or attending trade shows and industry events in their field.

The majority of the first cohort and the second cohort were not part of an enclave economy comprised of networks of firms with ethnic labour; they did not open businesses within an ethnically identifiable neighbourhood or target their businesses to customers from their ethnic group. However, a few entrepreneurs from both cohorts targeted their businesses to the Russian ethnic community, hired co-ethnic employees, and used co-ethnic suppliers to buy their products. Co-ethnics are an important source of customers for the goods and services of some businesses in the Russian community, such as food stores catering to a Soviet-Jewish clientele. As with other immigrant groups, some Soviet Jews relied upon the members of their community as a source of labour.

The majority of both cohorts either did not target their businesses to the Russian enclave community or expanded to other ethnic communities because they believed they could make more money selling their products in a variety of different communities. Most were concentrated in mechanical and technical fields where they manufactured and sold products to anyone in their field, regardless of ethnicity or location. In terms of hiring practices, the majority of the entrepreneurs did not hire co-ethnic employees because they based hiring on skills rather than ethnicity. High-technology firms, in particular, emphasize research and development, and as a result, employ people with technical training.

Even though both cohorts had a lot of work experience in the former Soviet Union, especially in engineering, only those in the second cohort could leave state-sector jobs and start businesses after the transition. As a result, the two cohorts became entrepreneurs in Toronto as a result of very different employment experiences in the former Soviet Union. Despite the variation in employment experience and source of training, both cohorts learned socialist entrepreneurial skills in the primary and secondary economy in Russia that helped them develop businesses in Toronto.

Since all immigrants in the first cohort had limited access to relevant home country business experience because Soviet black market experience, while valuable, is still different from business experience in Canada, Canadian business experience was vital to the success of their enterprises.

Second-cohort immigrants who lived in Russia during the transition and those from the first cohort who returned to Russia at that time obtained valuable cultural capital. They were likely to have built up transnational social networks, connections with state enterprise directors, state elites and business groups, which they used to good effect in Toronto.

The transnational entrepreneurs derive higher-than-average incomes. They succeeded because they actively looked for opportunities and market niches beyond the national boundaries of the receiving countries. They had a distinct advantage in forming transnational businesses with republics in the former Soviet

Union because they understood how to conduct business there, the government regulations, and the language, and they were able to link up with distributors and retailers in Toronto. The entrepreneurs with extensive and diverse international social networks were in a better position to initiate and sustain transnational entrepreneurship. They set up new joint private firms with entrepreneurs and managers of enterprises in Russia, who could take advantage of the combination of legalization of private businesses and the continued government regulation of prices, export, import and internal trade licensing.

In the case of the Russian immigrant entrepreneurs I interviewed, transnational entrepreneurship does not financially benefit the ethnic community, as these entrepreneurs seem to be only concerned with making millions for themselves.

Russian businesses have been networking internationally since the breakdown of the former Soviet Union. Some of the new Russian businesses started by Russian immigrants in Toronto are propelled by globalization and oriented towards transnational networking. These businesses differ from their predecessors in scale and structure. "Enclave" is no longer an appropriate word to describe these Russian businesses because their success depends on transnational linkages with Russia. Since these transnational entrepreneurs are economically successful, they may stimulate others to follow their example, thus expanding this mode of economic adaptation.

Research Contributions

This research has made the following major contributions.

First, I argue that the success of immigrant entrepreneurs in the two phases of entrepreneurship (pre-start-up and start-up) is influenced by a combination of the following factors: 1) social capital, 2) financial capital, 3) human capital, and 4) home country experience. To understand how the above four factors influence the success of immigrant entrepreneurs in the two phases of entrepreneurship, it is necessary to use a multi-level theoretical approach which includes the following perspectives: transitional economy, ethnic and class dimensions of entrepreneurship, and transnationalism. Rather than seeing class and ethnic resources as competing, when we use longitudinal analysis we can see how both class and ethnic resources are important at different times and stages of business development.

Second, studies in the past have not placed enough emphasis on the importance of social context in the origin country influencing business success in the host country. This study shows how past Russian cultural traditions and institutional arrangements influence and shape business practice and success in Toronto. I have explored a seemingly contradictory phenomenon, namely, how people who grew up in a context where entrepreneurship was forbidden could develop entrepreneurial skills and how they could transfer these skills to the modern context of market capitalism in Toronto. It is this historical context which makes Russian entrepreneurs unique.

Third, I focus on the emerging phenomenon of immigrants arriving with a lot of human capital, and some with a great deal of financial capital, establishing medium and large businesses. The Russian immigrants I interviewed all came with human capital; most of the second cohort had financial capital, management experience and business knowledge. In contrast to past research, which believed that medium and large businesses would be run by native-born Canadians and established immigrants who had worked their way up, my research demonstrates that as a result of globalization, the tendency of the immigrants I interviewed was to establish not only small businesses in an enclave market, but also medium and large businesses in a diversity of industries, many with transnational links to Russia.

Finally, I consider five diverse paths to entrepreneurship taken by the immigrants from both cohorts to establish successful businesses in Toronto. I demonstrate how human capital, social capital, financial capital, and home country experience influenced the paths they took during each stage of business development. I make an effort to move away from cultural or structural theories, such as the disadvantage hypothesis, as the sole explanation for the high rate of self-employment among these Russian immigrant entrepreneurs. The series of biographical narratives reveals the importance of agency.

Unanswered Questions and Directions for Future Research

One limitation of my study is that only 32 people were interviewed, so findings cannot be generalized to all immigrants from
the former Soviet Union who established businesses in Toronto.

Nor do I control for all variables. For example, I do not
control for the effect of different places of departure from the
former Soviet Union or the effect of age and gender. Future
research could involve a more representative sample of people
who emigrated from the former Soviet Union to Canada, including a larger sample that will take into account different immigration periods, places of departure, age cohorts, and differences
between males and females.

My study only included two female entrepreneurs. Future
research could have a more representative sample of male and
female entrepreneurs, so that we could discover whether the transitional economy, ethnic and class resources, and transnationalism affect male and female entrepreneurs differently during each
stage of business development.

My study focused mainly on the Russian immigrants who
consider themselves and who are considered by others to be successful rather than dealing either with failed businesses because
the central research question is not "why are Russian immigrant
entrepreneurs so successful that they can earn millions," but
rather, "how did immigrants who grew up most of their lives in
a state-controlled communist system where entrepreneurship was
forbidden learn to become so adept at starting businesses in a
market economy when they moved to Toronto." So, the central
research question that this study aimed to address was: How did
experiences in the former Soviet communist economy and in the
transitional economy affect the role that human capital, financial
capital, and social capital played in establishing businesses in
Toronto. And my explanation is a two part argument: first, it has
to do with the historical national and global moment (transitional
and global economy); and, second with the skill set or cultural
capital that these men acquired in Russia and honed in Toronto.
This is why I did not distinguish the successful entrepreneurs
from those that did not succeed, and why I did not compare the
successful with the failures in the empirical part of this study.
Future research could draw on a larger sample that includes both

successful and failed cases, which would include immigrants who started private companies/businesses, but their businesses either went bankrupt or they were forced to sell their businesses because they were not generating enough revenue; those who left their salary jobs in order to make more money establishing a business that ended up being unsuccessful; and those who opened up businesses in the former Soviet Union which were initially successful but then failed because of competition, legal changes, and the danger of doing business in Russia.

A final limitation is that my study considers only one metropolitan area, specifically, the city of Toronto, so this study may not be able to be generalized to other cities. Future research could involve a comparison of several cities in North America.

Future research on entrepreneurship should use a similar longitudinal multi-level analysis that incorporates the three theoretical approaches, including transitional economy, ethnic and class dimensions of entrepreneurship, and transnationalism to study how the success of immigrant entrepreneurs in the two phases of entrepreneurship (pre-start-up and start-up) is influenced by a combination of the following factors: 1) social capital, 2) financial capital, 3) human capital, and 4) home country experience.

Future research could compare how the success of immigrant entrepreneurs in several cities in different countries is influenced by a combination of social capital, financial capital, human capital, and home country experience, during the two stages of business development (pre-start-up and start-up), through the theoretical lenses of the transitional economy, ethnic and class dimensions of entrepreneurship, and transnationalism. It will be interesting to compare Russian and Chinese entrepreneurs who both grew up in contexts where entrepreneurship was forbidden and there was no privatization. How did they develop entrepreneurial skills and use these skills to establish businesses in the modern context of market capitalism in big metropolitan cities, such as Toronto?

In contrast to past research, which believed that medium and large businesses would be run by native-born Canadians and established immigrants who worked their way up, future research should pay more attention to immigrants who arrive with human capital, financial capital, management experience and business knowledge. As a result of globalization, they are establishing not only small businesses in an enclave market but larger businesses in diverse industries, many with transnational links to their home country.

Future research could compare the entrepreneurial strategies used by these Russian immigrants to establish successful businesses in Toronto to the entrepreneurial strategies of other immigrants in other cities.

Future research could also investigate the different paths to entrepreneurship to shed light on the apparent complexity of immigrant self-employment. The majority of the entrepreneurs I interviewed began in Toronto as salaried employees and gradually moved into self-employment; this suggests a career trajectory to self-employment that is relatively unexplored in the literature on immigrant entrepreneurs.

Future research could use ethnic and class dimensions of entrepreneurship, transitional economy, and transnationalism to consider the factors that influence the mature stage of a business in Toronto and other places, in other words after the business has survived for more than a couple years and is established. This usually involves the expansion of networks by using professional services and government agencies to generate more business and obtaining services or knowledge to improve the operation and build the company's image.

REFERENCES

Aldrich, H. 1999. *Organizations Evolving*. Thousand Oaks, CA: Sage.

Aldrich, H. 1979. *Organizations and Environments*. Englewood Cliffs, NJ: Prentice-Hall.

Aldrich, Howard and Philip H. Kim. 2007. "Small Worlds, Infinite Possibilities? How Social Networks Affect Entrepreneurial Team Formation and Search," *Strategic Entrepreneurial Journal*, 1, pp. 147-165.

Aldrich, Howard and Philip H. Kim. 2005. "Social Capital and Entrepreneurship," *Foundations and Trends in Entrepreneurship*, 1, 2, pp. 1-52.

Aldrich, H., and R. Waldinger. 1990. "Ethnicity and Entrepreneurship," *Annual Review of Sociology*, 16, pp. 111-135.

Aldrich, Howard, John Carver, Trevor Jones and David McEvoy. 1989. "From Periphery to Peripheral: The South Asian Petite Bourgeoisie in England." *Research in Sociology of Work*, 2, pp. 1-32.

Aldrich, H., C. Zimmer and D. McEvoy. 1989. "Continuities in the Study of Ecological Succession: Asian business in Three English Cities," *Social Forces*, 67, 4, pp. 920-44.

Aldrich, H. and C. Zimmer. 1986. "Entrepreneurship through social networks," in *The Art and Science of Entrepreneurship*, eds. D. Sexton and R. Smilor, pp. 3-23. Cambridge, MA: Ballinger Publishing.

Anwar, M. 1979. *The Myth of Return: Pakistanis in Britain*. London: Heinemann.

Aslund, A. 1995. *How Russia Became a Market Economy*. Washington, DC: The Brookings Institution.

Bailey, T.R. 1987. *Immigrant and Native Workers*. Boulder: Westview Press.

Bailey, T. and R. Waldinger. 1991. "Primary, Secondary, and Enclave Labor Markets: A Training System Approach," *American Sociological Review*, 56, 4, pp. 432-445.

Baker, W. 1990. "Market Networks and Corporate Behaviour," *American Journal of Sociology*, 96, 3, pp. 589-625.

Basch, I., N. Glick-Schiller and C. Blanc-Szanton. 1994. *Nation Unbound: Transnational Projects, Post Colonial Predicaments and Deterritorialized Nation States*. Langhorne, PA: Gordon and Breach.

Basu, E.O. 1991. "Profit, Loss and Fate," *Modern China*, 17, pp.227-259.

Bates, T. 1994. "Social Resources Generated by Group Support Networks May Not be Beneficial to Asian Immigrant-Owned Small Businesses," *Social Forces*, 72, 3, pp. 671-689.

Bates, T. 1985. "Urban Economic Transformation and Minority Business Opportunities," *The Review of Black Political Economy*, 13, pp. 24-36.

Batjargal, B. 2003. "Social Capital and Entrepreneurial Performance in Russia: A Longitudinal Study," *Organization Studies*, 24, 4, pp. 535-556.

Beaujot, R., P.S. Maxim and J.Z. Zhao. 1994. "Self-Employment Among Immigrants: A Test of the Blocked Mobility Hypothesis," *Canadian Studies in Population*, 21, 2, pp. 81-96.

Belliveau, M., C. O'Reilly, and J. Wade. 1996. "Social Capital at the Top: Effects of Social Similarity and Status on CEO Compensation," *Academy of Management Journal*, 39, pp. 1568-1593.

Berger, Brigitte. 1991. "The Culture of Modern Entrepreneurship," in *The Culture of Entrepreneurship*, ed. Brigitte Berger, ch. 1. San Francisco: ICS Press.

Berliner, J. 1957. *Factory and Manager in the USSR*. Cambridge, MA: Harvard University Press.

Birley, S. 1985. "The role of networks in the entrepreneurial process," *Journal of Business Venturing*, 1, 1, pp. 107-117.

Blalock, H. M. Jr. 1967. *Towards a Theory of Minority Group Relations*. New York: John Wiley.

Blasi, J., M. Kroumova, and D. Kruse. 1997. *Kremlin Capitalism: Privatizing the Russian Economy*. Ithaca: Cornell University Press.

Blau, P. M. 1977. "A Macrosociological Theory of Social Structure," *American Journal of Sociology*, 83, 1, pp. 26-54.

Bolcic, S. 1997-98. "Entrepreneurial Inclinations and New Entrepreneurs in Serbia in the Early 1990s," *International Journal of Sociology* 27, pp. 3-35.

Bonacich, E. 1993. "The Other Side of Ethnic Entrepreneurship: A Dialogue with Waldinger, Aldrich, Ward and associates," *International Migration Review*, 27, pp. 685-92.

Bonacich, E. 1973. "A Theory of Middleman Minorities," *American Sociological Review*, 38, pp. 583-594.

Bonacich, E. and J. Modell. 1980. *The Economic Basis of Ethnic Solidarity: Small Business in the Japenese-American Community*. Berkeley, CA: University of California Press.

Bonnell, V. E. and T.B. Gold. 2002. "Introduction," in *The New Entrepreneurs of Europe and Asia: Patterns of Business Development in Russia, Eastern Europe and China*, eds. Victoria E. Bonnell and Thomas B. Gold. New York: M. E. Sharpe.

Boojihawon, D.K. 2004. "International Entrepreneurship and Network Relationships: the International Marketing Communications Sector," in *Emerging Paradigms in International Entrepreneurship*, eds. Marian V. Jones and Pavlos Dimitratos, pp. 217-248. Cheltenham, UK: Edward Elgar.

Borjas, G. 1990. *Friends or Strangers: The Impact of Immigrants on the US Economy*. New York: Basic Books.

Borjas, G. 1986. "The Self-employment Experience of Immigrants," *Journal of Human Resources*, 21, pp. 485-506.

Bott, Helen. 1928. "Observation of Play Activities in a Nursery School," *Genetic Psychology Monographs*, 4, pp. 44-88.

Bourdieu, P. 1989. "Social Space and Symbolic Power," *Sociological Theory*, 7, 1, pp. 14-25.

Bourdieu, P. 1986. "The Forms of Capital," in *Handbook of Theory and Research for the Sociology of Education*, ed. J. G. Richardson, pp.241-58. New York: Greenwood Press.

Boyco, M., A. Shleifer, and R. Vishny. 1995. *Privatizing Russia.* Cambridge: MIT Press.

Breton, Raymond. 1964. "Institutional Completeness of Ethnic Communities and the Personal Relations of Immigrants," *American Journal of Sociology*, 70, pp. 193-205.

Brettel, C.B and K.E. Alstatt. 2007. "The Agency of Immigrant Entrepreneurs: Biographies of the Self-Employed in Ethnic and Occupational Niches of the Urban Labor Market," *Journal of Anthropological Research*, 63, 3, pp. 383-397.

Brym, R.J. 1993. "The Emigration Potential of Jews in the Former Soviet Union," *East European Jewish Affairs*, 23, 2, pp. 9-24.

Bunin, I. 1994. *Biznesmeny Rossii, 40 istorii uspekha.* Moscow.

Burawoy, M. 2001. "Neoclassical Sociology: From the End of Communism to the End of Classes," *American Journal of Sociology*, 106, 4, pp. 1099-1120.

Burawoy, M. and P. Krotov. 1992. "The Soviet Transition from Socialism to Capitalism: Worker Control and Economic Bargaining in the Wood Industry," *American Sociological Review*, 57, pp. 16-38.

Burt, R. 1992. *Structural Holes: The Social Structure of Competition.* Cambridge, Mass.: Harvard University Press.

Carter, N.M., W.B. Gartner and P.D. Reynolds. 1996. "Exploring Start-Up Event Sequences," *Journal of Business Venturing*, 11, 3, pp. 151-166.

Chan, J. and Y-W. Cheung. 1985. "Ethnic Resources and Business Enterprise: A Study of Chinese Businesses in Toronto," *Human Organization*, 44, 2, pp. 142-154.

Chin, K., I. Yoon and D. Smith. 1996. "Immigrant Small Business and International Economic Linkage: A Case of the Korean Wig Business in Los Angeles, 1968-1977," *International Migration Review*, 30, 2, pp. 485-510.

Chu, P. 1996. "Social Network Models of Overseas Chinese Entrepreneurship: The Experience in Hong Kong and Canada," *Revue Canadienne des Sciences de l'Administration*, 13, 4, pp. 358-365.

Cobas, J.A. 1986. "Paths to Self-Employment Among Immigrants: An Analysis of Four Interpretations," *Sociological Perspectives*, 29, 1, pp. 101-120.

Cohen, A. 1971. "Cultural Strategies in the Organization of Trading Diasporas," in *The Development of Indigenous Trade and Markets in West*

Africa, ed. Claude Meillassoux, pp. 266-81. London: Oxford University Press.

Cohen, R. 1997. *Global Diasporas*. Seattle: University of Washington Press.

Coleman, J. 1988. "Social capital in the Creation of Human Capital," *American Journal of Sociology*, 94, S95-S120.

Collins, J. 1998. "Cosmopolitan Capitalism: Ethnicity, Gender and Australian Entrepreneurs," Vols. 1 and 2, PhD diss., University of Wollongong.

Cooper, A.C., T.B. Folta and C. Woo. 1995. "Entrepreneurial Information Search," *Journal of Business Venturing*, 10, 2, pp. 107-120.

Cooper, A.C. 1986. "Entrepreneurship and High Technology," in *The Art and Science of Entrepreneurship*, eds. D.L. Sexton and R.W. Smiler, pp. 153-168. Cambridge, MA: Ballinger Publishing, pp. 153-168.

Coviello, N. and A. McAulley. 1999. "Internationalization and the Smaller Firm: A Review of Contemporary Empirical Research," *Management International Review*, 39, 3, pp. 223-56.

Djankov, S., E. Miguel, Y. Qian, G. Roland and E. Zhuravskaya. 2005. "Who are Russian's Entrepreneurs?" *Journal of the European Economic Association*, 3, 2-3, pp. 587-597.

Durand, J.F., A. Parrado and D.S. Massey. 1996. "Migradollars and Development: A Reconsideration of the Mexican Case," *International Migration Review*, 30, 2, pp. 423-444.

Emerson, M.O. and C. Smith. 2000. *Divided by Faith: Evangelical Religion and the Problem of Race in America*. Oxford: Oxford University Press.

Eyal, G., I Szelenyi and E. Townsley. 1998. *Making Capitalism without Capitalists*. London: Verso.

Filion, L.J., C. Ramangalahy, G.A. Brenner, and T.V. Menzies. 2004. "Chinese, Italian and Sikh Ethnic Entrepreneurship in Canada: Implications for the Research Agenda, Education Programmes and Public Policy," in *Emerging Paradigms in International Entrepreneurship*, eds. M.V. Jones and P. Dimitratos, pp. 295-318. Cheltenham, UK: Edward Elgar.

Foner, N. 1985. "Race and Color: Jamaican Migrants in London and New York City," *International Migration Review*, 19, pp. 708-727.

Fong, E. and C. Luk. Ed. 2007a. "Introduction." in *Chinese Ethnic Business*, eds. E. Fong and C. Luk, pp. 5-16. New York, NY: Routledge.

Fong, E. and C. Luk. Ed. 2007b. "Conclusion." in *Chinese Ethnic Business*, eds. Eric Fong and Chiu Luk, pp. 234-239. New York, NY: Routledge.

Fong, E. and L. Lee. 2007. "Chinese Ethnic Economies within the City Context," in *Chinese Ethnic Business*, eds. E. Fong and C. Luk, pp. 149-172. New York, NY: Routledge.

Fukuyama, F. 1995. "Social Capital and the Global Economy," *Foreign Affairs*, 74, pp. 89-113.

Galunic, C., and P. Moran. 1999. "Social Capital and Productive Exchange: Structural and Relational Embeddedness and Managerial Performance

Link," *Proceedings of the Academy of Management Meetings*, Chicago.

Gerber, T.P. 2002a. "Joining the Winners: Self-Employment and Stratification in Post-Soviet Russia," in *The New Entrepreneurs of Europe and Asia: Patterns of Business Development in Russia, Eastern Europe and China*, eds. Victoria E. Bonnell and Thomas B. Gold, pp. 3-38. New York: M. E. Sharpe.

Gerber, T.P. 2002b. "Structural Change and Post-Socialist Stratification: Labor Market Transitions in Contemporary Russia," *American Sociological Review*, 67, pp. 629-59.

Glazer, N. and D.P. Moynihan. 1963. *Beyond the Melting Pot*. Cambridge: MIT Press.

Gold, S.J. 2001. "Gender, Class, and Networks: Social Structure and Migration Patterns among Transnational Israelis," *Global Networks*, 1, 1, pp. 19-40.

Gold, S.J. 1997. "Transnationalism and Vocabularies of Motives in International Migration: The Case of Israelis in the United States," *Sociological Perspectives*, 40, pp. 409-427.

Gold, S.J. 1995a. *From the Workers' State to the Golden State: Jews from the Former Soviet Union in California*. Massachusetts: Allyn and Bacon.

Gold, S. J. 1995b. "Gender and Social Capital Among Israeli Immigrants in Los Angeles," *Diaspora*, 4, 3, pp. 267-301.

Gold, S. J. 1988. "Refugees and Small Business: The Case of Soviet Jews and Vietnamese," *Ethnic and Racial Studies*, 11, 4, pp. 411-438.

Goldman, M.I. 2003. *The Privatization of Russia: Russian Reform Goes Awry*. New York: Routledge.

Goldscheider, C. and A.S. Zuckerman. 1984. *The Transformation of the Jews*. Chicago: University of Chicago Press.

Gould, D.M. 1990. "Immigrant Links to the Home Country: Implications for Trade, Welfare and Factor Returns," PhD diss. University of California, Los Angeles.

Granovetter, M. 1985. "Economic Action and Social Structure: The Problem of Embeddedness," *American Journal of Sociology*, 91, 3, pp. 481-510.

Grasmuck, S. and P. Pessar. 1991. *Between Two Islands: Dominican International Migration*. Berkeley: University of California Press.

Greenfield, S.M., A. Strickon and R.T. Aubey. 1979. *Entrepreneurs in Cultural Context*. Albuquerque: University of New Mexico Press.

Greve, A. 1995. "Networks and Entrepreneurship – An Analysis of Social Relations, Occupational Background, and Use of Contacts during the Establishment Process," *Scandinavian Journal of Management*, 11, 1, pp. 1-24.

Greve, A. and J. Salaff. 2003. "Social Networks and Entrepreneurship," *Entrepreneurship, Theory and Practice*, 28, 1, pp. 1-22.

Grossetti, M. 2005. "Where do Social Relations Come From?: A Study of Personal Networks in the Toulouse Area of France," *Social Networks*, 27, 4, pp. 289-300.

Guarnizo, L.E. 1997. *The Mexican Ethnic Economy in Los Angeles: Capitalist Accumulation, Class Restructuring, and the Transnationalization of Migration.* La Jolla, CA: Center for U.S. Mexico Studies, University of California, San Diego.

Guarnizo, L.E., A. Portes and W. Haller. 2003. "Assimilation and Transnationalism: Determinants of Transnational Political Action among Contemporary Migrants," *American Journal of Sociology*, 108, 6, pp. 1121-1148.

Guarnizo, L.E. and M.P. Smith. 1998. "The Locations of Transnationalism," in *Transnationalism from Below*, eds. M. P. Smith and L. E. Guarnizo, pp. 3-14. New Brunswick, NJ: Transaction.

Guriev, S. and A. Rachinsky. 2005. "The Role of Oligarchs in Russian Capitalism," *Journal of Economic Perspectives*, 19, 1, pp. 131-150.

Hagen, E. 1962. *On the Theory of Social Change.* Homewood, IL: Dorsey.

Hankiss, E. 1990. *East European Alternatives.* Oxford: Oxford University Press.

Hanley, E., N. Yershova, and R. Anderson. 1995. "Russia: Old Wine in a New Bottle? The Circulation and Reproduction of Russian Elites, 1983-1993," *Theory and Society*, 24, pp. 639-68.

Hansen, E.L. 1995. "Entrepreneurial Network and New Organization Growth," *Entrepreneurship: Theory and Practice*, 19, 4, pp. 7-19.

Havrylyshyn, O. 2006. *Divergent Paths in Post-Communist Transformation: Capitalism for All or Capitalism for Few?* New York, NY: Palgrave Macmillan Press.

Head, K. and J. Ries. 1998. "Immigration and Trade Creation: Econometric Evidence from Canada," *Canadian Journal of Economics*, 31, 1, pp. 47-62.

Hill, S., M. Roderick, and A. Vidinova. 1997. "Institutional Theory and Economic Transformation: Enterprise Employment Relations in Bulgaria," *European Journal of Industrial Relations*, 3, 2, pp. 229-251.

Hoffman, D.E. 2002. *The Oligarchs: Wealth and Power in the New Russia.* New York: Public Affairs.

Howe, I. 1976. *World of Our Fathers.* New York: Bantam Books.

Ibarra, H. 1995. "Race, Opportunity, and Diversity of Social Circles in Managerial Networks," *Academy of Management Journal*, 38, pp. 673-703.

Itzigohn, J. 1995. "Migrant Remittances, Labor Markets, and Household Strategies: A Comparative Analysis of Low-Income Household Strategies in the Caribbean Basin," *Social Forces*, 74, 2, pp. 633-657.

Itzigohn, J., C. Dore, E. Hernandez and O. Vasquez. 1999. "Mapping Dominican Transnationalism," *Ethnic and Racial Studies*, 22, pp. 316-339.

Jones, A. and W. Moskoff. 1991. *Ko-ops: the Rebirth of Entrepreneurship in the Soviet Union.* Indiana University Press.

Kamm, J.B. and Nurick, A.J. 1993. "The Stages of Team Venture Formation: A Decision Making Model," *Entrepreneurship: Theory and Practice,* 17, 2, pp. 17-27.

Kanter, R.M. 1977. *Men and Women of the Corporation.* New York: Basic Books.

Kim, I. 1981. *New Urban Immigrants: The Korean Community in New York.* Princeton: Princeton University Press.

Kim, K.C., W.M. Hurh, and M. Fernandez. 1989. "Intra-Group Differences in Business Participation: Three Asian Immigrant Groups," *International Migration Review,* 23, 1, pp. 73-95.

Kim, K.C., and W.M. Hurh. 1985. "Ethnic Resource Utilization of Korean Immigrant Entrepreneurs in the Chicago Minority Area," *International Migration Review,* 19, pp. 82-111.

King, L. 2001. "Making Markets: A Comparative Study of Postcommunist Managerial Strategies in Central Europe," *Theory and Society,* 30, pp. 493-538.

Krackhardt, D. 1990. "Assessing the Political Landscape: Structure, Cognition, and Power in Organizations," *Administrative Science Quarterly,* 35, pp. 342-369.

Kryshtanovskaya, O., and S. White. 1996. "From Soviet Nomenklatura to Russian Elite," *Europe-Asia Studies,* 48, pp. 711-733.

Kurkchiyan, M. 1999. "The Transformation of the Second Economy into the Informal Economy," in *Economic Crime in Russia,* eds. Alena V. Ledeneva and Marina Kurkchiyan, pp.83-97. The Hague, Netherlands: Kluwer Law International.

Kyle, D. 1999. "The Otavalo Trade Diaspora: Social Capital and Transnational Entrepreneurship," *Ethnic and Racial Studies,* 22, 2, pp. 422-446.

Laguerre, M. 1998. "Rotating Credit Associations and the Diasporic Economy," *Journal of Developmental Entrepreneurship,* 3, pp. 23-34.

Laki, M. and J. Szalai. May 2006. "The Puzzle of Success: Hungarian Entrepreneurs at the Turn of the Millennium." *Europe-Asia Studies,* 58, 3, pp. 317-345.

Landolt, P. 2001. "Salvadoran Economic Transnationalism: Embedded Strategies for Household Maintenance, Immigrant Incorporation, and Entrepreneurial Expansion," *Global Networks,* 1, pp. 217-242.

Landolt, P., I. Antler and S. Baires. 1999. "From 'Hermano Lejano' to 'Hermano Mayor': The Dialectics of Salvadoran Transnationalism," *Ethnic and Racial Studies,* 22, pp. 290-315.

Ledeneva, A. 1998. *Russia's Economy of Favours: Blat, Networking and Informal Exchange.* Cambridge: Cambridge University Press.

Leonard, K. and C. Tibrewal. 1993. "Asian Indians in Southern California: Occupations and Ethnicity," in *Immigration and Entrepreneurship: Cul-*

ture, Capital, and Ethnic Networks, eds. I. Light and P. Bhachu, pp. 141-62. New Brunswick, NJ: Transaction Publishers.

Lever-Tracy, C. et al. 1991. *Asian Entrepreneurs in Australia.* Canberra: Australian Government Publishing Service.

Levitt, P. 2001. *The Transnational Villagers.* Berkeley, CA: University of California Press.

Levitt, P. and N. Glick Schiller. 2003. "Transnational Perspectives on Migration: Conceptualizing Simultaneity." Paper presented at the Conference on Conceptual and Methodological Development in the Study of International Migration, Center for Migration and Development, Princeton University, May 23-25.

Ley, D. 2006. "Explaining Variations in Business Performance among Immigrant Entrepreneurs in Canada," *Journal of Ethnic and Migration Studies,* 32, 5, pp. 743-764.

Li, P.S. 2007. "Business Owners and Workers: Class Locations of Chinese in Canada," in *Chinese Ethnic Business,* eds. Eric Fong and Chiu Luk, pp. 173-191. New York, NY: Routledge.

Li, P.S. 1998. *The Chinese in Canada.* Second edition. Toronto: Oxford University Press.

Li, W. 1997. "Spatial Transformation of an Urban Ethnic Community from Chinatown to Chinese Ethnoburb in Los Angeles," Ph.D. Dissertation. Department of Geography. University of Southern California.

Light, I. 2007. "Globalization, Transnationalism, and Chinese Transnationalism," in *Chinese Ethnic Business,* eds. E. Fong and C. Luk, pp. 89-98. New York, NY: Rouledge.

Light. I. 2001. "Globalization, Transnationalism and Trade," *Asian and Pacific Migration Journal,* 10, 1, pp. 53-79.

Light, I. 1992. *Immigrant Networks and Immigrant Entrepreneurship.* Los Angeles: Institute for Social Science Research, University of California, Los Angeles.

Light, I. 1985. "Immigrant Entrepreneurs in America: Koreans in Los Angeles," in *Clamor at the Gates: The New American Immigration,* ed. Nathan Glazer, pp. 161-78. San Francisco: Institute for Contemporary Studies.

Light, I. 1984. "Immigrant and Ethnic Enterprise in North America," *Ethnic and Racial Studies,* 7, 2, pp. 195-216.

Light, I. 1980. "Asian Enterprise in America: Chinese, Japanese, and Koreans in Small Business," in *Self-Help in Urban America: Patterns of Minority Business Enterprise,* ed. S. Cummings, pp. 33-57. Pt. Washington, NY: Kennikat Press.

Light, I. 1979. "Disadvantages Minorities in Self-Employment," *International Journal of Comparative Sociology,* 20, pp. 31-45.

Light, I. 1972. *Ethnic Enterprise in America: Business and Welfare among Chinese, Japanese, and Blacks.* Berkeley, CA: University of California Press.

Light, I., M. Zhou and R. Kim. 2002. "Transnationalism and American Exports in an English-Speaking World," *International Migration Review*, 36, 3, pp. 702-725.

Light, I. and S. J. Gold. 2000. *Ethnic Economies*. San Diego, CA: Academic Press.

Light, I., R. B. Bernard and R. Kim. 1999. "Immigrant Incorporation in the Garment Industry of Los Angeles," *International Migration Review*, 33, 1, pp. 5-25.

Light, I. and E. Roach. 1996. "Self-Employment: Mobility Ladder or Economic Lifeboat," in *Ethnic Los Angeles*, eds. R. Waldinger and M. Bozorgmehr, pp. 193-213. Berkeley, CA: University of California Press.

Light, I. and C. Rosenstein. 1995a. "Expanding the Interaction Theory of Entrepreneurship," in *The Economic Sociology of Immigration*, ed. A. Portes, pp. 166-211. New York: Russell Sage Foundation.

Light, I. and C. Rosenstein. 1995b. *Race, Ethnicity and Entrepreneurship in Urban America*. New York: Walter de Gruyter.

Light, I. and S. Karageorgis. 1994. "The Ethnic Economy," in *The Handbook of Economic Sociology*, eds. N. J. Smelser and R. Swedberg, pp. 647-671. Princeton, NJ: Princeton University Press.

Light, I., G. Sabagh, M. Bozorgmehr and C. Der-Martirosian. 1994. "Beyond the Ethnic Enclave Economy," *Social Problems*, 41, pp. 65-80.

Light, I., P. Bhachu and S. Karageorgis. 1993. "Migration Networks and Immigrant Entrepreneurship," in *Immigration and Entrepreneurship*, eds. I. Light and P. Bhachu, pp. 25-50. New Brunswick: Transaction.

Light, I., and E. Bonacich. 1988. *Immigrant Entrepreneurs: Koreans in Los Angeles, 1965-1982*. Berkeley: University of California Press.

Lin, N. 2001. *Social Capital: A Theory of Social Structure and Action*. Cambridge: Cambridge University Press.

Lin, N., J. Vaughan, and W. Ensel. 1981. "Social Resources and Occupational Status Attainment," *Social Forces*, 59, 4, pp. 1163-81.

Lo, L. and S. Wang. 2007. "The New Chinese Business Sector in Toronto," in *Chinese Ethnic Business*, eds. E. Fong and C. Luk, pp. 65-67. New York, NY: Routledge.

Lovell-Troy, L.A. 1980. "Clan Structure and Economic Activity: The Case of Greeks in Small Business Enterprise," in *Self-Help in Urban America: Patterns of Minority Business Enterprise*, ed. S. Cummings, pp.58-87. Port Washington, NY: Kennikar.

Luk, C. 2007. "The Global-Local Nexus and Ethnic Business Location," in *Chinese Ethnic Business*, eds. E. Fong and C. Luk, pp. 192-212. New York, NY: Rouledge.

Lynch, R. D. and V. V. Makoukha. 1996. "Entrepreneurs in Post-Communist Russia," in *Privatization and Entrepreneurship: The Managerial Chal-*

lenge in Central and Eastern Europe, eds. E. Kaynak, A.A. Ullman, Alfred Lewis, pp. 167-179. Haworth Press.

Mahler, S. J. 1995. *American Dreaming, Immigrant Life on the Margins*. Princeton, NJ: Princeton University Press.

Manski, C. 2000. "Economic Analysis of Social Interactions," *Journal of Economic Perspectives*, 14, pp. 114-36.

Marger, M. N. 2001. "The Use of Social and Human Capital among Canadian Business Immigrants," *Journal of Ethnic and Migration Studies*, 27, 3, pp. 439-453.

Marger, M.N. and C.A. Hoffman. 1992. "Ethnic Enterprise in Ontario: Immigrant Participation in the Small Business Sector," *International Migration Review*, 26, pp. 968-81.

Markus, R.L. and D.V. Schwartz. 1984. "Soviet Jewish Emigres in Toronto: Ethnic Self-Identity and Issues of Integration," *Canadian Ethnic Studies*, 16, 2, pp.71-88.

Marsden, P. 1990. "Network Data and Measurement," *Annual Review of Sociology*, 16, pp.435-463.

Marsden, P., and J. Hurlbert. 1988. "Social Resources and Mobility Outcomes: A Replication and Extension," *Social Forces*, 67, pp. 1038-1059.

Massey, D.S. et al. 1993. "Theories of International Migration: A Review and Appraisal," *Population and Development Review*, 19, 3, pp. 431-466.

Mata, R. and R. Pendakur. 1999. "Immigration, Labor Force Integration, and the Pursuit of Self-Employment," *International Migration Review*, 33, 2, pp. 378-402.

McFaul, M. 2002. "The Fourth Wave of Democracy and Dictatorship: Non-cooperative Transitions in the Postcommunist World," *World Politics*, 54, pp. 212-44.

McFaul, M. 1995. "State, Power, Institutional Change, and the Politics of Privatization in Russia," *World Politics*, 47, pp. 210-43.

McPherson, J. M., L. Smith-Lovin and J. M. Cook. 2001. "Birds of a Feather: Homophily in Social Networks," *Annual Review of Sociology*, 27, pp. 415-444.

McPherson, J. M and L. Smith-Lovin. 1986. "Sex Segregation in Voluntary Associations," *American Sociological Review*, 51, pp. 61-79.

Menzies, T. V., G. A. Brenner and L. J. Filion. 2003. "Social Capital, Networks and Ethnic Minority Entrepreneurs: Transnational Entrepreneurship and Bootstrap Capitalism," in *Globalization and Entrepreneurship: Policy and Strategy Perspectives*, eds. H. Etemed and R.W. Wright, pp. 125-51. Northampton, MA: Edward Elgar Publishing.

Min, P. G. 1996. *Caught in the Middle: Koreatown Communities in New York and Los Angeles*. Berkeley, CA: University of California Press.

Min, P. G. 1988. *Ethnic Business Enterprise: Korean Small Business in Atlanta*. Staten Island, NY: Center for Migration Studies.

Min, P. G. 1987. "Filipino and Korean Immigrants in Small Business: A Comparative Analysis," *Amerasia Journal*, 13, 1, pp. 53-71.

Min, P. G. 1984. "A Structural Analysis of Korean Business in the United States," *Ethnic Groups*, 6, pp. 1-25.

Min, P. G. and M. Bozorgmehr. 2003. "United States: The Entrepreneurial Cutting Edge," in *Immigrant Entrepreneurs: Venturing Abroad in the Age of Globalization*, eds. R. Kloosterman and J. Rath, pp. 17-37. Oxford: Berg.

Min, P. G. and M. Bozorgmehr. 2000. "Immigrant Entrepreneurship and Business Patterns: A Comparison of Koreans and Iranians in Los Angeles," *International Migration Review*, 34, pp. 707-38.

Model, S. 1985. "A Comparative Perspective on the Ethnic Enclave: Blacks, Italians, and Jews in New York City," *International Migration Review*, 19, pp. 64-81.

Moffitt, R. 2001. "Policy Interventions, Low-Level Equilibria and Social Interactions," in *Social Dynamics*, eds. S. Durlauf and P. Young, pp. 45-82. Cambridge, MA: MIT Press.

Morawska, E. 1999. "The Malleable *Homo Sovieticus*: Transnational Entrepreneurs in Post-Communist East Central Europe," *Communist and Post-Communist Studies*, 32, pp. 359-378.

Mouw, T. 2006. "Estimating the Causal Effect of Social Capital: A Review of Recent Research," *Annual Review of Sociology*, 32, pp. 79-102.

Mouw, T. 2003. "Social Capital and Finding a Job: Do Contacts Matter?," *American Sociological Review*, 68, pp. 868-98.

Nakao, K. 2004. "Social Resources and Occupational Status Attainment: Comparison of Japanese and American Employees' Personal Networks," *International Journal of Japanese Sociology*, 13, pp. 88-99.

Nee, V. 1996. "The Emergence of a Market Society: Changing Mechanisms of Stratification in China," *American Journal of Sociology*, 101, pp. 908-949.

Nee, V. 1991. "Social Inequalities in Reforming State Socialism: Between Redistribution and Markets in China," *American Sociological Review*, 56, pp. 267-282.

Nee, V. 1989. "A Theory of Market Transition: From Redistribution to Markets in State Socialism," *American Sociological Review*, 54, pp. 663-681.

Nee, V., J. Saunders and S. Sernau. 1994. "Job Transitions in an Immigrant Metropolis: Ethnic Boundaries and the Mixed Economy," *American Sociological Review*, 59, 5, pp. 849-72.

Nelson, R. and S. G. Winter. 1982. *An Evolutionary Theory of Economic Change*. Mass: Harvard University Press.

Ng, W. 1999. *The Chinese in Vancouver, 1945-80*. Vancouver: University of British Columbia Press.

Orleck, A. 1987. "The Soviet Jews: Life in Brighton Beach, Brooklyn," in *New Immigrants in New York*, ed. Nancy Foner, pp. 273-304. New York: Columbia University Press.

Park, K. 1997. *The Korean-American Dream: Immigrants and Small Business in New York City*. Ithaca, NY: Cornell University Press.

Podolny, J., and J. Baron. 1997. "Resources and Relationships: Social Networks and Mobility in the Workplace," *American Sociological Review*, 62, pp. 673-693.

Pontusson, J. 1995. "From Comparative Public Policy to Political Economy: Putting Political Institutions in Their Place and Taking Interests Seriously," *Comparative Political Studies*, 28, 1, pp. 117-147.

Poros, M.V. 2001. "The Role of Migrant Networks in Linking Local Labour Markets: The Case of Asian Indian Migration to New York and London," *Global Networks*, 1, pp. 243-60.

Portes, A. 1998. "Social Capital: Its Origins and Application in Modern Sociology," *Annual Review of Sociology*, 24, pp. 1-24.

Portes, A. 1995. "Economic Sociology and the Sociology of Immigration: A Conceptual Overview," in *The Economic Sociology of Immigration: Essays on Networks, Ethnicity, and Entrepreneurship*, ed. A. Portes, pp. 1-41. New York: Russell Sage Foundation.

Portes, A. and W. Haller. 2002. "The Informal Economy," revised version of a chapter published in the *Handbook of Economic Sociology*, eds. Smelser and Swedberg (1994).

Portes, A., I.E. Guarnizo and W.J. Haller. 2002. "Transnational Entrepreneurs: An Alternative Form of Immigrant Economic Adaptation," *American Sociological Review*, 67, pp. 278-298.

Portes, A. and M. Zhou. 1999. "Entrepreneurship and Economic Progress in the Nineties: A Comparative Analysis of Immigrants and African Americans," in *Immigration and Opportunity: Race, Ethnicity, and Employment in the United States*, eds. E.D. Bean and S. Bell-Rose, pp. 143-171. New York: Russell Sage Foundation.

Portes, A. and M. Zhou. 1996. "Self-employment and the Earnings of Immigrants," *American Sociological Review*, 61, 2, pp. 219-230.

Portes, A. and J. Sensenbrenner. 1993. "Embeddedness and Immigration: Notes on the Social Determinants of Economic Action," *American Journal of Sociology*, 98, 6, pp. 1320-1350.

Portes, A. and I.E. Guarnizo. 1991. "Tropical Capitalists: U.S.-Bound Immigration and Small Enterprise Development in the Dominican Republic," in *Migration Remittances, and Small Business Development: Mexico and Caribbean Basin Countries*, eds. S. Diaz Briquets and S. Weintraub, pp. 101-131. Boulder, CO: Westview Press.

Portes, A. and R. G. Rumbaut. 1990. *Immigrant America: A Portrait*. Berkeley, CA: University of California Press.

Portes, A. and J. Borocz. 1989. "Contemporary Immigration: Theoretical Perspectives on its Determinants and Modes of Incorporation," *International Migration Review*, 23, 3, pp. 606-30.

Portes, A. and L. Jensen. 1989. "The Enclave and the Entrants: Patters of Ethnic Enterprise in Miami before and after Mariel," *American Sociology Review*, 57, pp. 418-20.

Portes, A. and R. I. Bach. 1985. *The Latin Journey: Cuban and Mexican Immigrants in the United States.* Berkeley, CA: University of California Press.

Radaev, V. 1998. *Formirovanie novykh rossiiskikh rynkov: transaktsionnye izderzhki, formy kontrolia I delovaya etika (The formation of new Russian markets: Transaction costs, forms of control, and business ethics).* Moscow: Tsentr politicheskikh tecknologii.

Radaev, V. 1997. "Practicing and Potential Entrepreneurs in Russia," *International Journal of Sociology*, 27, 3, pp. 15-50.

Razin, E. 1992. "Paths to Ownership of Small Businesses among Immigrants in Israeli Cities and Towns," *The Review of Regional Studies*, 22, pp. 277-296.

Redding, S. G. 1990. *The Spirit of Chinese Capitalism.* New York: W. de Gruyter.

Rona-Tas, A. 1994. "The First Shall Be Last? Entrepreneurship and Communist Cadres in the Transition from Socialism," *American Journal of Socialism*, 100, 1, pp. 40-69.

Rona-Tas, A., and G. Lengyel. 1997. "Entrepreneurs and Entrepreneurial Inclinations in Post-Communist east-Central Europe," *International Journal of Sociology*, 27, 3, pp. 3-14.

Ruef, M, H. E. Aldrich and N. M. Carter. 2003. "The Structure of Founding Teams: Homophily, Strong Ties, and Isolation Among U.S. Entrepreneurs," *American Sociological Review*, 68, pp. 195-222.

Salaff, J., A. Greve, and S. L. Wong. 2007. "Business Social Networks and Immigrant Entrepreneurs from China," in *Chinese Ethnic Business*, eds. E. Fong and C. Luk, pp. 99-119. New York, NY: Routledge.

Salaff, J., A. Greve and S. L. Wong. 2001. "Professionals from China: Entrepreneurship and Social Resources in a Strange Land," *Asian and Pacific Migration Journal*, 10, 1, pp. 9-33.

Sanders, J. and V. Nee. 1996. "Immigrant Self-employment: The Family as Social Capital and the Value of Human Capital," *American Sociological Review*, 61, 2, pp. 231-249.

Sanders, J. and V. Nee. 1987. "Limits of Ethnic Solidarity in the Enclave Economy," *American Sociological Review*, 52, pp. 745-773.

Satzewich, V. and P. S. Li. 1987. "Immigrant Labour in Canada: The Cost and Benefit of Ethnic Origin in the Job Market," *Canadian Journal of Sociology*, 12, 3, pp. 229-241.

Schumpeter, J.A. 1942 [1975]. *Capitalism, Socialism and Democracy*. New York: Harper and Row.

Scott, J. 1991. *Social Network Analysis: A Handbook*. London: Sage Publications.

Scott, R.W. 1995. *Institutions and Organizations*. Thousand Oaks, CA: Sage.

Sedaitis, J. 1998. "The Alliances of Spin-Offs Versus Start-Ups: Social Ties in the Genesis of Post-Soviet Alliances," *Organization Science*, 9, 3, pp. 368-381.

Shane, S., and D. Cable. 2002. "Network Ties, Reputation and the Financing of New Ventures," *Management Science*, 48, 3, pp.364-381.

Simon, R. J. 1985. *New Lives: The Adjustment of Soviet Jewish Immigrants in the United States and Israel*. Lexington, Massachusetts: Lexington Books.

Smith, A. 1776 [1961]. *The Wealth of Nations*, ed. E. Cannan. London: Methuen.

Staniszkis, J. 1991. *The Dynamics of Breakthrough in Eastern Europe*. Berkeley: University of California Press.

Stark, D. 1996. "Recombinant Property in East European Capitalism." *American Journal of Sociology*, 101, 4, pp. 993-1027.

Stark, D. 1990. "Privatization in Hungary: From Plan to Market or From Plan to Clan," *East European Politics and Societies*, 4, pp. 351-392.

Stark, D. 1986. "Rethinking Internal Labor Markets: New Insights from a Comparative Perspective," *American Sociological Review* 15, pp. 492-504.

Steinberg, S. 1981. *The Ethnic Myth: Race, Ethnicity, and Class in America*. New York: Atheneum.

Szelenyi, I. 1988. *Socialist Entrepreneurs: Embourgeoisement in Rural Hungary*. Madison: University of Wisconsin Press.

Szelenyi, S., I. Szelenyi and I. Kovach. 1995. "The Making of the Hungarian Postcommunist Elite: Circulation in Politics, Reproduction in the Economy," *Theory and Society*, 24, 5, pp. 697-722.

Timmons, J.A. 1986. "Growing Up Big: Entrepreneurship and the Creation of High-Potential Ventures," in *The Art and Science of Entrepreneurship*, eds. Donald L. Sexton and Raymond W. Smiler, pp. 223-240. Cambridge, MA: Ballinger Publishing.

Tress, M. 1994. *Research Note: The Soviet-Jewish Refugee Populations in Germany and the United States Compared*. New York: HIAS.

Tseng, Y. 1997. "Immigrant Industry: Immigration Consulting Firms in the Process of Taiwanese Business Immigration," *Asian and Pacific Migration Journal*, 6, pp. 275-294.

Tseng, Y. 1995. "Beyond Little Taipei: the Development of Taiwanese Immigrant Business in Los Angeles," *International Migration Review*, 29, 1, pp. 33-58.

Tsukashima, R.T. 1991. "Cultural Endowment, Disadvantaged Status and Economic Niche: The Development of an Ethnic Trade," *International Migration Review*, 25, pp. 333-54.

Uzzi, B. 1999. "Embeddedness in the Making of Financial Capital: How Social Relations and Networks Benefit Firms Seeking Financing," *American Sociological Review*, 64, pp. 481-505.

Walder, A. 2003. "Elite Opportunity in Transitional Economies," *American Sociological Review*, 68, 6, pp. 899-916.

Walder, A. 1986. *Communist Neo-Traditionalism: Work and Authority in Chinese Industry.* Berkeley CA: University of California.

Waldinger, R. 1994. "The Making of an Immigrant Niche," *International Migration Review*, 28, 1, pp. 3-30.

Waldinger, R. 1986. *Through the Eye of the Needle: Immigrants and Enterprise in New York's Garment Trades.* New York: New York University Press.

Waldinger, R. 1985. "Immigrant Enterprise and the Structure of the Labor Market," in *New Approaches to Economic Life*, eds. Bryan Roberts, Ruth Finnegan and Duncan Gallie (eds.). Manchester, England: Manchester University Press.

Waldinger, R., H. Aldrich, R. Ward et al. 1990. *Ethnic Entrepreneurs: Immigrant Business in Industrial Societies.* Newbury Park, CA: Sage.

Walton-Roberts, M. and D. Hiebert. 1997. "Immigration, Entrepreneurship, and the Family: Indo-Canadian Enterprise in the Construction of Greater Vancouver," *Canadian Journal of Regional Science*, 20, pp. 119-140.

Ward, R.H. 1986. "Orientation and Opportunity: An Interpretation of Asian Enterprise in Western Society," paper presented at Annual Meeting of the American Sociological Association, New York, August 30 – September 3.

Weber, M. 1981 [1927]. *General Economic History.* New Brunswick, NJ: Transaction.

Wellman, B. 1926. "The School Child's Choice of Companions," *Journal of Educational Research*, 14, pp. 126-132.

Werbner, P. 1984. "Business on Trust: Pakistani Entrepreneurship in the Manchester Garment Trade," in *Ethnic Communities in Business*, eds. Robin Ward and Richard Jenkins, pp.168-188. New York: Cambridge University Press.

Wilken, P.H. 1979. *Entrepreneurship: A Comparative and Historical Study.* Norwood, NJ: Ablex.

Wilson, K. and A. Portes. 1980. "Immigrant Enclaves: An Analysis of the Labor Market Experience of Cubans in Miami," *American Journal of Sociology*, 86, pp. 295-319.

Wong, B. 2002. *Chinatown, Economic Adaptation and Ethnic Identity of the Chinese.* New York, NY: Holt, Rinehart and Winston.

Wong, B. 1998. *Ethnicity and Entrepreneurship: The New Chinese Immigrants in the San Francisco Bay Area*. Boston: Allyn and Bacon.

Wong, B. 1987. "The Chinese: New Immigrants in New York's Chinatown," in *New Immigrants in New York*, ed. N. Foner, pp. 243-72. New York: Columbia University Press.

Wong, L. L. 2004. "Taiwanese Immigrant Entrepreneurs in Canada and Transnational Space," *International Migration Review*, 42, 2, pp. 113-152.

Wong, L., and M. Ng. 1998. "Chinese Immigrant Entrepreneurs in Vancouver: A Case Study of Ethnic Business Development," *Canadian Ethnic Studies*, 30, 1, pp. 64-85.

Woodrum, E., C. Rhodes, and J. R. Feagin. 1980. "Japanese American Economic Behaviour: Its Types, Determinants, and Consequences," *Social Forces*, 58, pp. 1235-1254.

Wu, X. and Y. Xie. 2003. "Does the Market Pay Off? Earnings Returns to Education in Urban China," *American Sociological Review*, 68, pp. 425-42.

Xin, K., and J. Pearce. 1996. "Guanxi: Connections as Substitutes for Formal Institutional Support," *Academy of Management Journal*, 39, pp. 1641-1658.

Yang, K. 2002. "Double Entrepreneurship in China's Economic Reform: An Analytical Framework," *Journal of Political and Military Sociology*, 30, 1, pp. 134-148.

Yinger, J. M. 1985. "Ethnicity," *Annual Review of Sociology*, 11, pp. 151-180.

Yoon, I. 1995. "The Growth of Korean Immigrant Entrepreneurship in Chicago," *Ethnic and Racial Studies*, 18, 2, pp. 315-335.

Yoon, I. 1991. "Changing Significance of Ethnic and Class Resources in Immigrant Business: The Case of Korean Businesses in Chicago," *International Migration Review*, 25, pp. 303-331.

Young, F.W. 1971. "A Macrosociological Interpretation of Entrepreneurship," in *Entrepreneurship and Economic Development*, ed. Peter Kilby, pp.139-149. New York: Free Press.

Yurchak, A. 2003. "Russian Neoliberal: The Entrepreneurial Ethic and the Spirit of True Careerism," *The Russian Review*, 62, pp. 72-90.

Yurchak, A. 2002. "Entrepreneurial Governmentality in Post-Socialist Russia: A Cultural Investigation of Business Practices," in *The New Entrepreneurs of Europe and Asia: Patterns of Business Development in Russia, Eastern Europe and China*, eds. V.E. Bonnell and T.B. Gold, pp.278-324. New York: M. E. Sharpe.

Zhou, M. 2004. "Revisiting Ethnic Entrepreneurship: Convergencies, Controversies, and Conceptual Advancements," *The International Migration Review*, 38, 3, pp. 1040-1074.

Zhou, M. 1992. *Chinatown: The Socioeconomic Potential of an Urban Enclave.* Philadelphia, PA: Temple University Press.

Zhou, M. and J. Logan. 1989. "Returns on Human Capital in Ethnic Enclaves: New York City's Chinatown," *American Sociological Review,* 54, pp. 809-820.

Zhou, Y. and Y. Tseng. 2001. "Regrounding the 'Ungrounded Empires': Localization as the Geographical Catalyst for Transnationalism," *Global Networks,* 1, 2, pp. 131-153.

Zhou, X. 2000. "Economic Transformation and Income Inequality in Urban China: Evidence from Panel Data," *American Journal of Sociology,* 105, pp. 1135-74.

AUTHOR INDEX

Lynch, R.D. 1, 209, 221

M

Mahler, S.J. 54, 210
Makoukha, V.V. 209
Manski, C. 45, 210
Marger, M.N. 24, 42, 47, 61, 103, 145, 210
Markus, R.L. 1, 8, 9, 59, 85, 86, 87, 92, 102, 104, 122, 210
Marsden, P. 44, 210
Massey, D.S. 26, 52, 204, 210
Mata, R. 58, 210
Maxim 58, 59, 108, 202
McAulley, A. 204
McEvoy, D. 201
McFaul, M. 36, 76, 210
McPherson, J.M. 45, 46, 121, 210
Menzies, T.V. 43, 204, 210
Miguel, E. 204
Min, P.G. 9, 29, 42, 53, 55, 58, 59, 61, 62, 108, 122, 210, 211
Model, S. 58, 61, 65, 188, 207, 211
Moffitt, R. 45, 211
Moran, P. 44, 204
Morawska, E. 83, 101, 211
Mouw, T. 44, 45, 70, 211
Moynihan, D.P. 10, 43, 60, 122, 205

N

Nakao, K. 45, 211
Nee, V. 5, 21, 22, 24, 33, 34, 37, 43, 45,

47, 67, 70, 110, 131, 189, 211, 213
Nelson, R. 7, 83, 84, 211
Ng, W. 54, 55, 69, 211, 216
Nurick, A.J. 3, 91, 207

O

O'Reilly, C. 202
Orleck, A. 102, 212

P

Park, K. 69, 212, 215
Parrado, A. 204
Pearce, J. 89, 216
Pendakur, R. 58, 210
Pessar, P. 54, 205
Podolny, J. 44, 212
Pontusson, J. 5, 20, 34, 67, 110, 189, 212
Poros, M.V. 53, 56, 212
Portes, A. 4, 5, 9, 10, 13, 15, 21, 22, 24, 26, 27, 28, 29, 33, 40, 42, 43, 44, 47, 48, 53, 54, 55, 64, 67, 70, 109, 110, 122, 131, 188, 189, 206, 209, 212, 213, 215

Q

Qian, Y. 204

R

Rachinsky, A. 72, 206
Radaev, V. 73, 77, 78, 88, 91, 213
Ramangalahy, C. 204
Razin, E. 5, 213
Redding, S.G. 33, 213
Reynolds, P.D. 203
Rhodes, C. 216
Ries 55, 206
Roderick, M. 206

Roland, G. 204
Rona-Tas, A. 7, 37, 42, 67, 68, 81, 82, 84, 213
Ruef, M. 45, 213
Rumbaut, R.G. 10, 122, 212

S

Salaff, J. 13, 14, 22, 23, 26, 33, 41, 42, 43, 51, 52, 54, 89, 115, 136, 168, 205, 213
Sanders, J. 24, 43, 45, 47, 70, 131, 213
Satzewich, V. 58, 213
Schumpeter, J.A. 41, 214
Schwartz, D.V. 1, 8, 9, 59, 85, 86, 87, 92, 102, 104, 122, 210
Scott, J. 34, 214
Sedaitis, J. 89, 99, 214
Sensenbrenner, J. 43, 44, 212
Shane, S. 41, 214
Shleifer, A. 75, 203
Simon, R.J. 102, 214
Smth, A., 93, 214
Smith, C. 45, 204
Smith, D. 46, 121, 203, 210, 214
Smith, M.P., 54, 206
Smith-Lovin, L. 45, 46, 121, 210
Staniszkis, J. 35, 67, 214
Stark, D. 35, 42, 67, 89, 214
Steinberg, S. 64, 214
Strickon, A. 205
Szalai, J. 11, 35, 67, 82, 101, 207

SUBJECT INDEX